Good Arguments

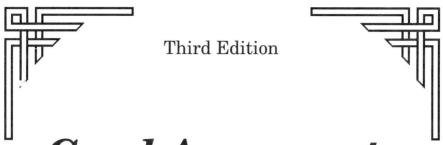

Third Edition

Good Arguments

An Introduction to Critical Thinking

C. A. Missimer

Prentice Hall, Englewood Cliffs, New Jersey 07632

Library of Congress Cataloging-in-Publication Data

MISSIMER, C. A.
    Good arguments: An introduction to critical thinking/C.A.
Missimer—3rd ed.

        p. cm.
    Includes index.
    ISBN 0-13-311804-5
    1. Logic.   2. Critical thinking.   I. Title.
BC177.M57   1995
169—dc20   94-29315
                                                                 CIP

Acquisitions editor: *Ted Bolen*
Cover design: *Bruce Kenselaar*
Buyer: *Lynn Pearlman*

© 1995, 1990, 1986 by Prentice-Hall, Inc.
A Simon & Schuster Company
Englewood Cliffs, New Jersey 07632

Printed in the United States of America
10 9 8 7 6 5 4 3 2 1

ISBN 0-13-311804-5

PRENTICE-HALL INTERNATIONAL (UK) LIMITED, *London*
PRENTICE-HALL OF AUSTRALIA PTY. LIMITED, *Sydney*
PRENTICE-HALL CANADA INC., *Toronto*
PRENTICE-HALL HISPANOAMERICANA, S.A., *Mexico*
PRENTICE-HALL OF INDIA PRIVATE LIMITED, *New Delhi*
PRENTICE-HALL OF JAPAN, INC., *Tokyo*
SIMON & SCHUSTER ASIA PTE. LTD., *Singapore*
EDITORA PRENTICE-HALL DO BRASIL, LTDA., *Rio de Janeiro*

Still dedicated to everyone who loves to
browse through books—
If that doesn't include you yet,
then I dedicate this book to you in advance.

Contents

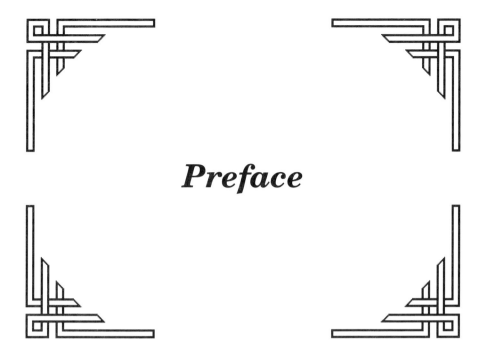

Preface

Students who approach this subject are far more timid than is warranted! The reason may be that to many ears critical thinking has a forbidding sound—"perfect, negative thinking," a new student of mine offered. If nothing else, I hope that this book will disabuse you of that impression. Critical thinking is the comparison of arguments on a subject to see which argument is likeliest, and this book is devoted to showing you how to do just that. There are a few basic concepts to master, along with the language in which these ideas are put, and the result is an endless array of subject-matter on which you can think critically. Indeed, I would argue that over the past centuries critical thinking has been responsible for the growth of knowledge in every field, from football to physics. Yet while critical thinking has produced good arguments that have vastly increased our store of knowledge, any piece of critical thinking is far from perfect. At least I would assume so, on the theory that if we don't search for even better arguments, for more evidence, we will never find them.

The idea of critical thinkers weighing arguments about an issue may sound remote from your life or interests, but I would argue that you think critically many times a day. Unless you reached into the closet out of habit, you made a decision what to wear today. You had reasons for your choice which you found better than those for things you left on the hangers. You made assumptions about the weather. Similarly, your choice of breakfast (or not to bother with one) entailed some quick critical thinking. Your discussion of which team was likely to win the playoff, or which political candidate would do a better job, would probably be critical thinking.

"Well," you might infer, "if I already do critical thinking, I don't need a course in it." Not so fast! In the areas you know well, you easily think critically. The purpose of this book is to back up a bit and show you exactly what it is that you have been doing so naturally, put names to the various *types* of thoughts you've had and how they are structured, so that it will be easy for you to apply the same good thinking in areas you're not as familiar with.

You may want to think about two assumptions underlying this book. One is that your time is best spent on a dozen basic workhorses of reason, rather than on learning many aspects of reasoning. In the vast majority of cases, even cases of complicated reasoning, these are features of thought which are used. There are many more concepts in informal logic, not to mention the rigors of formal logic. However, you will be best served by learning to manipulate these major mental gears.

The second assumption is that it is vital to practice the common phrases that indicate the structure of critical thinking. These phrases appear in boldface throughout the book.*

This new edition contains a new chapter on the reasearch paper, as well as expanded chapters on inference and evidence. In this connection, I gratefully acknowledge the assistance of Steve Carlson: Our conversations on the nature of evidence were clarifying and most enjoyable. I would also like to thank the following reviewers for their excellent suggestions: Diane M. Thiel, Department of English, Florida International University, Miami, Florida; Stephen T. Mayo, Department of Philosophy, Molloy College, Rockville Centre, New York; Amy Hayek, Department of English, Florida International University, Miami, Florida; and M. Kip Hartvigsen, Department of English, Ricks College, Rexburg, Idaho.

I hope that you will become at ease in recognizing the structure of critical thinking and enjoy a lifetime of fascination, reading others' good arguments, and creating your own across a wide spectrum of subjects. Have fun!

C. A. Missimer
Seattle, Washington

---

*This preface contains a few of the commonly used phrases that this book will show you how to use:

I would argue that
My reason is
You might infer that
[a claim has] little warrant
On the assumption that

1

Welcome to the Community of Thinkers

Actually, you're already a member. The fact that you were able to grasp what the preface was about indicates that you already possess critical thinking skills. In fact, you're far more skilled at critical thinking than you know. This book will help you to realize what you already know, and help you to build on it. And just as you've been a skilled thinker most of your life without necessarily being conscious of it, you have been a contributor to the community of thinkers, too. Members of this community address one another largely through the use of arguments, whether in conversations, articles, or books.

THE DOZEN BASICS

To argue is to try to convince someone else that your point of view is right. Everyone reading this book has made scores of arguments. Good arguments are structured with these twelve features:

1. definition and distinction
2. issue
3. conclusion
4. reasons
5. alternative arguments

6. evidence
7. truth
8. consistency
9. warranted inference
10. assumptions
11. implications
12. prescription

These are concepts which a critical thinker must be able to use in order to appraise arguments. You will be handling all of these features in their appropriate language with ease by the end of the book. They are the basic stuff of critical thinking. All arguments display most, if not all, of these features.

If these features are unfamiliar, you may doubt that you will be able to use a number of foreign concepts within a few weeks, all of them at the same time. You have, however, already learned to perform any number of involved tasks, much as a cyclist downshifts and makes a left turn at a busy intersection while watching out for cars and people. Almost everything that is difficult initially becomes easy with habit.

First, I want to make you aware of how often you use the notions of definition, distinction, and argument. You will find about twenty phrases in boldface in this chapter which show different ways that critical thinkers express these concepts. Try to get used to these phrases, start using them in everyday discussions, and be on the lookout for them. These phrases are the "noises" that critical thinkers make.

DEFINITION

How many times in your life have you said "What do you mean?" Or, perhaps, in informal talk, "Whaddyamean?"

> Linda: I thought that was a terrible game. Bah! 68–0.
> Sally: Whaddyamean, "terrible"? The score may have been 68–0, but the winning team made so many superb plays!

The same principle of "whaddyamean" applies in critical thinking. When you write, you should say "Whaddyamean" to yourself a lot. You define or explain the meaning of your main terms that might be misunderstood. Those last four words are important—you'd almost never need to define "oak tree" or "elephant." If you had to define every word you used, you'd end up defining your definitions and never even get around to making your point. By now you may be muttering, "Well, dang it, how much defining should I do and expect others to do?" As a rule of thumb, a writer should think about defining roughly one or two terms in a five-hundred-word essay. Abstract terms—the words for things you can't see, touch, or taste, such as "terrible," "justice," "natural," even "argument"—are more elastic and usually need defining.

So, *define what could be misunderstood, especially the abstract.* Here are some examples:

> **By the term** "community" in the chapter title, **I mean** participation in common.
>
> "Community" **means** participation in common.
>
> He used "community" **in the sense of** participation of people in a common activity.

Note the quotation marks around the term to be defined. Always use them. The quotation marks are important, emphasizing to the reader that the writer is setting up the ground rules to talk about "this important word."

You can get definitions from the dictionary, but one word about them. Because abstract terms such as "community" are harder to pin down, they are liable to have several dictionary definitions. Choose the one(s) you mean carefully.

DISTINCTIONS IN THE STRICT AND LOOSE SENSE

In *defining* a term you say for sure what's *inside* the limits of your term. When you draw a *distinction* between your term and another, you say what's *outside* the limits of your term. Together, definition and distinction are a pair of pincers that grab hold of a slippery term. For instance, here are a definition and a distinction, both taken from a dictionary:

> By "argue" in this book I mean "maintain" or "assert"; I would distinguish this sense of argue from "quarrel" or "bicker."

With a definition you show what you mean (within your term: here, maintain, assert); with a distinction you show what you don't mean (outside your term: here, quarrel, bicker).

> The author **makes a distinction between** "community" in the sense of participating in a common activity **and** "community" in the sense of living in the same district or city.
>
> She **drew a distinction between** being easygoing **and** being lazy.

In the baseball example above, Sally drew a distinction between Linda's definition of "terrible" (68–0) and hers (no superb plays). In everyday talk, people often make distinctions by responding, "But that's not the same thing!" Can you think of any instances in which you'd use that phrase to draw a distinction?

To sum up: In any discussion, show what you mean and what you don't mean by your major ideas, particularly the abstract ones; expect others to do likewise.

False Dichotomy: Distinction Run Amok

Someone who creates a distinction that doesn't in fact exist can be said to have created "a false dichotomy." For instance, if I claim that either you're a serious student or you love to party, I hope I have created a false dichotomy: You can be both academically ambitious and party-loving; you just can't fulfill both sides of your nature at the same time. Other examples are as follows:

> He argued that the slogan People, Not Profits **creates a false dichotomy between** making money **and** making people happy.
>
> In her speeches, she **raised a false distinction between** totalitarian **and** authoritarian regimes.
>
> The reader mistakenly thought that if ideas were expressed simply and enjoyably, they were not important. He **thereby created a false dichotomy between** the simple **and** the significant.

The following is an amusing claim of a false distinction:

> If you bet on a horse, that's gambling. If you bet you can make three spades, that's entertainment. If you bet cotton will go up three points [in the commodities market] that's business. See the difference?[1]

Failure to Make Distinctions

People can argue about whether a distinction is a valid one or is a false dichotomy. It can also be argued that a person has failed to make a distinction:

> While arguing that most people are selfish most of the time, the author **failed to make a distinction between** self-regarding acts, such as sleeping, **and** acts against others, such as stealing.
>
> In claiming that everyone over sixty-five should receive social security payments, the proponents of the bill are **confusing two groups:** those who really need these benefits and those who merely qualify for them but don't need them.

The key is to seek out and reflect on definition and distinction whenever an argument presents them.

ARGUMENT

In this book, we'll never mean "argument" in the sense of a quarrel; however, we will be using "argument" in two senses, because it often occurs in both ways. To keep them distinct,* I have called one the loose sense of argument and the other the strict sense of argument. Remember the phrases "in the loose sense" and "in the strict sense"—they'll come in handy when you make distinctions.

The Loose Sense

The loose sense of "argue" is the way it was defined above, to maintain or assert. Here are some examples showing how to use "argue" in this way:

> **He argued that** it is better to know some of the questions than all of the answers.[2]
>
> Lily Tomlin **made the argument that** reality is a crutch for people who can't cope with drugs.[3]
>
> **I would argue** with Goethe **that** the intelligent person finds almost everything ridiculous, the sensible person hardly anything.[4] (This phrase means "I am actually arguing that" or "I would *agree* with Goethe"; if you mean to disagree you'd say, "I would take issue with Goethe" or "I would argue against Goethe's position that. . . .")

Maybe . . . and Maybe Not   The term "argument" occurs frequently in this loose sense of making a claim about what is true. The word is wonderful in that it helps put the hearer in balance. While indicating that an assertion is clearly being brought forward, "argue" acknowledges that the assertion is just that—a claim that something is true. In fact, almost everything is a claim—or so I'm claiming!

The words "argument," "assertion," and "claim" help you to maintain that critical balance between accepting and rejecting an idea so that you can look it over at leisure. In short, use of the terms "argue" and "claim" helps you to think "Maybe that's true, but maybe not."

---

*See how useful distinctions are? "Argument" has been distinguished in three important ways.

Try This For the sake of developing your critical skills, and for the fun of it, try thinking of everything you hear and read as an argument, a claim, an idea to which you can respond "maybe; maybe not," rather than accept it as a given fact. It's impossible to actually think of every claim in that way, because of our overwhelming tendency to accept what we're told, but take this as a challenge (a "maybe not").* In the course of this book you will soon learn to sort out the likelihood of various types of claims (see chapters 4 and 11).

Your Next Move It's the addition of reasons that gives an argument needed backing. So when someone makes an argument or claim in the loose sense, your next move is to ask for reasons to support or back up the claim. Some ways of making that move:

> **"What are your reasons** for making that argument?"
> **"Why do you make that assertion?"**

Or, when analyzing a piece of writing in which the author made a claim but didn't give reasons why the reader should agree:

> The author argued that reality was just a crutch for people who can't cope with drugs, **but gave no reasons** to support this claim.

The Strict Sense

In its strict sense, to argue is to claim that something should be thought or done and to give a reason why it should be thought or done. For example, following this discussion I'm going to make an argument. I'll claim that reasoning with people is the best way to persuade them and then explain why I think so. A formal argument has at least one claim with at least one reason to support or back up that claim. *It's the addition of reasons that distinguishes an argument in the strict sense from an argument in the loose sense.* Reasons are needed to give most claims substance.

A Strict Sort of Argument You may have noticed that the common "noises of a critical thinker" in this book appear in boldface type. When you come to these phrases, repeat them, aloud if you can get away with it. Hearing information is a memory aid. Underlining is important too. Both come down to repetition, and the more you repeat, the easier it

---

*Some exceptions are greetings, such as "hello," or questions, "Is that a gefilte fish sandwich?" However, we're all aware of "leading questions" that contain claims, such as the famous "When is the last time you beat your wife?" And what about "Ow!"—is that a claim?

will be to remember these phrases. The following argument includes a number of crucial terms:

> Argument is by far the best way to get another person to believe or to do something. First, **let me define** the sense in which I mean "argument." **I mean it in the sense of** "reasoned persuasion to think or to act in a certain way." Others have **made the argument that** force or pure emotion are better ways to persuade, but I believe that those people are wrong, and I will in the course of the argument **make a distinction between** reason and these other techniques of persuasion.
>
> **My claim is this.** Reason is the best way to persuade anybody. **By** "reason" **I mean** "to explain why a thing should be done or accepted." When you reason with a person, you **by definition** respect both that person's mind and the idea you are presenting. You believe that your idea is compelling enough, is well-enough supported by good reasons for its truth, that another rational person, upon thinking about the idea, would accept it. You also permit that person to help you with your idea. The help can come in at least three forms. First, the person could come up with an even better idea based on your idea. Second, if your idea is flawed, the person could point out how that is the case and whether the idea can be salvaged by the support of better reasons. Third, by talking about the idea to other people you may be persuaded to abandon it in favor of a totally different, better idea.
>
> The major alternatives to argument are force and emotional blackmail. **Unlike*** argument, they respect neither the person's mind nor the idea enough to put these first. In fact, **I would argue that** force and pure emotion degrade both the idea and the mind of the person. (Incidentally, **I would accept the definition of** "pure emotion" as a type of force, but since it is rarely perceived in those terms, I'll deal with it separately.) People can be persuaded to act a certain way through force. For example, in a number of countries today, people who disagree with their governments are tortured or killed. Under that threat of death, the other people obey the dictates of their government. They don't obey because a reasoned and open discussion preceded some political consensus, but because they fear imprisonment or death. So the ideas that the government is promoting aren't trusted on their own merits, nor are the minds of the people.
>
> There are milder examples of persuasion by force, for example, fear of job loss, but even these are very powerful. Finally, to take a blatant example of force, the individual who holds a gun to the cashier's head while robbing the liquor store is not making an argument that the gunman deserves the money!
>
> The last alternative, pure emotion, can have almost as devastating effects as pure force. **I would distinguish** pure emotion from an argument that contains an emotional appeal. An emotional argument is still susceptible to reason. But just as with force, an individual exerting pure emotion over another wants that other to act or do a certain thing out of feeling. Thus, discussion is impossible, and failure to feel the same emotions is often seen as disloyalty. Emotional blackmail is often the result. "Emotional blackmail" **is here defined as** deliberately punishing a per-

---

*A handy term that points out a distinction.

son for not agreeing by withdrawing emotionally. **In effect*** the blackmailer is saying, "If you don't agree with me I won't love you any more."
Notice that in this case, as with force, the blackmailer does not appeal to
the person's mind nor to the rightness of the idea itself. Sometimes emotional blackmail can exist over relatively small things, such as a friend
threatening to cut off another friend for not agreeing (actually, if you're
the friend, it's no small thing to you). In one of the worst instances of force
by pure emotion in recent years, the Reverend Jim Jones convinced most
of his nine hundred followers that to oppose him was to betray him and
then led them to follow him in suicide as an act of loyalty. This kind of
blind loyalty **must be carefully distinguished from** the loyalty to others we demonstrate by arguing with them when we think they are wrong.

   In conclusion, reason by argument is the only means of persuasion that
respects both the person one is persuading and the idea. Therefore, it is
the best way to persuade.

Approach the Argument   You are either persuaded or not persuaded by this argument. In either case you should do some more thinking about it.

   If you are persuaded by the argument (or by the point of view that
is being argued), *what can you contribute* that would make the argument more persuasive? As stated in the preface, that assumption is that
arguments can always be made better, and it is assumed that you'll
operate on that assumption too. What does this argument need in the
way of further definitions, distinctions, or factual claims? What else do
you know that the author could have added? If you happen to think of a
factual claim you heard in your history class, say, that the three greatest mass murders of this century were all committed by governments
that didn't permit a loyal opposition, you can use that as contributory
information in your critique of the previous argument.

   Likewise, ask whether the author should subtract something, that
is, should eliminate some distinction or factual claim. Perhaps a term
should not have been defined in a particular manner. You already know
a lot that could be of critical assistance to the author, and even if you
agree, think of ways you could enhance the argument by suggesting that
the author remove something.

   If you're not persuaded and you know why, you're on your way. But
let's say that you just don't like the argument but don't know why. Take
a few minutes to think about it.

   Does it conflict with something you've experienced directly or
learned about? For example, you might just have come from a psychology class in which you've learned about the power of the unconscious.
You may be feeling uneasy because you're wondering how that information fits in with this argument that reasoning is the best way to per-

---

*A handy phrase for further defining.

suade. Use that "lack of fit" between your psychology class and the fore-going argument. Raise the unconscious as posing a difficulty for the argument.

To take another instance, you may be the parent of a two-year-old, and that experience may well be giving you grave doubts about reasoning as the best method of persuasion. That conflicting experience can be raised to challenge the author to take it into account, perhaps with a further distinction.

See? You can't lose, no matter what you think of an argument, and neither can the arguer who is willing to benefit from your critique.

Put Your Critique into Words   Here are some typical phrases to help you get started.

> **While I agree with Missimer's argument that** reason is the best method to persuade, **I think that the argument could have been stronger if** the author had:
>
> 1. **Defined** loyalty.
> 2. **Made a more careful distinction between** reason **and** force. After all, reason is a sort of force, isn't it? For instance, we speak of "the force of reason."
> 3. **Supported the argument. I disagree with Missimer's argument that** reason is the best method to persuade. The author **has not taken** the influence of the unconscious **into account.** Further, the author has **failed to distinguish between cases in which** adults have the time to reason with other adults, **and** those frequent instances when one person hasn't the luxury of reasoning with another, for instance when one has to deal quickly with people or when dealing with young children. Furthermore, Missimer has **created a false dichotomy between** reason and emotion.

Of course, you'd have to flesh out these comments with more examples, but you'd be well on your way to providing helpful criticism.

Agree to Disagree

Everyone has been stuck arguing in a circle with someone else: "Yes it is, no it isn't, *yes it is!*" It's clearly time to disengage. One way to back off would be, "Let's not discuss this any longer." That's better than getting into a fist fight, but it spells the death of communication on that subject. A better tack would be, "Let's agree to disagree until we get more information." Often people are disputing a fact, or a value judgment that hinges on a fact. Agreeing to disagree admits a sense of harmony and willingness on both sides to learn more and to resolve that dispute in the future.

SUMMARY

This chapter focused on three important concepts in critical thinking: definition, distinction, and argument.

1. The use and importance of "definition" and "distinction" were explicated: definition as an explanation of what is meant by a term; the importance of defining abstract terms; distinction as an explanation of some important difference within or between terms or ideas.
2. Two general uses to which critical thinkers put the term "argument" were discussed: argument in the loose sense of a "factual claim," a claim that something is true; argument in the strict sense of a "factual claim supported by a reason."

EXERCISES

1. Choose an appropriate critical thinking word or phrase from among those that appeared in **boldface type** throughout this chapter, and fill in the blanks. Try this example:

    James Thurber made an interesting remark. He _____ that "you might as well fall flat on your face as lean over too far forward."

    If you put in "argued" or "claimed," good! "Said" and "thought" are out for the time being, because you're supposed to choose from among words or phrases which appeared in **boldface type** in this chapter.

    Try these:
    a. In the course of his _____ , he defined "endurance" as the quality of withstanding hardship or stress.
    b. In his latest book, Byrne makes a careful _____ between "natural" in the sense of occurring in nature and "natural" in the sense of normal.
    c. In *The Open Society and Its Enemies,* Karl Popper _____ that "argument rarely settles a question, although it is the only means for learning—not to see clearly, but to see more clearly than before."[5]
2. Are the following arguments in the strict sense or the loose sense?
    a. He claimed that laughter could help cure illness.
    b. The doctor argued that babies start laughing when they're about ten weeks old and by four years of age children laugh about once every four minutes.
    c. She argued that laughter is beneficial, her reason being that when you laugh hard you stimulate the alertness hormone catecholamine.

   d. Nurses argue that because they spend more time with patients, they see the effects of humor on patients better than physicians do.
3. Consider making an argument that sports are violent. What terms would you have to define? What distinctions could you foresee needing to make? Do any analogous activities come to mind which would help you to make your argument?

READING

Sir Karl Popper's notion of the "rational unity of mankind" points, as he asserts, to our indebtedness to others for all we can possibly know or understand. These "others" are members of the community of thinkers, of which we're also part. The following selection is taken from a longer argument by Popper that persuasion by reason is best. As you read it, notice how carefully he crafts his definition of "reason." Don't be intimidated by this passage. Think (as always) about what you might contribute to the argument.

The conflict between rationalism and irrationalism has become the most important intellectual, and even moral, issue of our time. Since the terms "reason" and "rationalism" are vague, it will be necessary to explain roughly the way in which they are used here. First, they are used in a wide sense; they are used to cover not only intellectual activity but also observation and experiment . . . Secondly, I use the word "rationalism" in order to indicate, roughly, an attitude that seeks to solve as many problems as possible by an appeal to reason, i.e. to clear thought and experience, rather than by an appeal to emotions and passions. This explanation, of course, is not very satisfactory, since all terms such as "reason" and "passion" are vague; we do not possess "reason" or "passions" in the sense in which we possess certain physical organs, for example, brains or a heart, or in the sense in which we possess certain "faculties," for example, the power of speaking, or of gnashing our teeth. In order therefore to be a little more precise, it may be better to explain rationalism in terms of practical attitudes or behavior. We could then say that rationalism is an attitude to listen to critical arguments and to learn from experience. It is fundamentally an attitude of admitting that *"I may be wrong and you may be right, and by an effort, we may get nearer to the truth."* It is an attitude which does not lightly give up hope that by such means as argument and careful observations, people may reach some kind of agreement on many problems of importance; and that, even where their demands and their interests clash, it is often possible to argue about the various demands and proposals, and to reach—

perhaps by arbitration—a compromise which, because of its equity, is acceptable to most, if not to all. In short, the rationalist attitude, or, as I may perhaps label it, the "attitude of reasonableness," is very similar to the scientific attitude, to the belief that in the search for truth we need cooperation, and that, with the help of argument, we can in time attain something like objectivity. . . .

The fact that the rationalist attitude considers the argument rather than the person arguing is of far-reaching importance. It leads to the view that we must recognize everybody with whom we communicate as a potential source of argument and of reasonable information; it thus establishes what may be described as the "rational unity of mankind."[6]

Do you agree or disagree with Popper's argument? First reread "Put Your Critique into Words," above. Then write a paragraph in which you use some of these phrases to assess his argument.

NOTES

1. Blackie Sherrode, quoted in Andrew Tobias, *The Only Investment Guide You'll Ever Need* (New York: Bantam Books, 1983), p. 117.
2 Adapted from Robert Byrne, ed., *The 1,911 Best Things Anybody Ever Said* (New York: Ballantine Books, a division of Random House, Inc., 1988), p. 23.
3. *Ibid.*, p. 475.
4. *Ibid.*, p. 63.
5. Karl R. Popper, *The Open Society and Its Enemies* (Princeton, NJ: Princeton University Press, 1971), II, p. 227.
6. *Ibid.*, pp. 224–25.

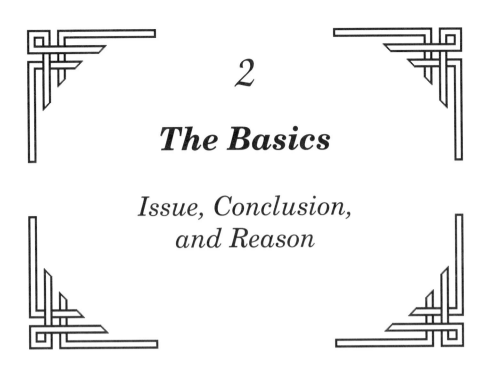

2

The Basics

Issue, Conclusion, and Reason

REASONS IN STRICT ARGUMENTS

To reiterate an important point made in Chapter 1, when critical thinkers hear a claim, the next move they make is to ask *why* they should believe that claim. For example:

> Claim: You should try to drive at or below 55 m p.h.
> Critical thinker's question: Why?
> Reason offered: Statistics show that there are fewer fatalities when people drive at or below this speed.

That is an argument in the strict sense. The claim is supported by a reason. It's the bare bones of a strict argument, and it's just one point of view on the subject. The reason may not even be true. But still, it is an argument. Here is "argue" as it appears in both loose and strict cases:

> Loose case: Fritz argued that you should try to drive at or below 55 m.p.h.
> Strict case: Martina argued that you should try not to drive over 55 m.p.h., **because** statistics show that when people drive at or below that speed, fewer deaths occur.

The *issue* Fritz is arguing is whether you should drive at or below 55 m.p.h. Fritz *concluded* that you should not drive over 55 m.p.h. He gave no reason for his claim. Therefore it is a loose argument, a claim without a reason.

Loose arguments are perfectly acceptable and are made all the time (for instance, right now!). You need only recognize them as such so that you can go on to ask whether they require supportive reasons. Most of the time they do.

Martina argued that you should try not to drive over 55 m.p.h., because statistics show that when people drive at or below that speed, fewer deaths occur.

The *issue* she argued is whether you should try not to drive over 55 m.p.h. She argued for the *conclusion* that you should try not to drive over 55 m.p.h. The *reason* that she gave in support of her conclusion *is that* statistics show that when people drive at or below 55 m.p.h., fewer deaths occur. A reason, be it that of Martina or anyone else, is a claim presented to defend or to justify a belief in a conclusion.

If the notions of issue, conclusion, and reason are still fuzzy, the rest of this chapter is calculated to set you straight. If, on the other hand, you feel confident about these features, skip to the exercises at the end of the chapter and try your skill.

FOR THE ISSUE, THINK "WHETHER"

A crucial ingredient in paying close attention to an argument is trying to figure out what question is being talked about. This is the issue, which permits alternative conclusions and is best approached by thinking "whether." The following are some common phrases:

> The author **deals with the issue whether**
> She **raised the question whether**
> The **issue under discussion is whether**

Everyone can find the issue in life and death matters. If someone were to walk into the room where you are now sitting and say, "Smoke is filling up the building," you would probably respond with something like, "What? Is there a fire?" You instantly seek out the significant question for you, namely, whether there is a fire and not just a hundred people smoking cigarettes, which may be the issue in the other person's mind. At the same time you are demanding to hear his conclusion ("Yes, there is a fire" or "No, there's no fire"). You thus make sure—before you run out of the building yelling—that you are not confusing your interpretation of the issue with the one the bearer of bad tidings has in mind. Better that both of you should run out of the building yelling!

It is in less than life and death matters that we should cultivate this same spirited interest. One very handy way of locating the issue is to say to yourself, "The issue is whether," and then fill in the ending with the author's or speaker's conclusion. Note that the issue is more precise than the topic, which is a word or phrase that is not in the form of a question. In the previous example the topic would be "smoke" or "smoky buildings," which is not helpful in arriving at any decision. In contrast, the issue you raised was whether there is a fire (another helpful issue might have been the factual question whether smoke was filling up the building).

Sometimes an author will come right out and tell us, "The question I'm going to address is whether abortion is right or wrong." Or, "at issue is whether there is better evidence for drinking coffee than tea." In other cases an author can rightly assume that we'll figure out what the issue is about without being told outright. When the argument is short, the presumption is that we can easily see what it's about; when the argument is long, say in a book or article, the issue is usually part of the title. Take for example, *Do Trees Have Standing?*, a clever title announcing the issue whether we have a moral obligation to forests. Whenever the argument is long and the issue is not part of the title, however, the author should come right out and say "**The issue is.**" Wherever the issue is found, in the title or in the body of the argument, it can always be found *embedded* in the conclusion, whether written or spoken. So it does not matter that you rarely find titles like *The Question whether Abortion Is Right or Wrong,* but titles like *Abortion: Scourge of Society* or *Abortion—Every Woman's Right.* Both of these titles state conclusions, which happen to be opposed to one another.

Let's look at some further examples of conclusions; then I can show you an easy way to get at the issue when it's not stated outright.

HOW TO FIND THE CONCLUSION

The conclusion is the *decision* that the thinker has made about an issue. Unlike the issue, the conclusion of an argument is usually stated outright. It is often preceded by words just meant to let us know that this claim is the conclusion, the main point the person has been driving at. When, near the end of the argument, the author says, "In conclusion," or "In sum," or "Therefore," it is tantamount to saying, "This is that major idea that I, the author or speaker, want you to believe." A conclusion word is almost mandatory in a good argument, if that argument is longer than a paragraph. The most popular word used to indicate a conclusion is "therefore." Other words that may show a conclusion are "in sum," and "so." Here is an example for each of them:

The weatherman said on the news this morning that it's going to rain today. In fact, when I walked outside I noticed that it was clouding up. **Therefore,** I'd better go back and get my umbrella.

The critical thinking instructor is notorious for giving tough quizzes. **So** I should spend all day Saturday studying.

The roof leaks, the floors are warped, the drains are clogged, the foundation is full of termites. **In sum,** this house needs a lot of work.

To get at the exact issue for these brief arguments, all you need do is substitute the word "whether" for the conclusion words.

Issue 1: **whether** I'd better go back and get my umbrella
Conclusion: Yes, I'd better go back and get my umbrella.
Issue 2: **whether** I'd better spend all day Saturday studying
Conclusion: Yes, I'd better.
Issue 3: **whether** this house needs a lot of work
Conclusion: Yes.

You can see by these examples how closely bound the issue and the conclusion are. Many people have a relatively easy time spotting conclusions, but it's harder for them to pull out the exact issue. This trick of exchanging the conclusion word for "whether" may help you to get started.

Perhaps you are wondering why you should bother pulling out issues when authors and people living their ordinary lives often don't. That's an excellent critical question! Look away from the book and think for a minute whether any of the claims made in Chapter 1 might relate to seeing arguments in a "whether" vein.

Any luck? How about the notion of "maybe . . . and maybe not"? If you still don't see the relationship, here is the argument for it:

One could argue that it is crucial for a critical thinker to start out by considering an argument in a balanced, "maybe . . . maybe not" stance. Digging the issue out of an argument brings alternative conclusions to the critical thinker's awareness. For instance, once a person becomes aware that an argument is about "**whether** I'd better spend all day Saturday studying," he or she is closer to the balanced start of "maybe I should study all day, but maybe I shouldn't," rather than being swayed too readily by the conclusion of the argument at hand to study all day. **Therefore,** extracting the issue from the argument is an important part of critical thinking.

Convinced? If not, you're welcome to take issue with the argument.

Conclusions at the Beginning

We're not out of the woods with conclusions yet. Conclusions almost always begin with words like "therefore" and "so" when they occur at the end of an argument. But were you aware that the conclusion of an argument often occurs right at the *start*? When it does, there is no telltale word. Imagine starting an essay with "therefore"! Here is a typical example of an argument that starts with its conclusion:

> Eating crackers in bed is a bad idea. First of all, you probably don't need the calories. Moreover, when you turn out the light and lie down, there are all these sharp crumbs which attack you. Then, you have to get up, stumble around in the dark, find the light switch, and either sweep them onto the floor—which is messy—or locate and use a whisk broom and dustpan—which is tedious.

The ideas which follow the opening sentence are all reasons supporting the conclusion that eating crackers in bed is a bad idea. One way to see whether the first statement of any argument is the conclusion is by putting it at the end of the argument, preceded by "therefore," and seeing if that makes sense:

> Eating crackers in bed is a bad idea. First of all, you probably don't need the calories. Moreover, when you turn out the light and lie down, there are all these sharp crumbs which attack you. Then, you have to get up, stumble around in the dark, find the light switch, and either sweep them onto the floor (messy) or get and use a whisk broom and dustpan (tedious). *Therefore, eating crackers in bed is a bad idea.*

And it fits the sense of the argument. Notice what happens if you try this "therefore" test with one of the earlier arguments:

> The weatherman said on the news this morning that it's going to rain today. In fact, when I walked outside I noticed that it was clouding up. I'd better go back and get my umbrella. *Therefore the weatherman said on the news this morning that it's going to rain.*

It doesn't make sense. The weatherman doesn't say it's going to rain because I'd better go and get my umbrella. Only a megalomaniac would think so. That first sentence isn't the conclusion of this argument.

Try your new techniques on Mario's argument, next. Find the sentence you believe to be the conclusion, "test" it if you need to by putting it at the end with "therefore," then see if you can pull out the issue using the term "whether":

> I really deserve to go to the movies tonight. I did several loads of wash (even studying while I was at the laundromat), went to class, and worked all afternoon. (Therefore, _____.)
>   Mario's conclusion is that _____.
>   His reason is that_____.
>   Mario's issue is whether _____.

The conclusion is almost always found at the very beginning or the end of an argument. In the clearest longer arguments it is found in both places.

VISUALIZE A STRUCTURE

Keep in mind that the basic structure of all arguments great and small is the same. The main issue is brought to a conclusion, with at least one reason to support that conclusion. This structure is really quite simple, and we're using it all the time (Figure 2-1).

The house is not a universal symbol for arguments, but it does provide a way to visualize them. Some form of schematization helps you to see the argument more clearly. This visual analogy is full of helpful figures of speech: A house is called a "structure"; we often refer to well-structured and well-supported arguments. Both houses and arguments can "collapse." It's not good for arguments or houses to "shift" without due notice. Finally, both need to "rest on solid ground."

But why visualize arguments as structures in the first place? If you can readily locate the structure when reading most arguments, by all means don't bother with the visualizations. However, novice critical thinkers are in the habit of seeing the claims in an argument as separate pieces of lumber lying about rather than as parts of a whole. Or they will read an argument the way one should read a story ("this was said, and then this, and then that"). They thus give each sentence equal importance and often fail to see that certain types of sentences are always going to be more important than others. To overcome this "line

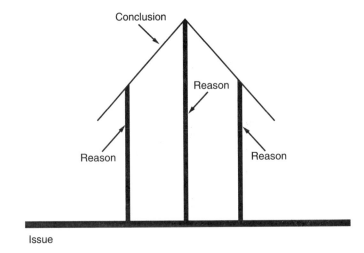

Figure 2-1   The Structure of an Argument

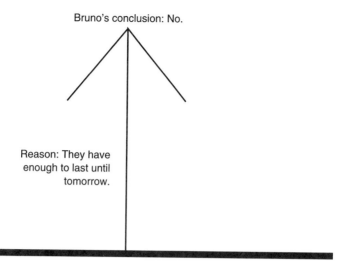

Issue: Whether Annie and Bruno need to buy food this afternoon.

Figure 2-2   Bruno's Argument

by line" habit, *think of yourself as always on a mission in search of the issue, conclusion, and reasons.* If you have to reconstruct the major features of an argument in a visual form, you will be forced to literally see the reasons supporting the conclusion, the way posts hold up the roof of a house.

Let's try this with some day-to-day examples:

Annie: Do we need to go to the market this afternoon?
Bruno: No.
Annie: Why not?
Bruno: We have enough food to last until tomorrow.

The visual structure of this discussion is shown in Figure 2-2; the verbal structure is as follows:

Annie: Do we need to buy food this afternoon? (*The issue* here is whether Annie and Bruno need to go to the market this afternoon.)
Bruno: No (*Bruno's conclusion*). We have enough food to last until tomorrow (*Bruno's reason* for claiming that they don't need to go to the market).

Annie raised the issue in this case, and Bruno made the argument. Let's continue the dialogue. Can you spot the issue, conclusion, and reason or reasons?

Bruno: Well, Annie, do you think we need to go to the market this afternoon?

Annie: No. I'd like to take you out to dinner tonight. Besides, we can always borrow whatever we want from the people next door.

Bruno raised the same issue, and Annie came to the same conclusion that he did (no, we don't need to go to the market); but Annie gave different reasons to support her conclusion. So Annie made a different argument:

Issue: Do Bruno and Annie need to buy food?
Annie's conclusion: No.
Annie's reasons: (1) She wants to take Bruno to dinner; (2) they can borrow whatever they need from the neighbors.

Figure 2-3 is a visual comparison of Annie's and Bruno's arguments. Notice that since the issue of the arguments is the same, the houses are both on the same "block." In fact, thinking of different arguments on a subject as being like different houses on a block isn't a bad way to imagine arguments.

Of course, arguing doesn't require two people. One can make an entire argument to oneself, as often happens. Ask yourself whether you need to go to the market today, make a decision (your conclusion), and notice your reasons for deciding the way you did:

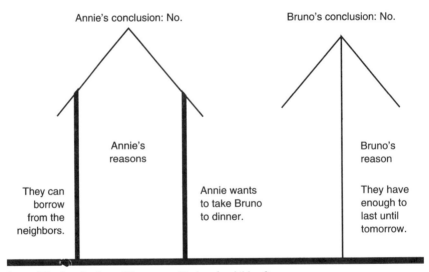

Figure 2-3   Annie's and Bruno's Arguments

Issue: Do I need to go to the market today?
Your conclusion: _____.
Your reason(s): _____.

Next, draw a structure to represent your argument.

If you live a simple life, your conclusion was probably a straightforward yes, or no, with one or two reasons. But what if you're not sure, or you think that maybe you'll need to go? Then "not sure" or "maybe" are your conclusions!

Here's an example of a person suffering through life's little aggravations. Hal is really not sure whether he should bother to go to the market, because he can't remember what's in his refrigerator. Then those are his conclusion and reason:

Hal's issue: Do I need to go to the market today?

Hal's conclusion: I'm not sure.

Hal's reason: I can't remember what's in my refrigerator.

People make literally thousands of arguments every day on the question of whether to go to the market. Here is an example of one of a myriad of "maybe" answers:

Agnes: Let's see . . . do I need to stop by the market today?

Agnes's conclusion: Maybe.

Agnes's reasons: If my brother has already gone to the market, then I don't need to go, because he will buy whatever we need. If he hasn't gone yet, then I do need to go.

Agnes has come to a "double" conclusion (maybe yes, maybe no); she has one reason for going and another for not going, but she needs to know an additional fact before making her final decision. What is that fact?

She needs to know whether her brother has gone to the market already. Her decision *hinges on that fact*. Agnes's needed fact can be visualized as a beam in the ceiling of the argument structure (see Figure 2-4). If you didn't find this fact on which both arguments hinged, don't worry about it. Examples of facts on which arguments hinge will be presented throughout the book. You'll have plenty of time to catch on.

DO THE REASONS MAKE SENSE AS REASONS?

It's easy to get careless and just slap down some statement as the reason because it could be a reason in some argument. That won't work here. You have to take a few minutes to think about whether that state-

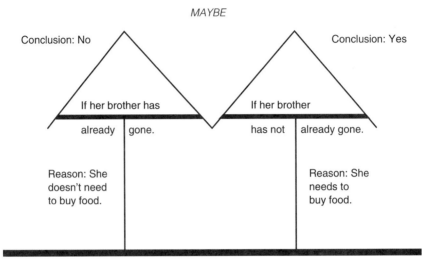

Issue: Whether Agnes needs to go to the market.

Figure 2-4   Agnes's Argument

ment you're writing down is the reason being offered *in the argument at hand.* Think of statements as analogous to pieces of lumber. Just as a board can be made a part of the wall or part of the ceiling, so a statement can be a reason or a conclusion. It depends on what the builder (arguer) decides to do with it.

You might want to say out loud, "The author concludes that . . . because," and see if what you've come up with makes any sense. If it doesn't, out of charity assume first that it may be your fault and look very carefully. Only then can you start wondering about the arguer's carefulness or sanity.

The following is an issue that most of us have to face. Al, the owner of a car 50,000 miles old, inspects the beloved object:

> Gee, I think I'd better get new tires for my car. With these threadbare tires I'm afraid I'll have a blowout on the freeway.

See if you can identify the issue, conclusion, and reason given by the car owner. Diagram the structure first, then analyze the language.

Al's issue is whether _____.
His conclusion is _____.
His reasons are that _____.

If you determined that the issue is whether Al should get new tires and his conclusion was yes; and if you wrote that his reason was that he's afraid that with his threadbare tires he'll have a blowout on the freeway, you've done well. If you decided that he gave two reasons, that his tires were threadbare and that he was afraid that he'd have a blowout, that's even better. But if you got it wrong, let's figure out how you can avoid the mistake in the future.

What, for example, if you had this:

> Al's issue: Whether with his threadbare tires he'll have a blowout on the freeway.
> Al's conclusion: Yes.
> Al's reason is that he thinks he'd better get new tires for his car.

Would Al have a blowout because he thinks he'd better get new tires? That would be a cosmic injustice to careful car owners; that's not Al's reasoning. You have to spend a couple of minutes pondering whether the reason makes sense. Say to yourself "Is that *really* the reason?" Most people who misidentify the reason just haven't stopped long enough to think it through.

BOOK TITLES AS CONCLUSIONS

Book titles offer the first clues about what a book will argue. The title of a book or article may give just the general topic, as opposed to specifying an issue within that topic. Let's inspect a few topic titles. Take, for example, a book entitled *Execution*. Notice that the issue is not clear: Is it a book about the incidence of execution, its rightfulness or wrongfulness, an evaluation of state-approved or gangland-style, or some bizarre how-to book? We'd have to look at the table of contents to see. Other topic titles: *On History, The Germans*. Here again, while the titles tell us the overall topic, we have no idea what the authors are concluding about history or about the Germans. For a precise issue, we must dig out an author's main conclusion and then place "whether" in front. In a well-written book, we need not dig deeply.

Often the title of a book or article contains the author's overall conclusion. When you pull the issues out of these title-conclusions it helps you to see that conclusions other than the ones the authors suggest are quite possible. Consider these examples: *You Can't Spoil Your Baby; I'm O.K.—You're O.K.; India: A Wounded Civilization; The Disappearance of Childhood; Winning Through Intimidation;* or *The Criminal as Victim.*

In these cases we know what the authors have concluded, but not why they have done so. From the last title we can infer that the author has concluded that the criminal is a victim, whereby we can helpfully turn this around to the issue of whether the criminal is a victim. But we don't yet know the author's argument. Why is the criminal a victim?

Will the argument be that it's because of the criminal's environment or genetic makeup or some other cause? The answer to that question will have to come as a result of browsing through the book or reading it.

WRITING ABOUT SEVERAL RELATED ISSUES

We will deal at length with complex arguments in Chapter 9, but start to familiarize yourself with the following phrases for the main issue:

> **The central question** that must now be asked is . . .
> In my opinion, **the foremost issue is** . . .
> The **fundamental problem** that we must first solve is . . .

Once the main issue has been discussed, the reader must somehow be alerted that a second issue is going to be raised. For the issue that's second in importance (or for the one that is dealt with next), a paragraph could begin with the following:

> There is **a second problem.**
> **Subordinate to** this **main issue is the question whether** . . .

Each time the issue changes, the reader should be alerted:

> There is still **a third difficulty.**
> Of **further** importance is the **question whether** . . .

SOME DISTINCTIONS

Arguments involve decisions of two sorts: what to do and what to think. The examples in this chapter have been about what to do in day-to-day life. The arguments which follow are all of the other sort, dealing with what to think. Obviously, there is considerable overlap between what one does and what one thinks, but the general distinction is useful. Some students will have more trouble with arguments about what to think. If you are one of them, review the first part of this chapter, keeping in mind that the structure is the same in both types of argument.

Another distinction regarding arguments is between those that make claims about what *is* the case and those that make claims about what *should be* the case. While there are a few examples of purely factual or purely directive arguments, much argumentation that at first seems purely factual is actually directive as well. Does this chapter, for example, argue (in the loose sense) about what the basic features of formal argument are, or does it direct you on what they should be? Both, actually.

SUMMARY

There are three basic features of argumentation in the strict sense: An issue is brought to a conclusion with the support of at least one reason. These basic features may appear anywhere in an argument. Therefore the critical thinker must actively seek them out by asking questions.

What is the author trying to have me think or do? That is, what is the author's conclusion? Tip-off terms may occur at the end of the paragraph: "therefore," "in conclusion," "to summarize." If not, the conclusion may well be at the beginning.

What is the exact issue? Try replacing the "therefore" word with "whether."

What are the reasons? If the word "reason" doesn't appear, look for "because"; whatever occurs after that word is a reason. See if it makes sense as a reason that supports the conclusion.

If you can't find these telltale terms, and you know that the author is driving home a point, see if any of these synonyms is doing the work:

Therefore	**Because**
in short	since
so	for (before a clause)
it follows that	for the reason that
it is believed that	the source is
shows that	
indicates that	
proves that	
we may conclude that	
necessitates	

Don't forget to check for the conclusion at the beginning.

EXERCISES

1. The following are brief arguments about human nature expressed clearly and cleverly. Whether you agree or disagree, you might become intrigued by them.

   a. People often think they are in love when they are not: The excitement of an intrigue, the emotional flutter of gallantry, natural delight in being loved, and the difficulty of saying no, all these conspire to persuade them that they are feeling passionate when they are merely being flirtatious.[1]

(1). Diagram the structure.

(2). Analyze the language.

The issue here is whether _____.

The author concludes that _____.

His reasons for making this argument are _____

_____.

The issue is whether people often wrongly think they are in love. **The author concludes that this is the case. His reasons are that** people confuse the excitement of an intrigue, the emotional flutter of gallantry, natural delight in being loved, and the difficulty of saying no for being in love (feeling passionate).

The language of your analysis doubtless varied somewhat from that above. Don't be concerned, as long as you have stated your answers in complete, grammatical sentences and have used "issue," "reason," and "conclusion" for the correct ideas. Study the phrasing that is in boldface, however. Repeat it a number of times, and think about copying it in your essays to expand your repertoire of critical thinking phrases. You might even copy the language used in the foregoing example when writing out the exercise which follows.

b. People hate injustice, not because it is inherently wrong, but because of the harm it does them.[2]

(1). Diagram the structure.

(2). Analyze the language. Provide a description of the basics, being careful to use the language of argument exemplified in boldface type. When you give the reason, be sure to say, "The reason is **that**." Never write, "The reason is because"; it is redundant.

It would be all right to ignore the statement, "It [injustice] is inherently wrong." You could also draw a falling wall-beam (a negation symbol is printed over it) to indicate that the author alleges that it is *not* the reason that people hate injustice (see Figure 2-5).

Just be certain that you did not put down, "Injustice is inherently wrong" as the *author's* reason, even though it might be your reason and might be true. One of the most important tasks is to separate your opinion from that of the person who is presenting an argument.

c. One of the most important things you must do as a critical

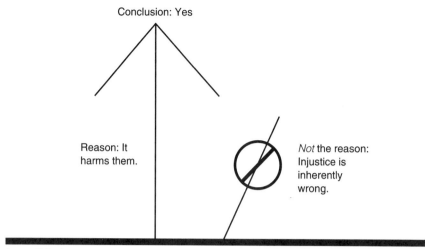

Figure 2-5   IDentify What is not the Author's Reason

thinker is to be aware of how your opinion differs from that of the person who is presenting you an argument. Otherwise, you will not learn this new opinion.

(1). Diagram the structure.

(2). Analyze the language.

The writer proposes the issue whether one of the most important things that you must do as a critical thinker is to distinguish your opinion from that of the person who is presenting an argument, **concluding that** this is the case, and **giving the reason that** otherwise you will not learn this new opinion. Notice that even though the reason contains a "not," it still is the author's reason, unlike the "injustice" example before it, in which the author was telling something that was *not* his reason.

Rule: If the word "not" goes in front of the word "because" or "reason," then it's not the reason. Otherwise, it is the reason. For example: He rewrote his essay not because he had to, but because he did not want to turn in shoddy work ("because he did not want to turn in shoddy work" being the reason argued).

Mull over this distinction until it makes sense to you.

d. When we have grown tired of loving, we are delighted at the other's unfaithfulness, for that releases us from having to be faithful.[3]

Hint: Watch the issue. Don't make it broader than the arguer does.

(1). Diagram the structure.

(2). Analyze the language.

The issue under discussion is whether we are delighted at the other's unfaithfulness when we have grown tired of loving. **The author concludes in the affirmative, reasoning that** it releases us from having to be faithful. Your statement of the author's issue must include "when we have grown tired of loving." Otherwise you are stating that the author is claiming that we generally delight in others' unfaithfulness to us. The author has, however, **qualified his statement.**

2. You're on your own! Identify the issue, reason, and conclusion, using the pictorial structure if it helps.

   a. We should not take offense when people hide the truth from us, since so often we hide it from ourselves.[4]

     (1). Diagram the structure.

     (2). Analyze the language.

     The issue at hand is whether _____.

     The author concludes that _____.

     The reason offered is that _____.

   b. Little is needed to make a wise man happy, but nothing can content a fool. That is why nearly all men are miserable.[5]

   c. I don't trust him. We're friends.[6]

     Is this last example a strict argument or just two factual claims side by side? Why?

3. Which of the following are loose arguments; which are strict?

   a. I saw him tiptoe across the lawn and steal softly into the house. It was broad daylight.

   b. Since I'm not in the business of giving advice, I refused to tell him which career to choose.

   c. When the stock market is down, buy more stock. When it's up, sell.

   d. Thinking about how to spend your time most efficiently is of vital importance.

   e. Thinking about how to spend your time most efficiently is of vital importance, because that's the only way you'll accomplish your major goals in life.

Answers: a. two loose arguments (just two claims, one not the reason for the other); b. strict argument; c. two loose arguments; d. loose argument; e. strict argument

4. What are the issue, conclusion, and reason(s) in the following two arguments?

1

Should there be a law requiring motorcyclists to wear helmets? Many motorcyclists would argue "No." They object to a helmet law because the helmet reduces peripheral vision and hearing acuity. Another reason is that helmets interfere with the freedom of being completely exposed to the elements.

2

Motorcycle accidents cause more than four thousand deaths and tens of thousands of brain injuries each year in the United States. In California alone $60 million to $100 million is taken from the public purse each year to pay medical bills of riders injured while they were not wearing helmets. So while some motorcyclists say "Let those who ride decide," I would argue that "Those who pay should have the final say," a helmet law.

READINGS

1. *Should we consider the welfare (interests) of animals as equal to that of humans? While admitting that "this suggestion may at first seem bizarre," Peter Singer makes a persuasive argument. What is his basic argument?*

The capacity for suffering and enjoying things is a prerequisite to having interests at all, a condition that must be satisfied before we can speak of interests in any meaningful way. It would be nonsense to say that it was not in the interests of a stone to be kicked along the road by a schoolboy. A stone does not have interests because it cannot suffer. Nothing that we can do to it could possibly make any difference to its welfare. A mouse, on the other hand, does have an interest in not being tormented, because it will suffer if it is.

If a being suffers, there can be no moral justification for refusing to take that suffering into consideration. No matter what the nature of the being, the principle of equality requires that its suffering be counted equally with the like suffering—insofar as rough comparisons can be made—of any other being. . . .

Racists violate the principle of equality by giving greater weight to the interests of members of their own race when there is a clash between their interests and the interests of those of another race. White racists do not accept that pain is as bad when it is felt by blacks as when it is felt by whites. Similarly, those I would call "specieists" give greater weight to the interests of members of their own species where there is a clash between their interests and the interests of those of other species. Human specieists do not accept that pain is as bad when it is felt by pigs or mice as when it is felt by humans.

That, then, is really the whole of the argument for extending the principle of equality to nonhuman animals.[7]

> *Analyze Singer's argument:*
> *Singer raises the issue whether* _____ .
> *He argues (concludes) that* _____ .
> *because* _____ .

2. *Philosopher Paul Weiss became curious about the deep love many people feel for sports. The book* Sport: A Philosophic Inquiry *was the result. Keep the following in mind as you read this excerpt from Weiss's book:*

   a. *Two of these paragraphs entail almost all factual claims; the third contains an argument. Which is which?*

   b. *One way to deal with a lot of closely related questions is to summarize them into one "umbrella" question.*

   c. *Look for the conclusion and then work backwards (a good ploy most of the time).*

Athletes usually submit themselves, often with enthusiasm, rarely with reluctance, to long periods of training. They do not seem to mind having to engage repeatedly in dull exercises and tedious practice sessions. Nor do they seem to take amiss the need to control their appetites, even those that are imperious and insistent. Willingly, athletes sacrifice opportunities to be lax, give up occasions to be irresponsible, and put aside a desire simply to enjoy themselves. At times they risk injury, and in some cases death. Fatigue is a familiar. Sooner or later every one of them comes to know . . . defeat, and perhaps humiliation. [The athlete's] days are numbered, successes rarely momentous, and glories short-lived; [one] works hard and long to prepare . . . for what may end in dismal failure. Why?

Why are athletes ready to give up so much that is desirable to accept what involves a good deal of wasted motion and boredom? Why are they willing to risk making their inadequacies evident, instead of enjoying the struggle of others from afar, or instead of plunging into a game without concern for how they might fare? Why do they subject themselves to the demands of a severe disciplining? Why are they so ready to practice selfdenial or to sacrifice their interest in other pursuits to prepare themselves for what may prove disastrous? Why are they so prone to accept advice, often from [others] not nearly so competent as they themselves are? Strong, with more than the normal amount of pride and impulsiveness, why do they docilely listen to criticism which is not infrequently phrased in brutal or scathing terms?

These questions are not often asked. But unless they are, we will not learn what it is that the athlete wants or . . . should get. The answer that I think should be accepted—[is that] sport attracts because it offers a superb occasion for enabling young [people] to be perfected . . . to have fine functioning bodies and thereby reveal [one dimension of what humans] can be and do. . . . [8]

Analyze Weiss's argument.

NOTES

1. LaRochefoucauld, *Maxims,* trans. Leonard Tancock (New York: Penguin Books, 1981), p. 74.
2. *Ibid.,* p. 117.
3. *Ibid.*
4. *Ibid.,* p. 105.
5. *Ibid.,* p. 108.
6. Bertolt Brecht, quoted in Robert Byrne, ed., *The 1,911 Best Things Anybody Ever Said* (New York: Ballantine Books, a division of Random House, Inc., 1988).
7. Peter Singer, *Practical Ethics.* Second Edition (New York: Cambridge University Press, 1993), pp. 57–58.
8. Paul Weiss, *Sport: A Philosophic Inquiry* (n.p.: Southern Illinois University Press, 1969), pp. 18–19.

3

How to Create Alternative Arguments

The basic structure of argument consists of issue, conclusion, and reasons—three of the twelve basics. You have also been alerted to a fourth fundamental feature, distinction. That leaves eight. At this point, there is no "correct" next move. Having discovered the three basics in any argument, you could proceed to consider any of the remaining features next. You might, for example, immediately proceed to generate alternative arguments (Figure 3-1); or you might pursue one of the other areas of argument shown in Figure 3-2. These will be thoroughly discussed in chapters 4 through 7.

Alternative arguments are presented next because they give you a lot to work with. The novice critical thinker, when faced with an argument to critique, often worries, "I can't think of anything to say." In a few weeks you will suffer from the opposite problem, wondering which of many approaches to take.

Most important, alternative arguments broaden your perspective on the issue to a greater extent than the other remaining tools. Ultimately you will come to see how **critical thinking is consideration of alternative arguments in light of their evidence.**

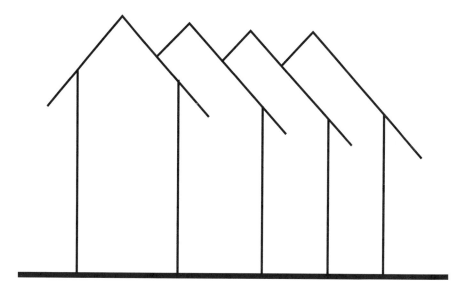

Figure 3-1   Generating Alternative Arguments

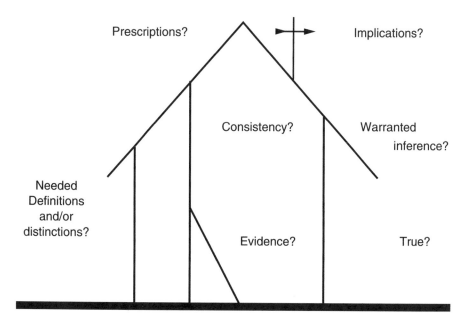

Figure 3-2   Areas of Argument

QUICK STARTS

Quick Start 1

The easiest way to get a second argument on an issue is to *oppose the conclusion* of the first and support that opposite conclusion with a reason:

> First argument: Students shouldn't underline in their textbooks, because they can sell them back to the bookstore for more money when the books have no writing in them.
>
> Second argument (oppose conclusion of first and back up with a reason): Students should underline in their textbooks, because doing so will help them to get better grades.
>
> Now you try. Think up a strict argument, then oppose it.

Quick Start 2

Another easy way to come up with a second argument is to *oppose the conclusion and oppose a reason* or reasons offered by the first:

> First argument: Students shouldn't underline in their textbooks, because they can sell them back to the bookstore for more money when the books have no writing in them.
>
> Second argument (oppose first conclusion and its reason): Students should underline in their textbooks, because once they've written their names in them, the bookstore buys them back at the same used price whether the students underline in them or not.

If the reasons for the foregoing arguments are true, questions still remain. For instance, we're still faced with the question whether students should write their names in their textbooks. But the issue has expanded, and the argument is making progress.

It would mean even more progress if the arguments could "speak directly to one another." Here, for instance, if underlining tends to help students get better grades (but how much better), should students go for better grades over a bigger refund (but how big is the refund)? We need to engage these arguments directly with one another to make the most enlightened decision about underlining textbooks. In the next two sections you'll see how to get arguments directly engaged in this way.

FACTORS FOR, FACTORS AGAINST

Say that someone argues that grades should be abolished because they create bad feelings in students who get poor marks. If a school were seriously considering eliminating grades, then students, school administra-

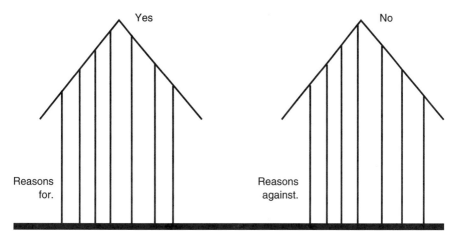

Issue: Whether grades should be abolished.

Figure 3-3 Generating Reasons

tors, teachers, and even businesses would have to consider a great many factors before being in favor of it. Brainstorm for a few minutes, listing as many factors as you can in favor of abolishing grades, and then do the same against the idea. Don't forget to include favorable and unfavorable factors from the point of view of nonstudents. For the moment, put down everything you can think of, no matter how zany it sounds.

In thinking up these factors, you will be generating *reasons* which you could use in arguments for and against grades (see Figure 3-3).

Now do the same for underlining in textbooks.

Winnow Out the Strongest Reasons

Do not censor yourself in coming up with factors, because sometimes a wild idea can lead you by association to a very good idea. In fact, sometimes the wild idea, upon further reflection, *is* a good idea. Many ideas considered nonsense in one century become common sense in the next.*

To prevent an argument from becoming unwieldy, it is best to reduce both sets of factors to the two or three strongest, most convincing reasons, in your opinion. If your wilder idea happens to convince you, by all means use it, and make it a convincing reason for others.

---

*Instances of ideas which when propounded seemed outlandish to most, but later drew millions of adherents: Christianity, Marxism, Einstein's theory of relativity (a wild idea winning general acceptance within twenty years, rather than a hundred); Freudian notions of the unconscious, neurosis, and repression; equality of the sexes.

ENGULF AND DEVOUR

Here is a wonderful three-part technique for developing a sophisticated argument. Its "point, counterpoint, point" structure really engages opposing arguments:

1. Strongest Reasons For   First, you make the strongest case you can for some position. First argue for, say, the importance of grades (or of an athletics requirement or capital punishment), offering your strongest reasons in support of this position.

2. Strongest Reasons Against   Then you argue against grades, offering the strongest reasons you can to abolish grades (athletics requirement, capital punishment).

3. Engulf and Devour the Second Argument   Taking the first position again, you argue that **even granting** the truth of the reasons offered in this second argument, say, against grades, the argument for grades is stronger because . . .

"Engulf and devour" is a very powerful form of argumentation because the arguer acknowledges the opposing point of view at its best and goes on to show how the first argument is still better. The following argument in favor of brainstorming illustrates "engulf and devour."

> Strongest reasons for: One of the best ways to get critical material is to play around with an argument, generating as many factors favorable or unfavorable to it as one can. Generating factors also helps the critical thinker to consider an issue in broad perspective, from many angles.
>
> Strongest reasons against: **On the other hand, one could argue that** this method of generating arguments is inadvisable because it is dishonest. The honest approach would be to gather evidence before ever entertaining a factor as part of an argument.
>
> Engulf and devour the second argument: **Yet even granting that** honesty in making arguments is necessary, it is possible to be honest and still to generate playfully as much of an argument as possible. One remains honest throughout this endeavor by realizing that the ideas so generated are exploratory, not final. And it is arguable that surveying the whole landscape of factors, rather than limiting oneself to an immediately demonstrable few, will result in a fuller and, therefore, more honest argument. **Moreover, accepting that the second argument offered that** evidence plays a vital role in finally deciding whether a factor is a strong reason for accepting an argument, **the fact remains that** most critical thinkers, scientists included, advance by making an imaginative leap beyond the evidence at hand and then looking to see if evidence exists in support of the new idea. In sum, with arguments as well as in many areas of life, it is better to leap before you look.

You can see that this three-part argument is a lot stronger than the first part of the argument alone.

One final note: Engulf and devour is a two-way treat. Someone might come along saying " **even granting all that has been said** about leaping before one looks, **still,** careful investigation should precede all argumentation **because,** " thus engulfing and devouring this example whole!

If It's Better, Accept It

If in the course of making a strong opposing argument, the arguer becomes convinced of the opposing argument, the arguer has learned something. There should be no shame in that, only in obtusely refusing to budge from one's original position in the teeth of better reasons. (See Chapter 10 for a distinction between deliberation, which allows you to gracefully embrace the opposite argument, and debate, which prohibits you from accepting the opposite argument under pain of "losing the debate.")

If you are in the middle of writing a paper and convince yourself of the opposite argument, just switch the placement of the argument and counterargument, enabling whichever position can engulf and devour to do so.

Of course, that second argument may persuade you intellectually while making you uneasy emotionally. Remember that in the interests of balance you can accept an argument provisionally—no cost, no obligation to act on it today.

A SIGNIFICANT EXCEPTION

In some cases one argument can engulf another, but many times this is not possible. You can't in conscience grant the truth of all of the reasons in an opposing argument. So engulfing is out. The next best approach is to try to think up the *strongest possible reason against* the argument. Again, generate a number of factors against a position and then winnow out the one or two most likely to change the opinion of a person who believed the position.

Take the issue of grade abolition. Say that someone has presented two strong factors in favor of abolition: (1) that many people would actually try harder, no longer feeling incompetent because of bad grades, and (2) that everyone would work for the correct reason, that is, the value of learning, rather than for an extrinsic reward.

Now, what is the strongest reason that can come up against those reasons? Another way of putting it is to ask, "What is the main reason that grades exist?" You may have thought of a better answer, but one answer is that grades are supposed to let both the individual and society (employers, graduate schools, etc.) know what level of skill an individual has attained in a given subject. This is, then, a factor in favor of grades. In countering the argument against grades, one could say:

> **However, in arguing that** grades should be abolished, the author **has failed to take the problem of** standards of preparedness **into account.**

or

> **The proponents of** grade abolition **must address the difficult necessity of** distinguishing those who are skilled from those who are not skilled in a subject.

Tactfully raising these important problems for the arguer is doing the arguer a great favor.

COUNTEREXAMPLE

This tack, of coming up with one significant exception, works especially well on arguments that at first seem so airtight as to be inevitable. Consider this argument about boredom:

> It's plain that boredom results from outside stimuli which are dull, repetitious, or tedious. People become bored because they are in such an environment.

Who could fight that argument? We've all been in such situations, and it's obvious that people get bored because they're in boring situations. But wait—just fool around trying to remember whether you've been in situations where boredom can't have occurred because of dull, outside stimuli. Rack your brain for a few minutes. Any ideas? If not, here's one approach. Think of any situations in which one person has been bored and another hasn't? We're searching for any exceptions to the claim that boredom has to come from dull, outside stimuli. Any situation in which some people get bored and others don't can be used to argue against the position that boring situations are just "out there" in the same way that boiling water is "out there" on the stove.
    If you can think up such an exceptional case, you can use it to back up your counterargument:

> **On the contrary, one could argue that** boredom **does not result** from outside stimuli which are dull, repetitious, or tedious. **For instance, ____.**

For instance, there are many people who would find a lecture on thermodynamics boring, while others would find it quite interesting.

Finding such exceptions can be a revelation. If you have always believed that a boring situation came from the outside world, attacked, and bored you, then you should now feel puzzled, wondering just how people do get bored. That puzzlement is good. It will lead you to deepen your awareness on the subject.

FALSE OR INSUFFICIENT REASONS

The first argument's reasons may be false, or they may be true but too flimsy to support the conclusion. Either of these factors is ruinous to an argument. Each will be dealt with at length: truth of reasons in Chapter 5 and strength of reasons in Chapters 4, 5, 11, and 12.

Examples of language used to criticize reasons:

> **It has been claimed that** the abolition of grades would result in greater efforts on the part of many students. **This argument does not hold because its reason is simply untrue. It is not the case that** students would try harder; if anything, a lot of students would stop trying entirely.

Taking the first argument's reasons head-on is a favored strategy when you are alone and trying to decide whether to accept an argument. It's easy to run the reasons through one's experience and past reasoning on the issue, coming to a decision. But accusing reasons of being false or flimsy is the least-favored method when arguing with someone else. The reason is due to the complexity of the human mind. Take the example of grades. The person who is convinced that grades should be abolished is probably already convinced of a lot of other things as well, perhaps that people are basically intellectually curious and that the carrot of academic enjoyment is better than the stick of bad grades. These other, deeper convictions beneath the argument at hand are called assumptions and are discussed in Chapter 6. A person's reasons for accepting an argument are normally much more complicated than the argument at hand would lead one to believe. In addition, people like what they believe, and feel a personal stake in it.

The complexity of human reason and the commitment to belief are two reasons why "engulf and devour" is such a powerful argumentative tool. When it can be used, it leaves all the apparatus of the person's beliefs intact, while enlarging them.*

---

*Big factor and significant exception also tend to enlarge the perspective of the other side, although not to as great an extent.

TIME OUT FOR FACT-FINDING
OR EXPERIMENTATION

You probably realized while reading the example of grade abolition that you had no statistics that would help you to decide whether, in fact, abolishing grades would help students to work harder or not. You doubtless have your suspicions about the matter, but if you're arguing with someone of opposite suspicions, you're stuck.

One approach would be to suggest researching for past or present cases in which schools have abolished grades:

> **The author has argued that** the elimination of grades will improve student efforts. **If we are to seriously entertain this possibility, thorough research** of the effect of grade abolition on other schools similar to ours **must be undertaken.**

or

> **More facts must be gathered on the question whether** to abolish grades **before it can be decided.**

When past and present cases cannot be found, an arguer can call for experimentation. Consider these examples:

> **Only experimentation will decide the question whether** searching students on high school campuses for weapons will reduce the incidence of violence.
>
> At the moment, the answer remains controversial. **It might be resolved by further experimentation.**

Notice that the second writer has decided to be more cautious about the role experimentation will play in deciding the issue at hand.

BALANCE AND BELIEF

If you happen to agree with an argument, it's going to sound terrific. If you violently disagree, an argument will sound like it's full of holes and just terrible. Both of these tendencies are hard on balance, and mean that everyone has to work to be tougher on arguments with which they already agree, more tender with those they initially feel opposed to. This may seem obvious, but it often gets lost in the flush of argument.

Don't infer that openness to counterarguments means to accept all arguments as equal. That would lead to *relativism,* the view that there is no ultimate truth. Openness to counterarguments is meant to defend against a different danger, that of *dogmatism,* the belief that one already has all the truth to be known on a subject. Dogmatism is the refusal to entertain a different point of view.

There is an intermediate, balanced view which has aided material as well as social progress—*progressivism*. It holds that the truth is real and that, thanks to the community of thinkers, we're getting closer to it on many issues. At the heart of progressivism is a willingness always to entertain counterarguments, even on positions on which near-certainty is felt.

The distinction among these three beliefs is crucial. As Figure 3-4 indicates, relativism makes fresh information to be of little consequence, and dogmatism locks it out.

Obviously, you do not have to agree.

I can't think of any alternatives beyond these three positions, but can you?

LOGOPHOBIA: THE FEAR OF ARGUING

If you slink away from an argument, it's often from fear that the conclusion is true. If that conclusion is right, you may feel that it could do violence to one or more of your deeply felt beliefs—and therefore violence could be done to you! So in a sheer panic of self-protection, you retreat.

Now, one can remain in permanent retreat or make a comeback—that is, get back into balance—either to make a counterargument or to defer making one. Let's make the case for the comeback. You may have noticed that the foregoing paragraph was an argument in favor of retreating. Imagine a second "you" talking to the "you" crouching in a corner:

> Look, you really should face up to this argument. No matter what happens, you stand to win, whether you become convinced by the argument or not.
>
> Say that you give the argument your most sincere efforts but aren't convinced. Chances are that you've seen flaws in it that will help you to find more points to make your original belief even stronger. So by looking at a counterargument you have enriched your original argument.
>
> On the other hand, assume that after giving the argument your sincerest efforts you find that you do become persuaded by that argument. You can easily define your experience as one of *changing* your beliefs as if having had violence done to your old belief. After all, the old belief isn't dead—as long as you leave yourself open to persuasion, you can take back your old belief any time you decide that it is more convincing to you.
>
> And just as violence is not really done to the belief, violence is not really done to you. It just seems that violence is going to be done to you, because you are experiencing fear that such a big belief change will turn you into an unknown quantity, maybe even cause you to lose your identity. It's true that your beliefs are an important part of you, but you are, in fact, more

Progressivism: The truth is real,
and we're on a
never-ending journey
towards it.

Dogmatism: The belief
that one has already
arrived at the truth and can
rest, complacently asserting
that no differing view
matters.

Relativism: The belief
that there is no ultimate
truth—only a random
wandering from one
position to another.

Figure 3-4   Three Beliefs

than the sum of your beliefs; you are a reasoning, feeling, many-faceted human being. And rather than the new belief having a power of its own that changes you, you, in fact, have been in charge all along, changing your belief! However, if you continue to hide over there, not making an informed choice between the belief you have and this one, you can hardly consider yourself in charge.

Remember, too, that you can always accept an argument *provisionally*— in fact you should. You can think, "I can't beat that argument at the moment, so I'll accept it for the time being. But I'm still uneasy with it, so I certainly won't act on it yet. But now I'm fascinated, so I will definitely keep thinking about it, and look for arguments others have made on the issue." Temporary acceptance pending further thought will not force you out into the street to act on that belief.

Welcome All Comers

If we can acquire the habit of seeing arguments as opportunities to acquire wisdom, with no possibility of "losing" an argument since we always "win" insight, it will be easy to cultivate a spirit of welcome for any ideas. Then no argument need scare us off—at least not for long. Or would you like to make the opposite argument? All you have to do is to turn the conclusion around, claiming "No, there are some positions that should never even be considered. My reason(s) for saying this are that _____. For instance (strongest exception), _____.

A Horrifying Issue

What assertion could we practice on that would displease nearly everyone? How about the argument that torture is right under certain circumstances? The most offensive argument on the subject would probably be that we should be constantly torturing one another. But one couldn't construct a good foundation for that conclusion. I'll make do by arguing that torture under a few circumstances is right. Note that this argument is as persuasive as possible because the **strongest case** has been taken.

Torture is not only right but a positive obligation in certain very limited circumstances. By "torture" I mean the willful infliction of physical pain on another, unwilling person.	*delimit scope of argument definition*
The decison to torture another person is a grievous one. I would rule out almost all cases of torture as inhumane and therefore highly immoral. Yet consider this frightening scenario: A man has hidden a plutonium bomb somewhere in New York City. When captured, the man claims that the bomb	*emphasize limited acceptability*
	strongest case: death to millions over pain to one

will go off in half an hour, that all New
Yorkers deserve to die, and that he will
not tell where the bomb is.

With millions of lives at stake, the   *strongest case:*
police sergeant surely has the right to   *recommend least pain*
apply a bit of pressure, perhaps start-   *necessary*
ing with the delicate fold of skin
between the man's thumb and index
finger and increasing the man's pain
until he reveals the bomb's location.

In fact, torture of this man will have   *strongest case,* even for
the effect of saving his life as well as   man tortured!
the lives the millions held in jeopardy.
But consider this statement: "The right
of one person to be free of pain is
greater than the right of millions, even
if that one person would take the lives
of those millions of people." Doesn't
that sound wrong? The right of many
people to live is in fact greater than the
right of one person to be temporarily
free of pain, especially if that one person has put the millions in jeopardy.

By "strongest case" you should recognize the significant exception,
the most persuasive example that you can imagine. Then to respond to
the argument, you might keep that strongest case in mind and generate
an argument "engulfing and devouring"—claiming why, even in that
strongest case, torture would still be wrong. For example,

> Don't accept even this compelling case. Once torture is permitted, where
> will the line be drawn? Should we torture one person who even *says* she's
> got a plutonium bomb and will hurt three people with it?

See? A strong case in the opposite direction.

Use Uneasiness to Generate Alternatixves

If you dislike both the argument and the counterargument, use that dislike to propel yourself into creating alternative ways of dealing with an
issue. In the case of a terrorist with a bomb, aren't the alternatives quite
limited? Perhaps, but it would be better to assume that the alternatives
are unlimited. Otherwise we wouldn't bother to think up alternatives,
possibly missing some very important solutions to our problems. For
example, consider how the Dutch have dealt with the terrorism that
plagued their country several years ago. The terrorists were a few of the

Moluccan immigrants to Holland from their islands near Indonesia. They wanted independence for their islands, which were once under Dutch rule but overtaken by Indonesia in the 1950s. In the late 1970s the Dutch Moluccans hijacked trains and executed a number of people until the government came up with a unique alternative. Why not send some Moluccans back to visit their islands? First, they would see that their quarrel was with Indonesia, not Holland. Second, life in Holland compares very favorably with life in the Moluccas, so they would not even want to go back to live in the Moluccas. The Dutch paid the fare for perhaps 10 percent of the 40,000 Moluccans living in Holland. The terrorism has stopped.[1]

Obviously, this won't work in a number of other terrorist hot spots. But maybe *some as yet unthought alternative* would.

MISCELLANEOUS ADVICE

When you hear an argument, think "Yes, maybe so, but." For the fun of it try to generate a counterargument or at least some reasons why the argument at hand may not be complete. Try to think of instances that don't fit the argument. Take the reason and imagine some exception. Or make a strong opposite case. Try to imagine what the person is arguing—both for and against.

Ask yourself *whether the argument needs more* support in the form of *evidence or reasons;* perhaps the argument needs the support of different reasons. Don't forget that there are times when the opposite case is better just because it's closer to the truth.

SUMMARY

The following tactics were discussed in this chapter:

1. *Quick starts:* Oppose the conclusion, come up with a reason; oppose the conclusion and reason(s).
2. *Factors for and against:* Brainstorm for as many factors as possible on either side, then winnow them down to the best few.
3. *Engulf and devour:* Accept the opposing argument, offering more powerful reasons to accept your argument.
4. *A big factor, a significant exception, the strongest case:* Search for missing elements that the arguer has not taken into account.
5. *Faulty or flimsy reasons:* The first position's reasons are false or insufficient to support the argument.
6. *Call for more factual evidence or for experimentation.*

Although these are different approaches, they can overlap.

EXERCISES

1. Use one of the quick start techniques on each of these arguments:
   a. Everyone should buy a few clothes every year because wearing something different adds spice to life.
   b. Fraternities and sororities are clubs whose sole purpose is to make their members feel superior to outsiders. These clubs should be banned from college campuses.
2. Factors for, factors against:
   a. Generate five reasons in favor of a flat, 15 percent federal income tax for every person and every business; then imagine five reasons against such an idea. Winnow the reasons on each side to two, then choose the strongest, explaining why it is strongest.
   b. Think of alternative ways, even zany ones, to tax people other than according to income.
3. Engulf and devour the following:
   a. It's a mistake to have children. They are expensive, difficult to train, and often end up ungrateful for parental efforts.
   b. Since no one can predict how the economy will be in ten years, one is better off spending money on desired items than saving it.
4. Think up a strongest case against the following:
   a. People want only what they cannot have.
   b. Laughter is the best medicine.
5. Make up an argument in favor of dogmatism, then see if you can engulf and devour it. Do the same for relativism and progressivism.

READINGS

1. *The best arguments are those which give a counterargument and then show how the case being argued is better. Two examples follow. In each, pick out the argument and its opposing view.*

Unhappily, biography has lately been overtaken by a school that has abandoned the selective [aspects of a person's life] in favor of the all-inclusive . . . . We are presented with the subject's life reconstructed day by day from birth to death, including every new dress or pair of pants, every juvenile poem, every journey, every letter, every loan, every accepted or rejected invitation, every telephone message, every drink at every bar . . . . I think this development is part of the anti-excellence spirit of our time that insists on the equality of everything and is thus reduced to the theory that all facts are of equal value and that the biographer or historian should not presume to exercise judgment. To that I can only say, if he cannot exercise judgment, he should not be in the business. A portraitist does not achieve a likeness by giving sleeve buttons and shoelaces equal value to mouth and eyes.[2]

Having grasped both arguments, do you agree with the author? One way to discovering whether you agree would be to imagine that there exist two biographies about someone whom you greatly admire: One presents every known fact—"every drink at every bar"—about that person; the other biography tells only about the major events in that person's life along with what the biographer has decided are interesting details. Which would you prefer to read and why?

2. *The following are an argument and counterargument on the merits of an artist's career by Dame Janet Baker, a famous opera singer. Can you tell when the counterargument begins? Is her conclusion the same in both arguments? Notice that she is careful to define her major term.*

If someone asked if my career has been "worth it," in other words worth the sacrifices made by me and members of my family, worth the separations, the agony of performing, of trying to keep perfectly fit, the undying battle against nerves, the strains and pitfalls of being a public figure, my honest answer would have to be "No."

This sounds a terrible comment to make on a career which, in terms of the world, has been a highly successful one. I have done everything any singer could dream of, yet the moments when the musical rewards have equalled the price one has to pay for them have been few.

But if someone were to ask me how I would choose to be born in order to learn about life, I would unquestionably reply, "As an artist." If it is, as many people suggest, a rather special privilege to be born one, the privilege lies in the opportunities such an existence provides for the individual to learn about himself; in the questions artistic life forces one to ask and try to answer; in the struggle to come to terms with performing and everything implied by an act of heroism, which demands the baring of the soul before strangers, and public judgment of this act; in the choices to be made as a result of loving something more than oneself and serving that something with the greatest integrity one is capable of. Yes, in these terms, my career has been "worth it," a thousand times over.[3]

3. *Social historian Norbert Elias gives a counterargument to the normal accounts one might give for eating with a fork:*

What is the real use of the fork? It serves to lift food that has been cut up to the mouth. Why do we need a fork for this? Why do we not use our fingers? Because it is "cannibal," as . . . the author of The Habits of Good Society said in 1859. Why is it "cannibal" to eat with one's fingers? That is not a question; it is self-evidently cannibal, barbaric, uncivilized, or whatever else it is called.

But that is precisely the question. Why is it more civilized to eat with a fork?

"Because it is unhygienic to eat with one's fingers." That sounds convincing. To our sensibility it is unhygienic if different people put their fingers into the same dish, because there is a danger of contracting disease through contact with others. Each of us seems to fear that the others are diseased.

But this explanation is not entirely satisfactory. Nowadays we do not eat from common dishes. Everyone puts food into his mouth from his own plate. To pick it up from one's own plate with one's fingers cannot be more "unhygienic" than to put cake, bread, chocolate, or anything else into one's mouth with one's own fingers.

So why does one really need a fork? Why is it "barbaric" and "uncivilized" to put food into one's mouth by hand from one's own plate? Because it is distasteful to dirty one's fingers, or at least to be seen in society with dirty fingers. The suppression of eating by hand from one's own plate has very little to do with the danger of illness, the so-called "rational" explanation. In observing our feelings toward the fork ritual, we can see with particular clarity that the first authority in our decision between "civilized" and "uncivilized" behavior at table is our feeling of distaste.[4]

NOTES

1. "Why Holland's South Moluccans Aren't Hijacking Trains Any More," *Wall Street Journal* (New York), May 24, 1984.
2. Barbara W. Tuchman, *Practicing History* (New York: Alfred A. Knopf, 1981), p. 89.
3. Janet Baker, *Full Circle* (London: Julia MacRae Publishers, a division of Franklin Watts, 1982), pp. 52–53.
4. Norbert Elias, *The History of Manners, The Civilizing Process* (New York: Pantheon Books, a division of Random House, Inc., 1978), 1, pp. 126–27. This book was published again in 1993 under the title *The Civilizing Process,* by Blackwell Publishers, London.

4

Deciding to Accept an Argument

Compare the Evidence

Are we at the mercy of authorities who serve up arguments which we must swallow whole because we don't know very much about a subject? No. At least, not if we take a bit of time to consider the type of evidence which that authority is depending on. In the best situation, we get to compare what this authority argues with the alternative argument of another authority to see which seems to have the better evidence.

No matter who is drawing conclusions, be they an authority or not, the question to ask of their judgments is "What kind of evidence are they relying on here?" An authority in the humanities will of necessity have a different sort of evidence to draw on than will a scientist.

But first, notice that the word "evidence" is sometimes used as another word for "reason," and at other times people use it to describe facts which support their reason. Back to our argument structure for a bit, let's see examples of both uses of the term "evidence."

EVIDENCE AS THE REASON

A piece of evidence can be the reason that a person comes to a conclusion, as in this example:

> **The evidence** Mr. Holmes **offered in his argument** that the heir died **is that** Holmes saw the man's body in the basement (Figure 4-1).

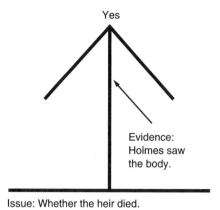

Issue: Whether the heir died.

Figure 4-1   Evidence as the Reason

EVIDENCE AS SUPPORTING THE REASON

In other arguments, evidence, rather than being the main reason, *supports* the reason in coming to some conclusion. Evidence usually refers to something *seen,* but evidence often refers to a collection of identical things which have been seen or heard, called data.

"Statistical evidence" usually refers to the totaling of similar things or instances. In some arguments the evidence can support a reason or reasons that in turn support the conclusion. For instance:

> The geologist **concluded that** that we will enter another ice age within one hundred years. Her **reasons are that** ice ages have occurred in recent geologic history every ten thousand years and that we are just a few years shy of the beginning of such an interval. She **produced** fossils **as the evidence** dating such climatic change over six ten-thousand-year cycles (see Figure 4-2).

You can see from these two examples that the English language isn't precise about the distinction between evidence as reason and evidence in support of a reason. The Concise Oxford Dictionary defines evidence as "the available facts . . . supporting . . . a belief. . . ."[1] It doesn't matter to the *structure* of an argument whether its author decides to call her supporting facts reasons or evidence. It will certainly aid in *clarity,* though, if an author who has a reason and data which support it calls the factual data "evidence."

As you read an argument containing evidentiary claims, ask yourself how the pieces of evidence fit into that argument. Sometimes an author leaves it unclear whether evidence is meant to support a reason or is supposed to stand on its own as a reason. In that case, your job is to

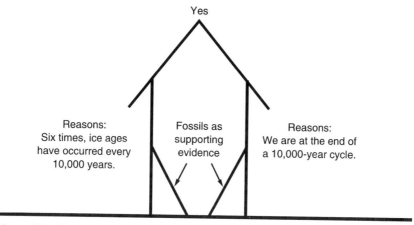

Issue: Whether we will enter another ice age within 100 years.

Figure 4-2   Evidence Supporting the Reason

realize that the argument could be interpreted either way. In most cases it doesn't make much difference to the argument. What does make a difference, however, is failure to pick up on an author's reason, mistakenly taking some evidence for the entire reasoning of an author (e.g., stating that the presence of fossil evidence is the geologist's sole reason for concluding that we will enter another ice age).

The ability to evaluate evidence skillfully is crucial to good decision making about arguments. Yet the subject is vast. First, the kind of evidence available varies according to the subject matter. Second, there is more information on more subjects than ever before.

In the teeth of this maze of subjects and evidence, what can we poor critical thinkers do? The following is meant as a useful sketch.

EVIDENCE AS DEPENDING ON THE ISSUE

Argumentation exists in all academic disciplines. All subject areas make an appeal to evidence in the course of their arguments, but the *kind* of evidence available to any given discipline varies.

Evidence in Science

When we hear arguments that have to do with the nature of the physical world, the evidence will be the result of direct, hands-on experimentation.

For instance, two thousand years ago Greek philosophers speculated upon the argument that the universe is made up of elementary particles (atoms). Other thinkers opposed this notion, with equally strong arguments. No experimental method had been devised to deal with this and other questions about the physical world. With the advent of the scientific method and its consistent application throughout the past century, however, we have amassed experimental evidence to support the notion of the atomic theory.*

Notice that scientists don't refer to atomic facts. A theory is a complex argument. Scientific method maintains the balance of "maybe not" by keeping the atomic argument (and all others) open to challenge, despite very strong evidence in its favor. Scientists search for facts but view them as factual claims. So evidence in science hews to the ideal of experimental method.

Examples of Scientific Questions   What is the physical basis of heredity? (Notice that this question does not involve the value judgment whether the theory of DNA or any other theories of heredity are good or bad.) What causes cancer?

Evidence in Philosophy

There are many other questions philosophers, ancient and modern, ponder, such as, "What is the most just society possible?" This question is still of intense interest to philosophers.[2] But unlike questions about the physical world, this one cannot be submitted to hands-on experimentation. What's there to experiment *on*? We are not involved here in a search for what is (facts) but in a search for what should be (values).

For this reason, the nature of evidence in philosophical argumentation is different from that in science. Philosophers try to explore by argumentation all aspects of values questions. Philosophers also concern themselves with many other sorts of arguments, about the nature of language, of knowledge, even offering alternative arguments about the nature of philosophy. They are fascinated by the assumptions which underlie other disciplines as well. The first task is to explore all these avenues intellectually. Each avenue could eventually evolve into an argument (theory).

One major tack taken by philosophers is to seek a general principle, then think about whether there are cases (evidence) which support that principle. If someone comes up with a counterexample (evidence contrary to the philosopher's position), then the philosopher must revise the principle to take that counterexample into account, or else explain how that contrary-seeming evidence is not so in fact. The philosopher thus uses a broad appeal to our reason and experience as evidence. Another source of evidence in philosophy and the humanities in general

---

*For further discussion of scientific and philosophical method, see chapter 11.

is to show how that one's argument is echoed by another, more famous authority. For instance, "No less an authority than the philosopher Leibnitz held that the simplest, most explanatory theory was better than a complicated argument that doesn't cover as many cases." As you read this you should realize that the philosopher Leibnitz was also relying on a broad appeal to reason and experience.

You've seen philosophical arguments twice, once with the Peter Singer argument for equal treatment of animals, and once with the argument about torture. Review each of these arguments for its general principle and significant supporting cases.

This general principle–significant cases technique is used in science too, but there one can always refer back to the hands-on evidence in a way that is not available for questions of value. With questions of value, the ultimate appeal for acceptance of the principle and cases offered is to the audience's reason and experience. *Evidence in philosophical argumentation is often an appeal to cases offered in support of a principle.*

Examples of Values Questions   How should you allocate money for medical research? Say you run a government agency that allocates money for medical research. There is a painful, devastating disease striking a few thousand people a year. There is another less devastating but more widespread disease. You want to allocate funds for research on both diseases. The amounts that are known about these diseases are about equal. The tasks of trying to eradicate the diseases are equally difficult. How do you put a dollar equivalent on this problem? If there is a conflict between telling the truth and maintaining social harmony, which should a society value more highly? What kinds of cases can be brought forward as evidence for either position?

Evidence Gathered after the Event

Social, behavioral, and medical scientists can run some experiments on humans. They might look at the metabolism of a new drug in human subjects or use people in learning experiments. But if an experiment has even a chance of being detrimental to a person, the research would be unethical. For example, imagine someone's abusing children to see if they become violent adults. Experiments of this sort would be immoral, only the stuff of horror movies. So in these areas researchers have to use a modified scientific method in the form of statistics-gathering and case studies after the fact. This approach has enhanced our understanding of correlations, but unlike strict scientific method, it can't fully explain how these correlations work.

Here's an example of evidence gathered after the event. A decade ago there was puzzlement whether vigorous exercise helped a person or hurt by causing a heart attack. Sports researchers suspected that people who exercise vigorously are at less risk, but how could they find out? Rather than using hands-on experimentation, keeping people in a laboratory under controlled conditions and *inducing* heart attacks, the researchers chose a humane but more laborious route. They looked at the medical records of thousands of people. Thus, they studied these heart attacks after they had happened.

In the earlier studies, the researchers eliminated any records that might confuse the evidence. For instance, they eliminated records of people with a history of heart trouble. After all, anyone born with heart disease who does not exercise much and who dies early is as likely to have died of the heart disease as of a lack of exercise.

All research, including two large new studies reported in the *New England Journal of Medicine* (December 2, 1993), have pointed in the same direction: Regular physical activity strongly protects people against an exertion-related heart attack, but sedentary people who suddenly exercise vigorously are fifty times more likely to suffer a heart attack than those who have built up their stamina by vigorous exertion such as slow jogging, speed-walking, tennis, or swimming several times a week. But couch potatoes will be happy to learn that even with this increased risk, a sedentary person is not very likely to have a heart attack within a hour of doing something strenuous like shoveling snow or digging up a garden. The absolute risk during that hour would be one in 10,000. Yet in the United States, at least 75,000 heart attacks a year, leading to 25,000 deaths, are related to exertion.

Despite this detailed evidence of the connection between exercise and cardiovascular health, we still don't know exactly how that connection works. Regular exercise reduces the tendency of the blood to clot, makes the muscles use oxygen more efficiently, improves one's cholesterol count, enables the heart to pump more blood with each beat, and during exertion dilates the arteries, as well as lowers heart rate and blood pressure. But we don't know which of these factors (all? a few? one?) causes the lower risk of heart attack. The sedentary—or the very busy—would like scientists to get down to the physical cause or mechanism, perhaps breeding mice which show only one of these features of exercise, then testing their resiliency on the exercise wheel. In a brave new world, maybe a pill could do the job that up to now can be done only by sweat.

Or consider cigarettes and cancer. There exist any number of after-the-fact case studies linking cigarette smoking and cancer, but there is no way to find out by case studies how cigarette smoke actually changes a normal cell into a cancer cell. That is, there's no way to study the *mechanism* between the two variables, smoking and lung cancer. The case study can show you very strong correlation, which would be very good evidence for the connection, but it doesn't give you any information about mechanism, which is necessary for pinning down the cause-effect relationship between the smoke and cancer. (In fact, laboratory experiments on whole animals and on living cells in culture have provided a theory for the mechanism.) *

Other Issues   Other issues which require after-the-fact investigation include whether there is a connection between genetic endowment and criminal behavior; whether there is a correlation between a growing middle class and political revolutions; whether inflation in a country is related to its balance of payments.

COMPARE THE EVIDENCE FOR ALTERNATIVES

The ability to evaluate evidence skillfully is crucial to good decision making about arguments. Yet the number of issues about which arguments or theories are raised is vast. How to cope?

I think that the best solution is to read widely enough to watch for alternative arguments to issues which interest you. How does the evidence of the argument you favor stack up against the evidence in favor of another view? Even an expert cannot evaluate a theory in his or her field without considering it in relation to comparable theories. We, too, should "comparison shop" for theories (arguments) which seem to us to provide the best evidence.

Further, since the evidence we learn about is, we hope, offered by experts skilled in experimental method, case studies, or philosophical discourse, we must for the most part trust that they made a good-faith effort. But the key is to trust a lot of experts a little bit, reading widely. For expert and novice alike, **critical thinking is the consideration of alternative arguments in light of their evidence.**

GOOD ARGUMENTS DON'T OVERSTEP THEIR EVIDENTIARY LIMITS

A good argument does not trick us into thinking that its evidence is better or of a different type than it is. Here are four rules of thumb:

1. *No matter how dazzling the evidence looks, be skeptical of any claim that an argument has been proven.* Beware of any claim that reads "This evidence proves that . . ." If you've looked at scientific journals, the

---

*For a further discussion of this example, see chapter 11.

authors of even the most exciting results write" **This evidence suggests that . . .**" or "**This evidence leads us to conclude that . . . ,**" but rarely "We have proven that. . . ."*

If scientists with their powerful experimental method won't use this term, we should be leery of claims like this one: "They have proven that there are ten personality types." It doesn't matter how much evidence this argument offered; don't accept that it's proven.

On the other hand, if the argument seemed to have some good points, don't reject it entirely.

2. *Shop around for counterarguments.* Upon reading an argument, think about other arguments or theories (here, of personality). If you are interested and energetic, do more reading on the subject. Expect to find arguments that conflict with the one in question. Weigh the evidence on the side of the "ten types" against the evidence for other theories.

3. *Evaluate the evidence.* Though we could totally accept or reject this argument, there are many options in between. Depending on how the argument stacks up against other arguments, we could use the following language to evaluate the evidence:

> **The argument presents little (no) evidence that** there are ten personality types.
> The argument **provides some evidence** that . . .
> The author **could marshal (should have marshaled) some evidence that** . . .
> The argument **provides good evidence that** ten distinct personality types exist.
> These data **constitute strong evidence that** . . .

4. *Evaluate the argument for how well it assesses its evidence.* Arguments that accurately assess their evidence usually contain evidence that was conscientiously and skillfully acquired. The "ten personality theories" argument would be a good argument if it dropped the "proof" claim, clearly described its basic structure while defining its major terms, included some good counterarguments, and honestly (even humbly) assessed itself as, say, quite speculative at the moment.

> My theory that there are ten personality types fits a number of situations that I and others have observed. **It is, however, quite speculative at the moment.**

Of course, arguments with stronger evidence than the alternatives are entitled to indicate as much.

---

*In mathematics, "proof" (of theorems) is a good term.

SUMMARY

Evidence exists in all subject areas. Evidence is material in support of arguments (theories).

The kind of evidence that it is possible to produce depends on the type of argument:

> For a theory about the material world, expect the strongest type of evidence, based on scientific method.
>
> For a theory about the behavior of human beings, whether as individuals or in social groups, normally expect evidence after the fact in the form of good case studies.
>
> For a theory about what should be, expect evidence in the form of an appeal to strongest cases and perhaps to other, more famous authorities.

There are four rules of thumb (for writers and critics):

1. Discount any claim "proving that." Keep every argument open to modification.
2. Shop around for counterarguments and alternative arguments.
3. Compare the evidence in light of that for alternative theories. Options range from no evidence to comparatively little evidence to some evidence to good evidence and, finally, to strong evidence.
4. Favorably evaluate arguments that carefully evaluate their evidence with an eye to alternative evidence.

EXERCISES

1. What kind of evidence would you expect in the following arguments?
   a. An argument that people who eat a special diet will have less chance of getting cancer.
   b. An argument that God exists.
   c. An argument·that human cells secrete some substance under certain conditions.
   d. An argument that stealing is unethical.
   e. An argument that owning a pet tends to lower one's blood pressure.

   Answers (a) evidence after the fact; (b) philosophical evidence (a general principle, for instance that the universe is orderly); (c) direct scientific experimentation; (d) philosophical evidence; (e) evidence after the fact

2. Underline the language in the following argument that you believe indicates that it does (or does not) admit its limits.

It's an obvious fact that living in the suburbs is better than city life. Everyone knows that cities are far more polluted and dangerous. And of course, people don't even know their neighbors. On the other hand, suburbs are peaceful havens from the workaday world.

READINGS

The following two articles show breathtaking advances in the ability to detect whether a person will suffer from a particular genetic disease. The first article contains references to all three types of evidence discussed in this chapter. Compare the language used to depict direct experimentation, after-the-fact evidence, and values questions.

Predictive Probes
by Jerry E. Bishop

Several years ago, Nancy Wexler's mother died of Huntington's disease, a hereditary and always-fatal affliction that strikes in midlife. Since then, Ms. Wexler, the 38-year-old president of the Hereditary Diseases Foundation in Santa Monica, Calif., has lived with the uncertainty of whether she, too, inherited the deadly gene.

That uncertainty may soon be resolved. A few months ago, scientists announced they were on the verge of completing a new test to detect the gene for Huntington's disease (formerly called Huntington's chorea). But deciding whether to submit herself to the test is an anguishing choice for Ms. Wexler. "If I came out lucky, taking the test would be terrific, of course," she says. "But if I came out unlucky, well . . ."

Her dilemma is an extreme example of the kind thousands of Americans will face in the not-too-distant future as scientists learn how to pinpoint genes that cause or predispose a person to a future illness.

The test to detect the Huntington's-disease gene should be ready within one to two years. Researchers already have detected some of the genes that can lead to premature heart attacks and, in the near future, hope to spot those that could predispose a person to breast or colon cancer. Eventually, scientists believe they will be able to detect genes leading to diabetes, depression, schizophrenia and the premature senility called Alzheimer's disease.

"Extraordinary Power" "This new technology has an extraordinary power to predict any disease where there is any kind of genetic

influence," Ms. Wexler says. "Instead of looking in a crystal ball to see your future, you'll look in your genes."

Doctors long have been able to crudely predict a person's future illness. By studying disease patterns, for example, they can say that heavy cigarette smokers have 10 times the risk of developing lung cancer as nonsmokers and that middle-aged men with high blood cholesterol levels have higher-than-normal risk of heart attacks. Geneticists also look at family medical pedigrees to determine the chances of children inheriting any of the 3,000 known genetic disorders.

But such predictions are similar to casino odds. Doctors can't predict which smokers will actually develop lung cancer, which individual will have a premature heart attack or which child actually inherited a defective gene.

Genetic probes, however, will change predictive medicine. The probes are synthetic versions of genes that cause disease. Tossed into a test tube with a small sample of a person's own genetic material—his DNA—the probes cling to and identify their natural counterparts.

"Raft of Questions" Proponents of predictive medicine cite its potentially tremendous benefit in that it will allow, in some instances, people to take preventive measures to ward off certain illnesses. "But it also raises a raft of questions on almost every level—social, psychological, personal, legal and ethical," says Ms. Wexler, a psychologist who has specialized in the problems of victims of genetic diseases. Such problems range from how and when to tell a seemingly healthy person he or she has a gene for a possibly fatal disease to whether employers, insurance companies, or even the government should know a person carries such a gene.

Nowhere are the social and ethical questions surrounding genetic probes more apparent than in the case of Huntington's disease.

Although the disease is caused by inheritance of a mutant gene, the symptoms usually don't show up until between ages 30 and 50. The disease is characterized by slow but steady mental deterioration that begins with moodiness and ends fatally with severe mental illness. One tragedy is that carriers of the fatal gene often don't know their condition before having children of their own. Children whose parents are known carriers grow up haunted by the 50% probability that they, too, carry the gene.

Late last year, however, a team of scientists from several institutions reported making a breakthrough that will lead to a test for the Huntington's-disease gene. With the aid of experimental genetic probes, James F. Gusella, a doctor at Massachusetts General Hospital, and his colleagues studied the genes of 135 members of a large family in

Venezuela that is plagued by Huntington's disease. While the team didn't find the gene itself, they did discover an unusual genetic variation that seems to accompany the mysterious gene when it is passed along. Hence, it might serve as a "marker" for the Huntington disease gene.

Preparing for Problems   Dr. Gusella and Integrated Genetics, Inc., a small biotechnology company he works with, are sifting through genes of Huntington's-disease families looking for a second genetic marker, which would make the test more than 99% accurate. They then must confirm the mutant gene as the only cause of Huntington's disease, meaning the test probably won't be available for a year or two.

Researchers, however, already are preparing for problems the test will create. At Indiana University, medical geneticists since 1979 have located and compiled medical and genetic information on 34,000 people from Huntington's-disease families, including 5,000 who are still alive. Once the test is perfected, each of those 5,000 persons at risk must decide whether to take it.

"Roughly half of them say they want to know, and the other half say they don't want to know," says Joe E. Christian, a physician and chairman of the medical-genetics department at Indiana. "Many people said, 'Don't take away my last hope' by telling them that they definitely have the gene."

Whether the spouse or potential spouse should be told is a matter to be addressed in a program planned by Huntington's-disease centers at Massachusetts General Hospital and Johns Hopkins University, Dr. Gusella says. "Nothing has been settled yet, but the consensus seems to be that the person being tested gets the information and it will be up to him whether anyone else should be told." In any case, he adds, "there will have to be a maximum of pre-test counseling and post-test support."

Another issue is whether employers or insurance companies paying for the test are entitled to know the results. Health-insurance data go into a central computer and are available to all insurance companies. As it is, says Ms. Wexler of the Hereditary Disease Foundation, persons at risk of Huntington's disease can buy life insurance from only a few companies and then only at almost prohibitive rates.

Such problems won't be unique to Huntington's disease much longer. Probes for other diseases are certain to raise similar questions. "An executive might be passed up for promotion if it became known that he carried the gene for familial hypercolesterolemia (inherited high cholesterol) with its high risk of premature heart attacks," says Arno Motulsky, a doctor and a geneticist at the University of Washington. "Could one blame an industrial company for such action? Do individuals who know they carry such a gene have the right to withhold such information from employers?"

Despite those thorny questions, the geneticists are hard at work. Among their targets are the genes that cause atherosclerosis, the clogging of the arteries with fatty deposits. Atherosclerosis is a slow, silent disease that can lead to heart attacks in the adult years. And recently it has become clear that the rapidity with which arteries clog is determined by defects or variations in any of at least eight genes that control the way the body uses and disposes of fats. Genetic probes will be able to detect these genetic defects and variations long before a heart attack develops.

An early demonstration of that new predictive power already is under way involving an inherited disorder called familial dysbetalipoproteinemia. Victims of the disorder, which is uncommon but not necessarily rare, have such high amounts of cholesterol and other fats in their circulation that the blood serum is actually cloudy. The consequences begin to show up in early adulthood in men and later in women when the arteries in the limbs and heart become severely clogged. Unless treated, the victims suffer heart attacks in their 20s or 30s.

Scientists now know that at least 95% of people suffering this rapid artery-clogging have two copies of a gene called the apo E-2 gene, having inherited one copy from each parent. Recently, Jan Breslow, a doctor at Rockefeller University, and some collaborators at Harvard University, where Dr. Breslow worked before joining Rockefeller, developed genetic probes that detect both normal and mutant forms of the gene. The probes now can be used to determine whether the new-found mutant genes are responsible for the disease.

Genetic probes will allow doctors to detect such atherosclerosis genes at birth by taking umbilical cord blood and looking for lesions at the DNA level, Dr. Breslow says. If the infant is found to have genes that predispose him or her to an early heart attack, "we can begin to practice true prevention," he says. Cancer researchers have similar hopes for genetic probes. Scientists now are finding evidence supporting a theory proposed a few years ago by Alfred G. Knudsen, a doctor at Philadelphia's Fox Chase Cancer Center. While studying a type of childhood eye cancer known to be inherited, he speculated it took two "hits," or events, for the eye cancer to occur. The first hit would be the inheritance of a gene (or the absence of a gene, as it actually turned out) that had the potential of causing cancer. Then a second hit had to occur before the gene (or lack of a gene) turned a cell malignant and led to a tumor. The hypothesis is holding up in the case of certain childhood cancers, Dr. Knudsen says, adding, "It's a good bet that at least some adult cancers are caused by the same mechanism."

Researchers note, for example, that daughters of breast-cancer patients have a 10% higher risk of developing breast cancer than other women. Thus, it seems that a predisposition to breast cancer can be inherited. But only a small portion of such daughters develop breast cancer. Dr. Knudsen's two-hit hypothesis would explain that situation. While perhaps a fourth of all women whose mothers or grandmothers had breast cancer carry a cancer-prone gene—the first hit—only a small portion actually suffer the still unidentified second hit that leads to malignancy.

If Dr. Knudsen's hypothesis is true, then genetic probes would tell a woman if she inherited the first-hit gene. Those who did would be fore-warned to have frequent breast examinations to catch the tumor in its early, curable stage.

As with breast cancer and other physical ailments, there is evidence that certain behavioral illnesses can be inherited. For example, studies indicate that a tendency to depression and manic depression can run in families. And now there is a growing suspicion that Alzheimer's disease, the senility and loss of memory that usually strikes its victims in their late 50s or early 60s, has a genetic aspect.

If that suspicion is borne out, and if probes can uncover the predisposing genes early, the question of how such probes should be used becomes complex. One question: Could persons carrying such genes be banned from managerial or executive positions or even high political offices where their decisions affect large numbers of people?

To the University of Washington's Dr. Motulsky, the notion of genetic screening isn't that farfetched. "As public bodies assume a more direct role in the health system in many countries," he said, "confidentiality may become eroded and genetic information may be used by social and health planners to assign individuals their niche in society."[3]

This article, written nine years later, provides a dramatic update of the power of genetic testing to predict when and how severely a person will become ill. We may all have the choice to learn whether we will get cancer or suffer a stroke. Would you want to know? The following contains several arguments for and against finding out, based on differing philosophical principles of what makes for a good or happy life.

New Test Tells Whom a Crippling Disease Will Hit—and When

Amy Jo Snider, a college senior, has put her career plans and romantic life on hold until she settles a gnawing question about her genetic legacy.

During her Christmas break, the Charleston, SC, student plans to be tested for a gene that causes ataxia, a disease without a cure that destroys the brain cells governing muscle control. The disorder crippled and ultimately killed her father in middle age. Because of a recent breakthrough in genetic research, the 21-year-old Miss Snider will be able to find out whether she inherited the disease, and, if so, how soon and how hard ataxia may strike her.

"I want to be tested before I start to show symptoms," she says unflinchingly. "I'm graduating in May, and I have to start planning my life." As agonizing as the knowledge might be, she says the uncertainty is worse. "If I'm in limbo, it's not fair to people around me," she says. "I can't deal with not knowing."

The Hunt for Flaws   In the immediate years ahead, millions of people will face similar dilemmas, as researchers continue to discover the flaws in human genes that cause diseases. The gene responsible for ataxia was identified earlier this year by Harry Orr at the University of Minnesota in Minneapolis and Huda Zoghbi at the Baylor College of Medicine in Houston. The researchers then made another significant discovery: The gene, known as SCA1, has a flaw, a strikingly visible mutation that is common to other inherited neurological disorders, as well as some cancers.

The mutation—which SCA1 shares with the genes that cause neurological diseases such as Fragile X, Huntington's Disease, Kennedy's Disease and myotonic dystrophy—consists of an abnormal repetition of three-letter segments of the genetic code, a kind of genetic "stutter."

The ability to identify these "triplet repeats" may greatly accelerate the discovery of other genes that cause disease, and provide clues to the mechanics of inherited disease. Last week, two research teams announced that they looked for such code repeats to discover the gene that can lead to cancers of the colon, uterus, and ovary. In short order, a blood test will be able to identify the one out of every 200 people who carry that cancer gene.

Judgment Day   Bearers of the cancer gene may be dismayed to find out they have it, but they will be in a position to get constant monitoring and early treatment, which could save their lives. For victims of an incurable genetic disease such as ataxia, testing is like judgment day. Moreover, they face a new and chilling kind of biological prophecy, because the number of triplet repeats within the SCA1 gene can be used to forecast roughly when and how severe the onslaught of ataxia may be.

The discovery of SCA1 crowned a fervent eight-year collaboration with a moment of quiet eureka.

In 1985, Dr. Zoghbi in Houston was studying ataxia in a large African-American family in Texas, while Dr. Orr in Minneapolis was tracking the disease in Midwestern clans, many of Dutch descent. In a field rife with fierce rivalries, the two researchers shucked their egos and shared their data.

The Zoghbi-Orr collaboration is a "spectacular story," says Robert Currier, a neurologist and ataxia specialist at the University of Mississippi. "They could have hidden information from each other. They could have gone at it tooth and nail. But they shared it all the way."

"Neither lab could move through it alone," Dr. Orr explains. He likens their gene quest to the job of a plumber who gets a service call from "somewhere in the United States," and then must locate the trouble spot in the right state, city, block and house. First, they mapped the area using certain DNA markers—unique segments of genetic code—narrowing their search to a part of chromosome six. They cloned great swatches of genes in yeast for further study.

In early 1993, Drs. Orr and Zoghbi divided up their target area, using probes to examine it bit by bit. Smack in the middle, they spied a peculiar gene in which three chemical building blocks of DNA—cytosine, adenine and guanine—came together to spell our "CAG" over and over again. In a comparative analysis of DNA from healthy and sick people, they found normal genes held 25 to 36 of these 'CAG' repeats, while mutant genes expanded, containing 43 to 81 CAG repeats—blatant typos in the biological blueprint.

"That was when we knew we had the gene," remembers Dr. Orr. "I phoned her and said: 'I think we've got it.'"

"This is the sort of thing you dream about as a scientist," he says. "When it happens, it leaves you speechless."

Chilling Discovery   Their elation was tempered by the sober discovery that they could count the 'CAG' repeats and predict—to within a decade or two—how soon and how hard the disease would strike. The more CAG repeats, the earlier and more severe the ataxia. While the link wasn't perfect, Dr. Orr says, "You could certainly say whether [the ataxia] is going to be a juvenile case, a mid-adult case, or a late-adult case."

"We were amazed by it," says Dr. Zoghbi. "I decided to put it on a graph. When I saw what it looked like, I said, 'Oh my goodness.' It was chilling."

Scientists had earlier observed links between such "triplet repeats" and time of diagnosis in Huntington's Disease. But these earlier links were not as clearly predictive as the ones found by Drs. Orr and Zoghbi, says C. Thomas Caskey, a noted Baylor geneticist. "Their data is beautiful."

The growing significance of triplet repeats in human genetics has helped solve a puzzle that has long stumped classical geneticists schooled in the tradition of the monk Mendel with his sweet peas. Since genes were supposed to be stable, how could inherited diseases worsen from generation to generation? One answer: mutations that grow. In the

SCA1 gene, research has shown that the number of triple repeats can increase from generation to generation, triggering a worsening of the illness.

"The concept that genes can expand, causing [increasingly] severe disease, is a phenomenon that's new to us," says Arnold Gale, a neurologist and spokesman for the Muscular Dystrophy Association.

"It's gratifying and a bit alarming to find the five diseases pop up with this same genetic mechanism," adds David Nelson, another Baylor geneticist. Beyond linking SCA1 with the retardation of Fragile X, the movement disorder and dementia of Huntington's and the muscular degeneration of Kennedy's and myotonic dystrophy—and with colon cancer—experts feel more such genes may soon be unearthed.

No Firm Numbers "I can't begin to tell you how much excitement there is. Finally, after all these years, there is hope" for better diagnosis and treatment, says Donna Gruetzmacher, spokeswoman for the National Ataxia Foundation, which represents about 150,000 patients suffering from 60 types of ataxia. There are no firm figures on how many people suffer from SCA1 ataxia, which often results in complete disability and death.

"I'd like them to find the gene and remove it—cut it out, so I would be fine," says Tereess Bastion, a 30-year-old marketing specialist in Long Beach, Calif. Ms. Bastion lost her mother and brother to ataxia, before the disorder unhinged her own sense of balance.

Her wish for a procedure to disarm the ataxia gene seems a long shot at best. The neurons targeted by ataxia are tucked away in the cerebellum and brain stem, beyond the reach of current gene-therapy tools, says Dr. Orr.

He is more optimistic about drug therapy. He and Dr. Zoghbi are genetically engineering a mouse strain to study how the SCA1 gene produces a protein that kills brain cells. If such a protein is found, researchers might design molecules to block it.

Fear of the Unknown Until such designer drugs are devised, the SCA1 gene test acts as a kind of biological crystal ball. Rather than waiting for loved ones to stumble and slur their speech—the first symptoms of ataxia—families at risk can be screened. But the test may simply replace fear of the unknown with fear of the known.

"A lot of people are scared to find out. Put yourself in their place," says Jim Devlin, leader of an ataxia support group in Marina Del Rey, Calif. Wheelchair-bound and fiercely articulate, the 57-year-old Mr. Devlin forces out a painful question: "If I were your brother," he asks, "would you want to know?"

For those without symptoms, a genetic prophecy like SCA1 resembled an evil spell from a fairy tale. "For these people the spell is cast," says Larry Schut, a Minneapolis neurologist whose family tree was blighted by ataxia. "It may be 20 or 30 years, but they will get it." Career, family and insurance decisions hang in the balance. "I liken it to telling someone they have an HIV-positive blood test, but no signs of AIDS," says Dr. Schut. "We're dealing with people who are perfectly normal . . . but who will become ill. You don't know who's going to jump off the bridge, or who will take it well."

A Tragic End   That's why Dr. Currier in Mississippi approaches screening gingerly. Ten years ago, long before a precise gene test was available, he gave a gifted young guitarist a rough prognosis of ataxia, based on older tissue-typing technology. Still healthy, the youth took it stoically, then later fired a gun into his chest.

Emotional turbulence unleashed by testing can rend families. In a recently tested Pacific Coast clan, one family member who has the gene lashed out at relatives who tested negative, accusing them of collusion with researchers.

Such ruptures are "very poignant and very predictable," says Nancy Wexler, a Huntington's expert. "Imagine the rifts in the nuclear family. It's explosive. People who are unaffected feel guilty. People who are affected feel enraged."

She adds, "Pre-symptomatic screening needs to be done with extreme caution [and] extensive counseling." Joseph Martin, a neurologist who is chancellor at the University of California at San Francisco, believes that "absent treatment, only a minority of people will want to know."

Jane Blakely, a telephone company employee in Tacoma, WA, was one of that minority. A single woman of 45 who has spent the last dozen years caring for an elderly mother with ataxia, she says, "I wanted to know . . . We had to do some [family and financial] planning."

So when the test became available this past summer, Ms. Blakely submitted her blood sample—and got good news. "Mine was normal. I was just ecstatic," she says. But her relief is bittersweet. "I chose not to have children. I shied away from any involvements," she says. Had she known her genetic fate sooner, she adds, "I might have acted differently."

A Different Choice   Conversely, some ataxia patients now are choosing to conceive children—only to face a prenatal testing dilemma.

In Waynesboro, MS, Pam Shima, a court reporter with mild ataxia who already had two sons, became pregnant again this year. She underwent prenatal screening, but miscarried just after her fetus tested negative for the gene.

Ms. Shima now says she won't test her sons, aged two and 13. Life abounds with risks, she reasons: "When my teenager gets behind the wheel of a car and says 'See you after midnight,' then I'll be worried— more so than whether he'll be in a wheelchair at age 45."

For now, she admits, "I'm more worried about whether I'll be around to see my youngest son play baseball."

In Long Beach, Calif., Dawn Dizon, a 31-year-old aircraft engineer, is happily expecting her first child in February. She suffers from early ataxia, and strives to keep it in check with tremor-controlling drugs and exercise. But she didn't undergo prenatal screening of her fetus.

"Our child has a 50–50 chance of getting it," she concedes. But she thinks that "by the time it's old enough to have symptoms, there will probably be a treatment." Besides, she says, life is a gift, even when illness is part of the legacy. "I wouldn't have wanted my parents not to have me just because I happen to have ataxia."

Previewing one's genetic fate strikes some as a way to rational, ordered existence, and others as a road to spiritual ruin. "I'm very sure I can deal with the knowledge," says Ms. Snider, the Charleston college student, of her forthcoming test. "It's not going to ruin my life. But it will change it." Testing positive may mean forgoing having children, or giving up her dream of becoming a speech therapist. Above all, she acknowledges, it may shorten her life.

"If I know I'm going to be contracting symptoms," she declares stoutly, "I'll have to achieve things sooner."

But to Wanda Cox, a Los Angeles computer specialist who was surprised by ataxia when she fell off her bike at age 40, a predictive test might have hurt more than it helped. "If you're told you'll be sick by age 40, you'll look for symptoms," she says, arguing that determinism leads to despair.

"If I knew I was going to be hit by a car next week, life would be irrevocably changed," says Ms. Cox. "Do I want to know? Hell, no."[4]

NOTES

1. *Concise Oxford Dictionary* (New York: Oxford University Press, 1992), s.v. "evidence."
2. See John Rawls, *A Theory of Justice* (Cambridge, Mass.: Harvard University Press, 1971); Robert Nozick, *Anarchy, State and Utopia* (New York: Basic Books, 1977); Michael Walzer, *Spheres of Justice* (New York: Basic Books, 1984).
3. *Wall Street Journal* (New York), September 12, 1984, p. 1, col. 1.
4. *Wall Street Journal* (New York), December 8, 1993, p. 1 col. 1.

5

Warranted Inference

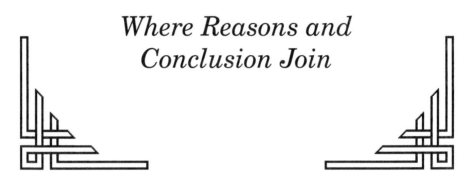

Where Reasons and Conclusion Join

This chapter links several of the ideas you have learned in foregoing chapters, and adds a powerful tool: the concept of inference.

The framework of an argument is an issue being brought to some conclusion with the support of reasons or evidence. As the earlier chapters implied, the structural strength of arguments can vary. Another way of saying this is that you consider an inference (conclusion) to be warranted, or "deserved," because you find its evidence stronger than (or as good as) supporting alternative arguments. In contrast, you could call competing conclusions with inferior evidence unwarranted inferences. To pursue the house analogy, you have found that some posts strongly support their roofs, while other roofs cave in. The inference is thus the roof and the spot where the posts join the roof.

TWO CONSIDERATIONS ARE TRUTH
AND CONSISTENCY

When you consider an inference warranted and thus worthy of your acceptance, you assume two things: 1) that the reasons are true, and 2) that the conclusion *flows* or follows from the reasons. We will look at each of these factors in turn.

Are the Reasons True?

For the conclusion, and therefore the argument, to be warranted, the reason or reasons supporting it must be true. If the reasons are false or misleading, the argument collapses. That pat-sounding statement needs explanation by way of historical example. History is full of inferences which people found well warranted, but which subsequent evidence showed to be unwarranted. Take the conclusion, shared by most of past humanity that men are more intelligent than women. In general, women didn't appear as mentally capable as men. Therefore, most men and women concluded that men are more intelligent. That inference was considered warranted. It failed to take into consideration that women as a rule were denied formal education, the very means to attaining the intellectual skills which made men appear so mentally superior! This misunderstanding is generally true of non-Western societies as well. In Muslim Kashmir, for example, men were considered the only ones capable of doing elaborate needlework, so boys received the training. In any case, the general perception that men appeared more mentally capable was true, but misleading. What is startling today is to see how unwarranted such an inference was, yet how pervasive it was throughout the world. When the nineteenth century British philosopher John Stuart Mill dared to claim in an essay that women were the intellectual equals of men, he was roundly mocked. Does this example lead you to infer that there may be some inferences we now hold as warranted which future evidence will show to be mistaken? Rather than reason for anxiety or despair, I find that reason for excitement at what we have yet to learn.

Unfortunately, we can't literally see arguments collapse when their reasons fail, although they are frequently described as doing so. Here is an example from the history of medicine:

> The nineteenth-century view of tuberculosis was that it was strictly psychosomatic. It was thought that people who were too artistic or angelic for this world were its primary victims. This theory collapsed with the discovery of the tubercle bacillus.

According to this author, on the issue whether tuberculosis is a psychosomatic disease, the nineteenth-century view was in the affirmative, the reason (evidence) being that extremely artistic or angelic people had a greater tendency to contract it. This inference is not warranted in light of current evidence. Instead, our reason for believing that people contract tuberculosis is that certain bacteria called tubercle bacilli have infected their lungs. The twentieth-century layman's view of the cause of tuberculosis is physical.

This is "the layman's view," the ordinary argument that we make in thinking about the cause of tuberculosis. But as you know from Chapter 4, this argument is based on more complicated evidence and assumes the provisional acceptance of that evidence until better comes along.

Although the layman's argument is as short as the nineteenth-century view, it is at the moment a lot better supported by evidence. Since it is well supported, its inference is, for the time being, warranted. By the same token, there is no evidence to support the notion that angelic or artistic people are more prone to tuberculosis, and so that inference is not warranted unless further evidence comes along.

The language of truth assessment is illustrated in the following examples:

> Because it is **not the case that** more artistic people die of tuberculosis, the author's **conclusion is not warranted.**
>
> **It is not true that . . . Therefore . . .** the author's **conclusion is not justified** by these reasons.
>
> The author claims that most people are dissatisfied with their jobs. **This, in fact, is not the case.**
>
> **It is not true that** job dissatisfaction is rampant.

Does the Conclusion Flow from the Reasons?

Not only must the reason or reasons be true, but they must directly lead, by logic or evidence, to that conclusion. The usual way of putting it is to say that **the conclusion follows from the reasons.** Other, related conclusions require their own reasons.

It can be easy to jump the track. For instance, once aware that tuberculosis is a well-understood and easily cured disease when caught early, you might be tempted to draw the additional inference that TB is not a health problem in the United States. That might well be the case, but it doesn't directly follow from the argument of what the cause of tuberculosis is. And unfortunately, despite good understanding of the disease and readily available medication, the government's Centers for Disease Control and Prevention reports that 26,673 people in the United States developed TB in 1992. Because some of those infected are not taking their antibiotics readily, they have developed drug-resistant strains of this highly communicable disease. So just because the cause and cure of TB are known, **it does not follow that** tuberculosis is not a health problem.

Nor is it proper to infer from known evidence about the tubercle bacillus that every lung disease is understood or curable. For example, there is a lung ailment, sarcoidosis, which causes a TB-like inflammation, but whether the cause is genetic or infectious is not known. It does not follow that because some diseases are understood, all diseases, including sarcoid, must be understood. Therefore, as you read or hear an argument, be sure to ask yourself, "Does this conclusion really follow from *these* reasons?"

To complicate matters, people who come up with new theories often meet with rejection, because of the strangeness of the new idea in comparison to the old one, which people have come to accept as obvious. As Nobel prizewinning physiologist P.D. Medawar put it: "The mind takes to a new idea the way the body takes to a microbe: It rejects it." In one sense, this rejection of new inferences as unwarranted might not be an altogether bad strategy. As another writer put it, "About 95% of new ideas don't work out anyway, so you have statistics on your side if you reject all new ideas." Yet it's regrettable that so many people reject that last 5% as well, those breathtaking inferences from true ideas that change the entire course of thinking in a field. The problem is telling the wheat from the chaff, and nobody has come up with a wheat-detector for new ideas. Some new ideas are just too strange, and without a lot of evidence most people find them unwarranted, as was the case for Newton's theory of motion, Darwin's theory of evolution, or the theory of continental drift. These theories, which form the basis of modern physics, biology, and geology, all met fierce headwinds of opposition for decades, even among experts. But what finally won the vast majority of people over is the overwhelming *evidence* that accumulated in favor of these theories, making their old rival theories less and less likely.

Put Down Your Money and Make Your Inferences

If experts make such mistakes, how can we ever know if those inferences which we believe to be warranted are, in fact, warranted? We can't. There is no litmus test outside of looking at the alternative arguments available and weighing for which seems more warranted. We're all probably making a number of inferential mistakes, if history is any judge. But knowledge grows by some people coming up with strange new ideas, and vast numbers of people thinking critically about them over time. Miraculously, the arguments or theories which garner superior evidence on their side seem to win, eventually. Your participation is vital, both as creator of new ideas and voter on those ideas which are already here!

It may be a comfort to learn that people who generate great ideas also hold unlikely ones. No less a thinker than the philosopher Francis Bacon, who is considered the theoretical father of modern scientific method, could also write around 1610 that the heart of an ape worn near the heart increases courage. This seems quite improbable today—luckily for the apes and your cleaning bill. Similarly, an idea common in the United States early in the last century was that if the butter didn't firm properly from the churning, someone standing nearby was responsible and probably was a witch. This idea was held by people who doubtless made other well-warranted inferences.

The point is that it is no sin to make unwarranted inferences as long as one has weighed them in the balance with alternatives, remaining open to new evidence. Although humanity has been wrong (or half-right) about many things over the centuries, my view is that only by means of the comparison of alternative arguments or theories, that is, only by critical thinking, have we been able to stair-step our way to greater knowledge.

THE ANATOMY OF INFERENCE—DEDUCTION AND INDUCTION

Just as you can breathe without knowing how your lungs work, so you can think without being aware that your thought ranges from particulars to generalities and back again. The ancient Greeks discovered these thought processes over two thousand years ago and gave us the concepts of deduction and induction. While these thought processes are illuminating, they rarely appear in the language of critical thinking, because people are more interested in the *likelihood* of an argument, and take for granted that both inductive and deductive thought processes played a role in its formation. Even critical thinking experts don't say in the midst of an argument, "And here I am arguing deductively," for example. So although this chapter contains a number of examples involving the phrase "warranted inference," you will see no language in boldface for deduction and induction.

Deduction Rounds the Circle

We often perform the mental operation of drawing a more particular conclusion out of an *all*-encompassing reason.

For instance:

> All-encompassing reason: All the people in this class are friendly.
> Particular conclusion: Therefore, the person sitting next to me in this class must be friendly.

The conclusion about a particular classmate was *deduced* from the general idea that all the people in the class are friendly.

Figure 5-1 shows by a much thicker wall beam that the reason is more general—*all* classmates—than the conclusion, which involves one particular classmate. Let's call her Frenelda.

Take a moment to realize that if the reason is true, then the conclusion has to be true too. If all our classmates are friendly and

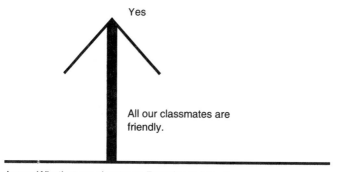

Issue: Whether our classmate Frenelda is friendly.

Figure 5-1   Structure of Deduction

Frenelda is a classmate, she has to be friendly, given the way the argument is set up. This is really the essence of a valid deduction: The conclusion is necessarily the case if the reason is true. That particular instance of Frenelda as friendly is already a part of the notion that everyone in the class is friendly. The conclusion is actually contained inside the reason. That is why the conclusion "roof" is planted firmly on top of the reason.

Now comes a surprise. Even if it is not true that all our classmates are friendly, this deduction is technically valid. That is because the logic still follows, that is, supposing that all our classmates are friendly, classmate Frenelda has to be friendly by logical necessity. When the reasons of a valid deduction are not true, that deduction is unsound, and the inference is not warranted. The ideal, of course, is to strive for true reasons and a valid deductive (all-encompassing) form.

There are an infinite number of things one can fit into this deductive scheme. The key is in the use of "all," "every," and "only" as adjectives in front of the major reason in an argument. For example, granting the notion that all ripe oranges taste good, you would have to conclude that any ripe oranges you eat this year will taste good. You start with the inclusive idea (any ripe oranges) and fit a smaller group (the ripe oranges you will eat this year) inside of it. Of course, the "smaller" group can be quite large. For instance, from the notion that all oranges taste good, I can deduce that all the ripe oranges consumed by Americans over the past fifty years tasted good. That is a lot of oranges.

Another common deductive mode is to be *all-exclusive.* For instance:

> Because no person is a louse and Francie is a person, Francie is not a louse (at least not in the literal sense).

Again, the deduction is valid because the two categories, person and louse, are claimed to be totally excluded from each other.

Here is a famous deduction, in a form called a syllogism:

All men are mortal (first reason, also called the major premise).
Socrates is a man (second reason, or minor premise).
Therefore, Socrates is mortal (conclusion).

This form of writing is seldom found in ordinary prose. It does serve, however, to lay bare the logical bones of an argument.

The previous two examples reflect the two commonest valid deductive forms:

All X are Y.
Z is an X (or all Z are X; or some Z are X).
Therefore, Z is a Y.*

No X are Y.
Z is an X (or Z is a Y).
Therefore, Z is not a Y. (Therefore, Z is not an X.)

You might want to amuse yourself by concocting deductions to fit these patterns. Remember,

In a valid deduction, the conclusion *inevitably follows* from an all-encompassing reason or reasons.
Deductions can be valid (logical) without their reasons or conclusions being true.
A deduction must be valid and true for its conclusion (inference) to be warranted.

The Limits of Deductivism   The beauty of a valid deduction is its mathematical inevitability. The weakness of a deduction is that the reasons may not be true, or in time may become untrue. To take deduction's most time-honored syllogism, a breakthrough in biology might make it the case that men are no longer mortal! No matter how perfect the deduction, it is hollow if the premises are untrue or misleading. Although the mind naturally moves from a generalization to its particular cases, without a method for constantly reviewing those generalizations, deductive thinking is sterile. Luckily there is such a method, called induction.

---

*Notice that the following deductive form is invalid:
All X are Y.   All men are mortal
Z is Y.   Fido is mortal.
Therefore, Z is an X.   Therefore, Fido is a man.

Induction Works up from Particulars

The mind also notes particular instances and builds on them. I see one person in my class and note that he is friendly. Then I meet a second. Over time I meet everyone and arrive at the conclusion that everyone is friendly. My thought process was inductive. I moved from a number of particular cases to a general conclusion. Take the example of the class again. Rather than starting out with the reason that all the people in the class are friendly, you might be wondering about that very point. So you speak to your neighbors on either side of you and to the person sitting in front and behind you. On the basis of friendly discussions with several neighbors, you come to the conclusion that most of the people in this class seem friendly (see Figure 5-2).

Notice that the roof is floating just above the posts. This is meant to symbolize that moving from particulars to a generalization involves a leap, called the "inductive leap." The same leap is, of course, true in any case of "most." Assume here that there are more than four students in this class and that these four are a fraction of the total, say twenty. Here you have actually "polled," or "tested," four particulars to leap to the conclusion about most. Notice how crucial that "most" is; it's hard enough to leap from "some" to "most"; given this small sample, one may not conclude that all the students are likable.

Unlike this classroom situation, however, the number of particular cases is often far greater than we can ever encounter. For example, what about the induction to the conclusion that people in the United States

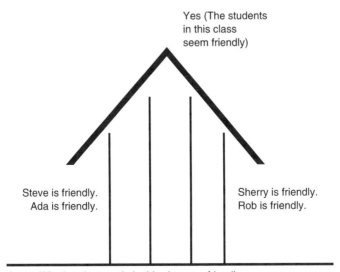

Yes (The students in this class seem friendly)

Steve is friendly.
Ada is friendly.

Sherry is friendly.
Rob is friendly.

Issue: Whether the people in this class are friendly.

Figure 5-2 Structure of the Inductive Leap

are friendly, or that every single ripe orange is delicious? It would be impossible to track down every orange or to meet two hundred and forty-five million people, and in any case some of them would not be sweet. And yet when we want knowledge about large groups of people and things, induction is the means to this end, and precise inductions rely on statistical methods. Believe is or not, the history of statistics is fascinating, showing the struggle of great minds during the past four centuries to develop ways to make accurate generalizations from far fewer particulars. In the nineteenth century the ability to closely predict the number of marriages or murders in a country was so startling that it created great debates about whether individuals had free will. This question no longer vexes philosophers, perhaps because we have become so accustomed to this inductive technique.

INDUCTION BREEDS A SENSIBLE CAUTION

Since there are many issues in which it would bend the truth to make a reason all-encompassing, for instance to claim that *all* the people in the South have southern accents. But it is true to claim that *most* people in the South have southern accents. So the warranted inference can be made that the next person encountered on the street in New Orleans is *likely* to have a southern accent. Because "likely" is used, even if the next person met doesn't have a southern accent, the inference is still good. The only way in which the inference will fall apart is that "Most people in the South have southern accents" is not true (e.g., if there have been so many people from other parts of the United States or abroad moving to the South). This "most" is a very useful tool.

Think of the benefits you enjoy daily from inductive reasoning:

1. The question whether it is safer to wear a seat belt could be answered either way. You may know of accidents in which people needed to get out of their cars quickly to avoid being caught in fires, who would have been trapped by their seat belts. Yet you've heard of other cases in which the belt kept people from flying out of the window to graver injury. The only way to resolve the question is to find out how a representative sample of individual accidents fared under each course to learn which is likelier to keep you safer. Most of the time, seat belts will keep you safer.

2. The question whether to invest in the stock market after a Democrat is elected president is best answered by checking on past stock market performances during the presidencies of individual Democrats (the answer, based on most past cases, is "Invest!").

3. Questions about the healthiest diet are based on large-scale studies of people who have eaten certain diets and their consequent rate of dis-

ease. From such studies have come the tentative conclusions that diets high in fat more likely lead to heart disease, or that diets high in fiber tend to protect against colon cancer.

Don't be confused by the fact that you can put these ideas into deductive form:

Most car trips are made safer if passengers wear seat belts.
I am going to be a passenger in a car today.
I will most likely be safer it I wear a seat belt.

Here you've started with the end point of the inductive work described in the first example above. The most important distinction between deduction and induction is that *deduction begins with a generalization* and works down to particulars; *induction begins with particulars* and builds up to a larger conclusion. It's the direction in which the thinker is proceeding that tells whether the thinking is inductive or deductive.

Deduction and Induction

The mind can rapidly make deductions and inductive leaps, all within a few seconds. Most intellectual endeavor is a complicated combination of deductive and nondeductive thought. You may baffle yourself if you think about your present opinion of oranges or anything else, wondering how your mind traveled (all-inclusive general belief, fitting a more particular conclusion? particular oranges to a more general conclusion about them?). Doubtless it has done both, about oranges and countless other issues.

Just keep in mind that anything you thought about deductively can be thought about inductively—it's whether you started from a general idea ("He acts nasty every time I see him") and deduced a particular conclusion ("He will be nasty when I see him today"); or you worked from a particular number of ideas ("Last Monday, Tuesday, Thursday, and Friday he acted nasty") to a generalization ("I guess it wasn't just a passing mood; he acts nasty every time I see him").

THINGS CAN GO WRONG WITH DEDUCTION AND INDUCTION

Both inductive and deductive arguments can collapse. Here are some quick tests for strength:

For deduction: When an argument gives an all-encompassing reason and a more particular conclusion, ask

1. Is that generalization true, as best you can figure? Can you think of counterexamples to the reason?
2. Then, accepting the truth of the reasons for the moment, does the conclusion have to follow? Or could it be otherwise?

Both items 1 and 2 must obtain for a warranted inference.

For induction: When an argument reasons from "most" or a number of particulars, ask

1. Are the particular cases or the claim of "most" true, as far as you know?
2. Are there enough particular cases to justify making a generalization?
3. Does the generalization seem to follow from those particulars?

Items 1, 2, and 3 are required for a warranted inference.

Under no circumstances go from one instance to all or always. For example,

I know of a man who wore his seat belt and was in an auto accident but didn't suffer any injuries. Therefore anyone who wears a seat belt and is in an auto accident will not suffer many injuries.

Safe Inductive Leaps

With inductive leaps you want to ask, "Have I got enough individual cases to safely generalize about this matter?" If I like four people in my class, is it a warranted inference (safe generalization) that most of the people in my class are likable? If the four people I picked as individual cases were the dear friends with whom I enrolled in the class, my generalization is not warranted. If I tried to walk up to four classmates, more or less at random, to speak to them, my chances are better (though not excellent) for assessing the general likabillity of people in the class.

This is common sense. What is not commonsensical, but an impressive feat, is the way statisticians can take a small sampling of people and predict how vast numbers will probably behave, say, in the voting booth. This powerful prediction technique has only developed over the last century.

Statisticians' methods are complex and vary from task to task. Thanks to their efforts, we are provided with daily information from surveys and other collections of data. For reasons discussed in Chapter 4, the behavioral sciences are particularly dependent on statistical data.

The key idea behind the success of this method is to make the small sample (the particulars) reflect as accurately as possible the large group under study. So, for example, to successfully predict how an election will turn out, one needs samples of people that represent a cross section of all voters. If the voting public is a certain percentage of low-income people (and it's been found beforehand that income affects voting in a certain way), then the same percentage of low-income people must be in the sample. Of course, because surveying people takes time and money, the fewer the people or events or things needed, the better.

Inductive leaps of this sort, called *predictions,* are based on probability theory, which is a branch of mathematics. Over time and with trial and error, these predictions have been greatly refined.

As critical thinkers reading about the results of some survey or poll, we're in scant position to be able to judge how faithful the polltakers were to these statistical requirements. But assuming reputable and knowledgeable data-gathering, we can still critically evaluate the results of a survey if we know what questions were asked. For instance, if a survey claims that people are not concerned about tropical deforestation, but the kinds of questions asked could lead people to give the answers they did because they didn't know about the incidence of tropical deforestation, the conclusion that people don't care is not warranted by the data from the survey.

So the main task in assessing a statistically gathered collection of data is to ask, "Does the generalization seem to follow from those particulars?" In other words, were the questions asked which would warrant the inference?

Calling Attention to Unwarranted Inference

Chapter 12 is devoted entirely to fallacies and problems of inconsistency. For the time being, however, notice the language often used to point to an unwarranted inference:

> It is **not immediately apparent how** the **reason offered** by the author that there is unrest in the Middle East is **relevant to** the **question whether** the United States should spend less money on its space program. Therefore, the author's conclusion that less money should be spent is unwarranted.

> Smith's **conclusion** that we should turn the other cheek **is not consistent with** her earlier claim that we should always act to defend our rights. She **must reconcile** these ideas; at present, her inference is not warranted.

> X's inference that people should take their grievances to court **is unwarranted, because** it is **inconsistent with** his **reasoning that** people are by nature unfair to one another. If people are so unfair, X has failed to explain why a judge and jury would be any different.

Keeping A Flexible Mind

The critical mind has fun constantly sorting things out, trying out new ideas, and seeing if particular situations fit. If the particulars don't seem to fit, a new general idea is called for.

People can suffer from two types of inflexibility. Some seem to hate generalizations. As the saying goes, they can't see the forest for the trees. Have you ever met someone who talks only about disconnected particulars, say, giving you every nattering detail about some conversation about which you have no interest? If only that person would tie those details to some useful generalization, for example, the way that Americans in their twenties interact with one another or use slang in a certain way, anything that will lift this material into something worth thinking about. Either of these topics might also bore you, but at least you have a chance to get to another topic of more general interest. It is very hard to pull out of the nose dive into a thicket of unrelated details. The world is full of an infinite number of details, and life is short. If you get stuck listening to such a conversation, you might try to find a spot to come in with "Well, that's very interesting. Do you think that the way she swore at him is characteristic of the way women speak to men these days?" Asking whether something is characteristic or typical or often done is a quick way to get to a bigger picture.

At the other extreme, some people generalize without letting the breeze of fresh events blow in. There is the pompous type who can speak only in opinionated conclusions and never seems to let some new or unusual occurrence modify his stale deductions. His mind's made up; don't confuse him with factual claims. Particular events need some general notions to make them significant; general ideas need constant testing against particular instances to make sure that they're right. You could critically evaluate the foregoing argument by using your reason and experience.

"LINCHPIN" CLAIMS AND WARRANTED CONCLUSIONS

There are many controversial arguments whose conclusions hinge on the truth of some additional claims, the certainty of which is hard to know. Those "linchpin" claims are fascinating to tease out. It's important to realize that the argument will hold (i.e., will be warranted) only if such additional facts are true. Do you remember Agnes's dilemma in Chapter 2 about whether she needed to go to the market? Her conclusion hinged on the question whether her brother had already gone. These kinds of arguments have the same structure.

Take, for example, the loose argument that the world will run out of oil. One might take issue, replying, "That inference is warranted only if other energy sources don't supplant oil." Can you think of any other fact or facts which would have to be true to warrant this inference? Or take the controversial question whether the Democratic or Republican political philosophy is better for the country. One might argue that the Democrats' inference that social programs are necessary for economic improvement is warranted only if the private sector cannot or will not provide jobs for anyone who is willing to work hard. One could also argue that the Republicans' inference that there should be a minimum of government interference in private enterprise is warranted only if such minimum interference results in greater benefits for all of society.

Do you agree that these inferences are warranted only if these additional facts must be true? Can you think of other necessary facts in these cases?

Decide and Do With Balance

Don't infer from the foregoing that you're supposed to keep an eternally suspended judgment about controversial areas that hinge on hard-to-verify facts. Quite the contrary—it is hoped that you will use the techniques described in this book to decide issues and act accordingly. Otherwise, what's the point of learning to think critically?

Base your decision on the available evidence, on your reasoning powers, and on your experience—your personal experience and claims you've heard and read from among the community of thinkers and believe to be reliable.

Just because you decide and then act doesn't mean that you are not still in balance, still open to future arguments as to why you should change your mind and act differently.

CHECK FOR CONSISTENCY

Most people who carefully review an argument can detect major errors of irrelevance and inconsistency, thereby seeing that the conclusion does not follow from the reasons. When an instructor tactfully points out an inconsistency in a student's paper, that student usually laughs—a healthy response. The point is to get into the habit of careful checking of both one's own work and that of others.

As you read, constantly ask yourself "Does this conclusion really follow from the reason(s) offered? Really?" Asking this question requires a lot more mental effort than passive absorption of the material.

On the assumption that humor, besides being enjoyable, can effectively show inconsistency, let's look at a wacky argument that doesn't obey these rules of consistency and relevance. What's wrong with this picture?

> Money is not everything, but it is better than having one's health. After all, one cannot go into a butcher shop and tell the butcher, "Look at my great suntan, and besides I never catch colds," and expect him to hand over any merchandise.[1]

The issue is whether having money is better than having health. Suggest the reason(s) for the argument. Do you feel foolish suggesting reasons? Whether you can get food for free by proclaiming yourself healthy is not *relevant* to the issue of whether having money is better than having health.

But while it's necessary that the reasons be relevant to warrant a conclusion, relevance alone is not sufficient. Here's an example showing why:

> It's important for people to make sacrifices for one another. One reason is that it's vital for people to do what they want every moment of their lives.

Do you detect any inconsistency? If you don't, reread the example and think about these two ideas, self-sacrifice and doing what one wants. You probably realize that these two ideas are often in opposition. They are therefore relevant to one another, but they are inconsistent and belong in opposing arguments.

In short, a reason that is irrelevant is off the issue entirely; an inconsistent reason is on the issue but does not fit the conclusion. (For a further discussion of consistency, see Chapter 12.)

Circular Reasoning

One might call this problem "overconsistency." A person offers the conclusion as the reason for the same conclusion. Children often like to sing, "We're here because we're here because we're here." For instance,

> Money is better than poverty, if only for financial reasons.[2]

Think for a minute. Is the argument relevant and consistent? It is. But since the reasons (financial) are identical with the term "money," there are actually no reasons (you can't hold up your roof with more of the roof). This statement is not a strict argument even though it pretends to be by offering a reason. Such an attempt to support a conclusion by using the conclusion itself as the reason is called circular reasoning.

HOW WE ALL BLOCK WARRANTED INFERENCES

Every human being who has lived to hear arguments has probably chosen wrongly at some point, against a warranted inference. It seems that we have a number of natural defenses against views with which we don't agree. Two educational researchers have detected seven ways in which students and experts in a field deal with evidence which contradicts their favored theory.[3] Interestingly, only one of these seven responses is to accept the new evidence and change theories:

1. Ignore the data—"No, I didn't read that article, book, etc."
2. Reject the data—"There must be something wrong with the experiment, survey, etc."
3. Exclude the data—"That data has nothing to do with this issue. It is not relevant here."
4. Holding the data in abeyance—"I'm not sure how this data fits with my theory, but I still think my theory is better."
5. Reinterpret the data—"Yes, the study is right, but it shows that *my* conclusion is correct."
6. Peripheral (slight) change—"Okay, . . . these studies convince me that I can't hold that all arrogant people are insecure, but I still maintain that *most* overbearing people are insecure."
7. Total theory change—"Amazing! That evidence is so strong that I can't help believing that this other theory must be right."

These tactics have their good side, too. They not only deflect warranted inferences, but they come in handy to block unwarranted inferences as well! Recall that the vast majority of new theories and preliminary evidence are not going to live up to their promise. Perhaps it is for the better that we have so many ways to block inferences contrary to those we favor. Of course, for knowledge to grow, some creative people such as Newton, Darwin, and Plato must rush in and give themselves over to a new theory before much evidence is in. Their first converts may be more reckless than most, adhering to that new theory because they find it more accurate, of greater scope, consistency, and perhaps simpler, a great advantage. But most of us most of the time need a whole lot of evidence for the contrary-sounding view, but then happily we too become converts: There is much evidence in the historical record that people will believe undesirable evidence if they cannot refuse it.[3]

While these seven responses to anomalous data are fascinating, there is no formula for their use, such as "Whenever you encounter an abortion argument, use 4." No person is prescient enough to know what inferences which we now take for granted will hold for the next five hundred years and which will come to be seen as grossly unwarranted. The critical thinker is not a perfect being, but an ordinary mortal who struggles, pleasurably most of the time, with competing arguments, blocking and admitting inferences as seems right.

HOW TO DISAGREE WITH GOOD ARGUMENTS

It is entirely possible to see that an argument is strongly supported, its inference(s) warranted, and still disagree with it. You might disagree because you can think of *even stronger* reasons in support of a different conclusion (the engulf and devour of "even granting"). "Stronger reasons" mean reasons that are still consistent with the conclusion, yet more relevant, taking in more factors, and more likely to be true as far as you can figure at the moment. An argument with such reasons is therefore, in your opinion, better supported.

Be wary of instances in which you can see that an argument is strongly supported but disagree with it without being able to strongly support your disagreement. You may be entirely right to disagree, but you should be certain that you have not yet worked out why you disagree, and therefore you don't yet know whether you're right to reject the argument. You know only that it doesn't seem right. You might either file it away under "doesn't seem right, I don't agree, will perhaps take it up later" or think about it right away. In the interest of truth, however, it's not fair to say "I disagree, so the argument must be wrong." That is a whopper of an unwarranted inference.

By the same token, it is entirely possible to agree heartily with the conclusion of an argument and not agree that the reasons are relevant or true or consistent with the conclusion, or even consistent with one another.

Pure Dislike

In all the discussion of deduction, induction, and statistics, pure like or dislike will never justify preferring or rejecting an inference. The question is where I find the better evidence for a conclusion. The following, therefore, is always unwarranted:

> I don't like this conclusion.
> Therefore, it is probably not true.

On the other hand, objecting to an inference but not being sure why is fine if you make this clear:

> **I feel that something is amiss with** argument A, **although it appears to be more warranted** than arguments B or C. At the moment **I can't offer a better alternative**. I will continue to research the matter.

This is a frank admission of discontent, but of the superiority of the argument.

SUMMARY

A warranted inference is a conclusion that is deserved because of the strong reasons which support it. Strong reasons are reasons which are true and which directly lead to the conclusion.

There are two types of inference, deduction and induction:

> In deduction, your mind moves from an all-encompassing reason to a more particular conclusion. In a warranted deduction, the conclusion inevitably follows from an all-encompassing reason. The reason(s) must be true.
>
> In induction, your mind moves from a number of particular to a "most likely all" or "most likely this" conclusion. In a warranted inductive leap, there are a sufficient number of particulars which make up the reason. These particulars are true.

READINGS

1. *Here is a theory to explain accounts reported in many places around the world of the killing of people by casting evil spells. Do you believe that the author's inference is warranted? Can you think of another explanation of this eerie phenomenon?*

An individual who is aware that he is the object of sorcery is thoroughly convinced that he is doomed according to the most solemn traditions of his group. His friends and relatives share this certainty. From then on the community withdraws. Standing aloof from the accursed, it treats him not only as though he were already dead but as though he were a source of danger to the entire group. On every occasion and by every action, the [society] suggests death to the unfortunate victim, who no longer hopes to escape what he considers to be his ineluctable fate. Shortly thereafter, sacred rites are held to dispatch him to the realm of shadows [death]. First brutally torn from all of his family and social ties and excluded from all functions and activities through which he experienced self-awareness, then banished by the same forces from the world of the living, the victim yields to the combined effect of intense terror, the sudden total withdrawal of . . . the support of the group, and, finally, to the group's decisive reversal in proclaiming him—once a living man, with rights and obligations—dead and an object of fear, ritual and taboo. Physical integrity [the body] cannot withstand the dissolution of the social personality.[4]

2. What do you think of the following argument by Edward de Bono about humor?

Humor provides an escape from the rigidity of the YES/NO system [of normal logic in which an idea is either right (yes) or wrong (no)]. . . . Humor has its own rules. In humor you are allowed to say things which are obviously wrong or at best unlikely. . . . [Yet an] explanation is funny because it does have a surface plausibility. The explanation has meaning for we can see the crazy logic involved. The ideas do fit together as ideas even though they do not reflect reality.[5]

3. A fundamental moral and philosophical principle is that lying is wrong. Yet are there ever exceptions, and when would such exceptions be warranted? The following paragraph makes the claim that to validate children one should overestimate their talents and beauty, in effect, lie. Assuming that such validation works, do you think that the conclusion that one should use it is warranted? Why?

"Validation" does not mean "reflecting accurately." Parents think wonderful things of their very young children. They invest them with giant talents and beauty. They see normal development as miraculous. And very young children, it seems, need this irrational appreciation of them in order to develop with confidence and self-love. They need to be fed irrational appreciation in order to gain a normal appreciation of themselves. An adolescent's need, for all her nit-picking honesty, is not all that different. A mother does not validate her daughter by seeing her accurately, as she "really is." Where mothers and daughters are concerned, the more accurately the mother views the daughter—the more objective her assessment of the daughter's abilities, skills, and characteristics—the less she is able to validate her.[6]

4. The philosopher Sissela Bok has wrestled with the question when it might be moral to lie. She is quite conservative on the topic, arguing against most of the lying we do for the purported good of others. And although wary of "paternalistic lies," falsehoods told to protect the young, she does offer a principle by which we might decide whether to lie. Do you think her principle is warranted for the validation of children described in the foregoing passage?

It is rare that children, friends, or spouses will have consented in advance to being deceived for their own good. A variation of the requirement for consent is therefore sometimes brought forth: implied consent. Some day, this argument holds, those who are rightly deceived will be grateful for the restraints imposed upon them for their own good. And those who are wrongly deceived will not. This expectation of future gratitude is likened to the ordinary consent given in advance of an action in the following way: If those who are now being deceived for what is truly their own good were completely rational, sane, adult, or healthy, they would consent to what is being done for them. If they were in the liar's position, they, too, would choose to lie out of this altruistic concern.

Can "implied consent" be used as a test of all the paternalistic lies told—in crises, under more trivial circumstances, to shelter or encourage or heal? It would then close the gap between the perspectives of liar and deceived: Their aims—to benefit the deceived—would coincide. The way to tell rightful paternalistic lies from all the others would then be to ask whether the deceived, if completely able to judge his own best interests, would himself want to be duped. If he becomes rational enough to judge at a later time, one could then ask whether he gives his retroactive consent to the deceit—whether he is grateful he was lied to.[7]

NOTES

1. Woody Allen, *Without Feathers* (New York: Ballantine Books, a division of Random House, Inc., 1991), p. 109.
2. *Ibid.*
3. Clark A. Chinn, and William F. Brewer, "The Role of Anomalous Data in Knowledge Acquisition: A Theoretical Framework and Implications for Science Instruction," *Review of Educational Research,* Spring 1993, Vol. 63, No. 1, pp. 1–49.
4. Claude Levi-Strauss, *Structural Anthropology* (New York: Basic Books, a division of Harper Collins 1967), pp. 167–168.
5. Edward de Bono, *Practical Thinking* (New York: Penguin Books, 1992), p. 138.
6. Terri Apter, *Altered Loves: Mothers and Daughters During Adolescence* (New York: A Fawcett Columbine Book Published by Ballantine Books, 1990), p. 128.
7. Sissela Bok, *Lying: Moral Choice in Public and Private Life* (Vintage Books, A Division of Random House, 1989), pp. 226–227.

6

Other Connections

Assumptions and Implications

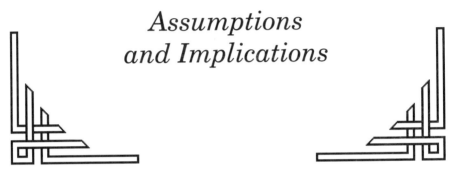

One of the most exciting facts about arguments is that they contain parts which are frequently invisible unless sought out. Assumptions lie beneath the argument and constitute the basement of the structure; implications are a weathervane which points above and beyond the structure, pointing to areas outside the argument that the argument will affect (see Figure 6-1).

THE BEST ARGUMENTS EXPOSE
THEIR MAJOR ASSUMPTIONS

Each argument has an enormous number of assumptions, for instance that the world exists and that the argument is comprehensible. But these assumptions don't affect our acceptance of an argument (that the world exists doesn't affect my views of a theory that capital punishment is a deterrent to criminals). But there are assumptions beneath arguments for capital punishment (for instance, that criminals are as rational as non-criminals), which would affect my acceptance of a theory of capital punishment. These types of assumptions are the major assumptions of an argument. *A major assumption is a claim, which, if you knew it, would be a significant factor influencing your decision to accept that argument.*

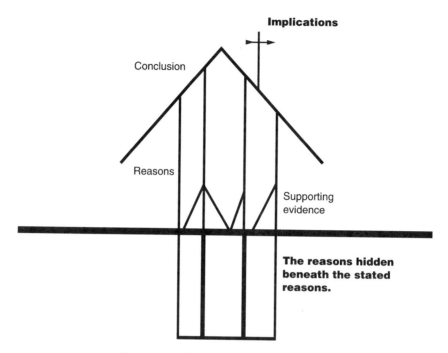

Figure 6-1   Structure of Assumptions

If an author is exposing an assumption, it will be with some form of these terms: "assumes," "presupposes," or "presumes." These words should convey the sense of something *beneath the reasons* that is different from them. Here is the language commonly used:

> I am **assuming that** . . .
> **The presupposition** here **is that** . . .
> **The presumption is that** . . .
> **Given the assumption that** . . .
> The author's claim is **predicated on the assumption that** . . .

BUT MANY ARGUMENTS DO NOT DISPLAY ASSUMPTIONS

Locating and bringing up hidden assumptions for scrutiny is enlightening. But notice the wording: "bringing up." If "assumes," "presupposes," or "presumes" isn't used somehow in a statement, then the statement is probably not an assumption. This cannot be stressed enough. Don't light on some hapless reason sitting innocently in the argument and label it the assumption.

There are two good ways to flush hidden assumptions from below. One is to think of a counterargument; the other is to seek a pivotal term.

TURN A COUNTERARGUMENT ON ITS HEAD

Oddly enough, thinking of a counterargument can often help you to see the assumptions beneath an argument you are inspecting. For example, say that you hear a senator arguing that taxes should go up because we need to pay off the national debt. How do you figure out a major assumption here? If you know a different argument, that taxes should not be increased because keeping taxes low will encourage businesspeople to make and sell more products which government can tax, thus collecting more money, you can argue that the senator may be assuming that keeping the tax rate low will not stimulate business sufficiently to reduce the national debt. You took the reason for the second argument and put a "not" in front of it. Or if someone else argues that we don't need to pay off the debt because it has no effect on the economy, you can say that the senator seems to assume that paying off the national debt *would help* the economy.

This technique, of turning the reason of an alternative argument on its head, may explain why it is easier to locate assumptions beneath arguments we don't agree with. Discovering one's assumptions can be a delightful or unsettling surprise, and it often leads to an enlarged understanding.

SEEK THE PIVOTAL TERM

Let's examine this standard argument:

> Abortion is murder because it involves the killing of a fetus.

Is there a word that does most of the persuading here? If you were going to counterargue, with which word would you most take issue? Underline it.

Definitions for the terms "abortion," "killing," and "fetus" could probably be found to meet the approval of both pro- and anti-abortionists. But what about murder? "Murder" is defined as the unlawful killing of one human being by another.[1] From this definition we can see that the arguer is assuming that a fetus is a human being rather than merely human tissue (otherwise it couldn't be murder).

The standard counterargument runs as follows:

A pregnant woman is morally entitled to exercise choice and abort the fetus.

In light of the term "human being," what would you suppose that this side is assuming about the fetus? The assumption is probably that the fetus is merely human tissue, a potential human being rather than an actual one. To claim that the pro-choice advocate *probably* assumes that the fetus is not an actual human being is to hedge, because almost everyone in our society assumes that all human beings have an equal right to life: One human being has no right to kill another human being.*

Unearthing Assumptions Engages Arguments All of this additional insight into the abortion example came from careful investigation of the pivotal term, "murder." But where is it getting us? *Both arguments are forced into closer communication.* You'll realize that this is no small feat if you've noticed how polarized the arguments about abortion often are. Now the pro-life side has to convince the pro-choice side that a fetus is a human being by appealing to some evidence that clinches the issue; for example, "The fetus has a heartbeat by the fifteenth day, so it must be a human being at that time." The pro-choice side for its part must convince the pro-lifers that a fetus is not (yet) a human being; for example, "Brain function and the capacity for suffering don't appear until the fourth month, so it's not human until that point." Do you notice that concessions have been imaginatively wrung from both sides?

Practice With Pivotals See if there's a pivotal word in the following argument:

> Education is merely a subtle form of manipulation. Students are encouraged to acquire a certain set of facts and values, with grades constituting reward or punishment, depending upon how well a particular student has been conditioned.

Presumably, nobody has trouble understanding "education," in the sense of schools, classes, and the like. The same applies to "grades"; good grades are rewards, poor grades are "dings" for not being up to snuff. One pivotal term here is "manipulation." Another is "conditioned,"

---

*It is fascinating to learn how many cultures have not acted out of this assumption that all members have an equal right to life. Of course, it is always possible to consider the fetus to be a human being yet sanction aborting it on the grounds that a woman's freedom from the burden of birthing is more important than the life of a human being. I would assume this position is rare.

which is a synonym for manipulation. These terms carry the weight of the argument. Both the counterarguer and the arguer will need to give a careful definition to that term "manipulation," convincing the other side that it does or does not fit into the larger definition of education.

In sum, the discovery of pivotal terms uncovers definitional assumptions, clarifies arguments, and gives counterarguments a chance to engage one another more directly. Pivotal terms are trapdoors through which you can fall to the basement. And once you're down there and can see what is shoring up a controversial argument, you realize that those particular assumptions need not necessarily be made; without explicit awareness of assumptions, it is all too easy to accept them without even being aware of it. Pivotal terms occur frequently in arguments, and you should be on the lookout for them.

VALUES ASSUMPTIONS

Many arguments proceed on the assumption that one value is more important than another. Here is a brief list in which the terms can be switched (e.g., an argument can assume that social order is of greater value than political freedom):

Assumes That . . .	Is of Greater Value Than . . .
political freedom	social order
personal gain	consideration for others
social harmony	personal expression
equality of opportunity	racial quotas
seriousness	humor
leisure time	making more money
thrift	generosity

Did you spot any possible false dichotomies? Did you wish that some of these terms were defined? Don't fall into the pat answer, "All of these things are valuable." Perhaps they are. But the important question is how much of which under what precise circumstances.

What Values Assumptions are Predominant? Have you ever caught yourself operating on an assumption which you had never even considered? It is really an eye-opener to discover these assumptions. The following assumptions were held by many people in the past two decades. Do you agree with them, and do you think that most people accept them these days?

The new, the shocking in art is more valuable than the traditional.
Social forces shape the individual more than he shapes himself.
Values are relative to time and culture, not absolute.

Sunday-Monday Syndrome Very different arguments are erected on diametrically opposed values assumptions. What is interesting is catching ourselves believing both. For example, on Sunday someone barges in front of you in line. You mentally argue, "Oh, well, forget it. That person just wasn't paying attention, and probably has lots of problems." Sunday's assumption: The best way to live is to turn the other cheek. On Monday someone barges in front of you in line. You mentally argue, "What nerve! That so-and-so can't do that to me; I was here first." Monday's assumption: The best way to live is to stick up for your own rights.

Unexamined values assumptions tend to make beliefs and decisions automatic. (It can be assumed that that's bad.) Because we live in a pluralistic society, we have more opportunity to encounter people with different values assumptions (and as long as those values don't include harming others, it can be assumed that that's good).

FACTUAL ASSUMPTIONS

We make arguments and base decisions not only on what we believe should be, but on what we believe is, the case. Here are some examples of factual assumptions examined in the language of argumentation:

> I would agree with the **author's assumption that in fact . . .**
> The author **is assuming that** in expressing anger one will get rid of it; in fact, studies have shown that . . .
> Is the author **assuming that . . . is in fact the case?**
> I would **question the assumption that** . . .
> This argument **rests on the assumption that** . . .

Sometimes you will read, "The underlying assumption is that . . ." but since assumptions by definition "underlie," the word is redundant.

Assumptions Take the Most Work, But are Worth it Unearthing assumptions is a skill that takes more practice and thought than any of the other twelve basics of critical thinking. Beginners often claim that the reasons of an argument are its assumptions (and sometimes in informal conversation reasons *are* called assumptions, just to complicate matters). But assumptions should cast a new light on the argument, not rehash the argument or be irrelevant to it. It is fascinating that in any group of people digging up assumptions, some will come up with assumptions that you would never have thought of—a piece of evidence for the importance of the community of thinkers.

IMPLICATIONS GO BEYOND THE ARGUMENT

The press uses "implicate" in its most lurid incarnation: to be involved intimately or incriminatingly, as when a newspaper informs us that someone is involved in a scandal. "Rock Star Implicated in Affairs with Twenty Cocaine Dealers," it blares.

But in its older, more interesting sense, "implication" means to interweave or entangle; entwine. We constantly entangle ideas. Implication has come to mean the way a conclusion might affect (entangle) other areas outside the argument. Here is an example:

> As long as women continue to work, the American family will remain small. For the first time in many generations, there will be far fewer people under eighteen years. **The implications** of this demographic change **are numerous.** As the average age rises, everything from advertisements to government policy will change to cater to this aging majority.

An implication is often a *practical upshot,* or outcome, of a conclusion. The foregoing passage argues quickly to the conclusion that there will be fewer children, then goes on to explore the outcome of this conclusion for society at large. The implications discussed might be favorable or unfavorable. When the implications are positive, they function as additional reasons for an argument.

But implications can also be negative, neutral, or unclear. It is not clear, for example, whether the writer above thinks that such catering to the majority is a good thing.

Or say that you are arguing against increased taxes, claiming that one implication of heavier taxation would be the bankrupting of many small businesses. This is an unfavorable implication and one that could be offered as a reason in a counterargument.

Remember that *implications arise beyond the argument at hand.* They are additions to an argument's main reasons. Implications should be easy to spot, because when they're mentioned, they are identified.

Language

> **The implications** for the atmosphere from tropical deforestation **are immense**.
> **There are a number of implications** to this idea.
> **Important implications are at stake** with this argument.

Here's another example of implication: Say that you're an unemployed computer whiz who worked hard to become skilled at writing. You find the following claim in a computer magazine:

> Informal surveys indicate that the average microcomputer owner buys nine to twelve books about that computer within six months of purchase.

What might the financial implications be for you? What other implications might there be for publishing houses, businesses, or others? If you hit upon the possibility of writing a book about microcomputers, then you saw an implication in the facts that you were given.

Notice that these implications are just possibilities—you haven't collected your royalties yet. Implications are usually predictions whose truth has yet to be established. Furthermore, implications can themselves become conclusions of different arguments, with all the same structural properties of arguments (e.g., it is arguable whether advertisements would change to cater to an aging population).

SUMMARY

Assumptions Defined

A student came up with a clever definition of assumptions: "the (hidden) reasons for the reasons given in an argument."

Look for the following:

1. pivotal, significant terms
2. alternative arguments whose reasons you can turn around

Types of Assumptions

1. values assumptions
2. factual assumptions

Assumptions are hidden unless stated as such.

Implications Defined

Implications are possible outcomes that follow from an argument. Unless explicitly mentioned, they are factors outside of the argument at hand.

EXERCISES

1. What is assumed by the claim that criminals can be rehabilitated by being put in a humane environment?
2. What is assumed by the claim that a humane environment won't rehabilitate criminals?
3. Consider the adages, "Good guys finish last," and, "Give them an inch and they'll take a mile." What is assumed in these proverbs about human nature: Is it good, bad, or neutral?
4. Can you think of other adages that entail assumptions about human nature?
5. Answer the following, giving values and factual assumptions if you can. What do most Democrats assume about taxing the wealthy? What do Republicans generally assume about it?
6. List all possible implications you can think of if intelligent beings from another galaxy were to come for a visit. Do a number of implications hinge on some important fact about these beings?

READINGS

1. There are numerous assumptions beneath any given argument, for instance, that the world exists, that the argument in question exists, and that argument is a valuable way to persuade. Some philosophers, concerned about this vast basement full of hidden assumptions and their effect on arguments, have claimed that we should try to construct arguments with few or no assumptions. Karl Popper counters this argument by pointing out its own "colossal assumption":

Since all argument must proceed from assumptions, it is plainly impossible to demand that all assumptions should be based on argument. The demand raised by many philosophers that we should start with no assumption whatever . . . and even the weaker demand that we should start with a very small set of assumptions ('categories') are both in this form inconsistent. For they themselves rest on the truly colossal assumption that it is possible to start without, or with only a few assumptions, and still to obtain results that are worthwhile.[2]

2. Even arguments that discuss assumptions have still more hidden assumptions. What assumptions remain hidden in this argument?

Some Pernicious Assumptions About I. Q.

Many people reason as follows: "I studied hard but didn't do well on that test, so I must not have the mental ability to do well in that subject." This argument is based on the questionable assumption that each person is endowed with a fixed mental ability, some people having more, and others (always including the person worrying) having far less.

I.Q. was never meant to measure "mental ability." I.Q. is merely a measure of how schoolchildren are achieving vis-à-vis children their age. I.Q. is totally meaningless for adults (presumably because everyone is learning something different). Further, since test-taking is inextricably bound up with an individual's motivation toward, and past exposure to, a subject, it is also meaningless as a measure of a child's ability, only measuring that child's achievement as compared with the achievement of other children that age in that subject area.

A far more pleasant assumption would be that most people are born with almost equal mental abilities. Then motivation, self-confidence, and opportunity to learn are the operant factors in the different performances among most people.

This assumption probably has no firmer evidence to support it than does the notion of a large range of innate abilities among people. But the implications of accepting the "equality" assumption are vastly different from the "innate-range-as-measured-by-I.Q." assumption.

The implications of concluding that each time one fails one has overreached his mental abilities are that this person will not continue to strive in that area. The person's feeling of inadequacy may spread to other endeavors as well.

On the other hand, if a person regards himself as having the same mental abilities as those who succeed in a subject, he will suppose that he did not have enough exposure to the subject or wasn't properly motivated. Not only is there considerably less sting to this interpretation, but the person is far more likely to try again, and harder. The implications for a happier, more striving society are clear if more people would operate out of this assumption of general mental equality.

3. *This is a stunning argument by Margaret Visser, not because of its unusual structure (which is one conclusion with a mass of evidence), but because it points to the overwhelming use of corn in our society. What implications can you imagine flow from this argument?*

You cannot buy anything at all in a North American supermarket which has been untouched by corn, with the occasional and single exception of fresh fish—and even that has almost certainly been delivered to the store in cartons or wrappings which are partially created out of corn. Meat is largely corn. So is milk: American livestock and poultry is fed and fattened on corn and cornstalks. Frozen meat and fish has a light corn starch coating on it to prevent excessive drying. The brown and golden colouring which constitutes the visual appeal of many soft drinks and puddings comes from corn. All canned foods are bathed in liquid containing corn. Every carton, every wrapping, every plastic container depends on corn products—indeed all modern paper and cardboard, with the exception of newspaper and tissue, is coated in corn.

One primary product of the maize plant is corn oil, which is not only a cooking fat but is important in margarine (butter, remember, is also corn). Corn oil is an essential ingredient in soap, in insecticides (all vegetables and fruits in a supermarket have been treated with insecticides), and of course in such factory-made products as mayonnaise and salad dressings. The taste-bud sensitizer, monosodium glutamate or MSG, is commonly made of corn protein.

Corn syrup—viscous, cheap, not too sweet—is the very basis of candy, ketchup, and commercial ice cream. It is used in processed meats, condensed milk, soft drinks, many modern beers, gin, and vodka. It even goes into the purple marks stamped on meat and other foods. Corn syrup provides body where "body" is lacking, in sauces and soups for instance (the trade says it adds "mouth-feel"). It prevents crystallization and discolouring; it makes foods hold their shape, prevents ingredients from separating, and stabilizes moisture content. It is extremely useful when long shelf-life is the goal.

Corn starch is to be found in baby foods, jams, pickles, vinegar, yeast. It serves as a carrier for the bubbling agents in baking powder; is mixed in with table salt, sugar (particularly icing sugar), and many instant coffees in order to promote easy pouring. It is essential in anything dehydrated, such as milk (already corn, of course) or instant potato flakes. Corn starch is white, odourless, tasteless, and easily moulded. It is the invisible coating and the universal neutral carrier for the active ingredients in thousands of products, from headache tablets, toothpastes, and cosmetics to detergents, dog food, match heads, and charcoal briquettes.

All textiles, all leathers are covered in corn. Corn is used when making things stick (adhesives all contain corn)—and also whenever it is necessary that things should not stick: candy is dusted or coated with corn, all kinds of metal and plastic moulds use corn. North Americans eat only one-tenth of the corn their countries produce, but that tenth amounts to one and a third kilograms (3 lb.) of corn—in milk, poultry, cheese, meat, butter, and the rest—per person per day.[3]

4. *An assumption about time in Western, industrialized countries is that people live in a present which is moving towards an indefinite future. So it was a pleasurable shock to learn that in traditional African cultures people assume that they are living in a present which is moving forward into the past. If you think about it for a minute, this view is every bit as logical (Didn't you just create some past for yourself as you read this last sentence?). The following is African philosopher John Mbiti's account of this assumption about time. Note the implications he infers for the individual and society.*

. . . according to traditional concepts, time is a two-dimensional phenomenon with a long past, a present, and virtually no future. The linear concept of time in Western thought, with an indefinite past, present and infinite future, is practically foreign to African thinking. The future is virtually absent because events which lie in it have not taken place, they have not been realized and cannot, therefore, constitute time. . . . Actual time is therefore what is present and what is past. It moves "backward" rather than "forward"; and people set their minds not on future things, but chiefly on what has taken place.

This time orientation, governed as it is by the two main dimensions of the present and the past, dominates African understanding of the individual, the community and the universe . . . Time has to be experienced [as opposed to anticipated, as in the West] in order to make sense or to become real. A person experiences time partly in his own individual life, and partly through the society which goes back many generations before his own birth. Since what is in the future has not been experienced, it does not make sense; it cannot, therefore, constitute part of time, and people do not know how to think about it—unless, of course, it is something which falls within the rhythm of natural phenomena.

. . . People expect the years to come and go, in an endless rhythm like that of day and night, and like the waning and waxing of the moon. They expect the events of the rain season, planting, harvesting, dry season, rain season again, planting again, and so on to continue forever. Each year comes and goes, adding to the time dimension of the past. Endlessness or "eternity" for them is something that lies only in the region of the past. . . .[4]

5. *What implications can you draw for the individual and society from the Western assumption of time?*

Of course, the illogical sounding view of time is the scientific theory that time is directly related to speed. Ironically, this strangest view has the best evidence in its favor. For example, exquisitely sensitive clocks placed at the equator and north pole exactly follow Einstein's mathematical predictions of millionths of a second difference, the clock at the north pole running ever so slightly faster due to the greater speed of land rotation there. But perhaps because the speed-time connection is not part of ordinary human experience, we must live by other assumptions about the nature and importance of the past and the future.

NOTES

1. *The American Heritage Dictionary,* Third edition (Boston: Houghton Mifflin Company, 1992), s. v. "murder."
2. Karl R. Popper, *The Open Society and Its Enemies* (Princeton, NJ: Princeton University Press, 1971), II, p. 230.
3. Margaret Visser, *Much Depends on Dinner: The Extraordinary History and Mythology, Allure and Obsessions, Perils and Taboos of an Ordinary Meal* (New York: Collier Books, a division of the Macmillan Publishing Co., 1988), pp. 22–24. Reprinted by permission.
4. John S. Mbiti, *African Religions and Philosophies* (New York: Doubleday & Company, Anchor Books Edition, 1970), pp. 21, 23, and 27.

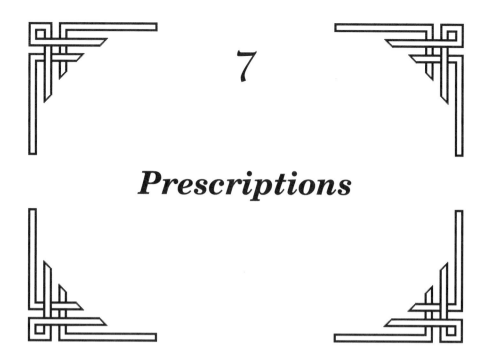

7

Prescriptions

A FINAL TOUCH

Some arguments give an issue, reasons, conclusion—and stop there. Other arguments add a final touch in the form of a solution, usually a recommendation that something be done. Here's a brief example:

> The dramatic increase in deaths from teenage drunk driving leads to the inescapable conclusion that the problem of drunk driving in this population has worsened. Therefore, we believe that all advertising of alcohol should be banned.

The recommendation to ban advertising of alcohol is really an additional conclusion which goes beyond the basic conclusion that the problem of drunk driving among teenagers has worsened. This second conclusion forms a second, higher roof-line of an argument (see Figure 7-1).

In this type of argument, the solution usually lies at the end of the essay or book. If a solution is proposed at the beginning, chances are that the argument is purely prescriptive. Notice that you can agree with the argument without having to agree with the prescription, and vice versa.

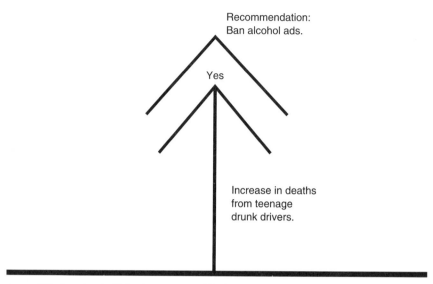

Issue: Whether drunk driving has worsened in the teenage population.

Figure 7-1   Structure of Prescriptions

PRESCRIPTIVE ARGUMENTS

Unlike the foregoing, some arguments are all "final touch." Their only conclusion is a recommendation of what should be done. Their structure is just like that of the arguments we've seen in the five preceding chapters. In fact, a number of purely prescriptive arguments have been presented in those chapters. Do you remember them?

Prescriptive arguments are values arguments, telling us what should be done. At the opposite extreme lie descriptive arguments that claim that something is the case (see Chapter 4).

Prescriptive Language

The solution seems to lie in . . .
The only way (or **one way**) **out of this dilemma is** . . .
The advice I would give for this problem is . . .
In light of the seriousness of the issue, the author **recommends that** . . .

Countering a prescritive conclusion:

It is arguable whether we should ban all alcoholic beverage ads.
Although the author's argument is sound, **it is not a foregone conclusion that** her **prescription is the best** one.

Countering a factual conclusion:

> **It is arguable whether ... is the case.**

Detached Advice

There are paragraphs, even books, full of loose arguments that are prescriptive. (For a review of factual claims and argument in the loose sense, see Chapter 1.) Rather than being argument structures, these more closely resemble detached pieces of lumber:

> It's a good idea to marry later in life. Just keep company with a number of friends in your twenties, relax, and enjoy your youth. Don't worry that if you don't accept the first person who seems interested in you you'll have lost your chance for romance. That is just not true. Don't grab the first person who comes along. My advice is to wait until you're at least in your thirties, then get married.

This paragraph makes sense, and is built around the advice (here the conclusion) to marry in your thirties. But notice that the other sentences don't support the conclusion. They are *related pieces of advice* (i.e., to have a number of friends, not to worry about finding a mate). If you try to turn these into reasons supporting the conclusion, it doesn't work: It's a good idea to marry later in life because you should just keep company with a number of friends in your twenties. While there is meaning and continuity of thought, one thought doesn't constitute a reason or get its support from another in that paragraph. On the other hand, watch this:

> It's a good idea to marry later in life. Too many people in their late teens and twenties don't yet know who they are and make fatal mistakes in choosing mates.

That is a brief formal argument. See the difference?

More Hybrids

For more evidence that life is complex, observe that much of what we read is a combination of strict and loose argumentation. A stack or two of descriptive or prescriptive lumber is followed by an argument, then perhaps more facts.

Sometimes a small argument nestles among a number of factual claims. See if you can find one here:

> In medieval society people generally blew their noses into their hands, just as they ate with their hands. That necessitated special precepts for nose-

cleaning at table. Politeness, "courtoisie," required that one blow one's nose into the left hand if one took meat with the right. But this precept was in fact restricted to the table [in all other situations, people blew their noses into both hands]. It arose solely out of consideration for others. The distasteful feeling frequently aroused today by the mere thought of soiling the fingers in this way was at first entirely absent.[1]

In the midst of this colorful description, the author argues briefly that the reason for nose-blowing into the left hand at table was consideration for others.

SUMMARY

Some arguments contain a second conclusion, called the solution or prescription. The reader should evaluate the prescription on its own merits, separately from the conclusion.

Some arguments contain only one conclusion, which happens to be prescriptive.

Sometimes arguments nestle among factual claims.

EXERCISES

1. Take any three arguments presented in the first six chapters and invent a prescription that is consistent with each of the arguments.
2. Make a formal argument that detached pieces of advice are not as valuable as formal arguments. Include a prescription in your argument.

READINGS

1. Bertrand Russell has some wonderful advice about how to avoid feeling envy:

Of all the characteristics of ordinary nature, envy is the most unfortunate; not only does the envious person wish to inflict misfortune and do whatever he can with impunity, but he is also himself rendered unhappy by envy. Instead of deriving pleasure from what he has, he derives pain from what others have. If he can, he deprives others of their advantages, which to him is as desirable as it would be to secure the same advantages himself. . . . Fortunately, however, there is in human nature a compensating passion, namely, that of admiration. Whoever wishes to increase human happiness must wish to increase admiration and to diminish envy.

What cure is there for envy? . . . The only cure for envy in the case of ordinary men and women is happiness, and the difficulty is that envy is itself a terrible obstacle to happiness. . . .

Merely to realize the causes of one's own envious feelings is to take a long step towards curing them. The habit of thinking in terms of comparison is a fatal one. When anything pleasant occurs it should be enjoyed to the full, without stopping to think that it is not so pleasant as something else that may possibly be happening to someone else. "Yes," says the envious man, "this is a sunny day and it is springtime and the birds are singing and the flowers are in bloom, but I understand that the springtime in Sicily is a thousand times more beautiful, that the birds sing more exquisitely in the groves of Helicon, and that the rose of Sharon is more lovely than any in my garden." And as he thinks these thoughts, the sun is dimmed and the birds' song becomes a meaningless twitter and the flowers seem not worth a moment's regard. All the other joys of life he treats in the same way. "Yes," he will say to himself, "the lady of my heart is lovely, I love her and she loves me, but how much more exquisite must have been the Queen of Sheba! Ah, if I had but Solomon's opportunities!" All such comparisons are pointless and foolish; whether the Queen of Sheba or our next-door neighbor be the cause of discontent, either is equally futile. With the wise man, what he has does not cease to be enjoyable because someone else has something else. Envy, in fact, is one form of a vice, partly moral, partly intellectual, which consists in seeing things never in themselves but only in their relations. I am earning, let us say, a salary sufficient for my needs. I should be content, but I hear that someone else whom I believe to be in no way my superior is earning a salary twice as great as mine. Instantly, if I am of an envious disposition, the satisfactions to be derived from what I have grow dim, and I begin to be eaten up with a sense of injustice. For all this the proper cure is mental discipline, the habit of not thinking profitless thoughts. . . . You can get away from envy by enjoying the pleasures that come your way, by doing the work that you have to do, and by avoiding comparisons with those whom you imagine, perhaps quite falsely, to be more fortunate than yourself.[2]

2. *Find the formal argument(s) in this advice to keep a budget, delivered in delightful style:*

If you do take the time to plan your financial future and to track your progress as it unfolds, don't be slavish about it. Who cares if you forget to jot down every last expense? Who cares if you go over budget from time to time? The idea isn't to account for every penny (although it would be an intriguing experiment for three months to see exactly where the money goes). The idea is to spend less than you earn each year, get out of debt, and build a secure, comfortable future.

The trick is to live a little beneath your means. Sounds glamorous, no? Okay, no. But if, earning $23,000 a year, you can force yourself to live as if you were earning $18,000 or $20,000 (people do, you know); or if, earning $140,000, you can live as if you were making $115,000—your life in the long run will be far more secure and, soon, more comfortable to boot. Your money begins to work for you, your savings swell, and you can pay for things with cash. The other way, living a bit above your means, you get deeper and deeper into hock, and life costs an extra 18% in finance charges. One way you're motivated by the carrot (saving up in great anticipation of whatever it is you're saving up for), the other way by the stick (having to pay for it—even though it wound up raining the whole time you were there).

Living beneath your means is tough. (Living within your means is tough!) Making a game of it helps. Seeing it as a challenge helps. "Paying yourself first" helps (direct the first 10% or 15% of every paycheck to a savings account or mutual fund). But tough as it is, as you begin to see results, it gets easier. And if you want to get ahead of the game, you're more likely to succeed this way than by buying lottery tickets each week, hoping to win big.

One way or another, the future will come. With a little planning, you can have a say in how it looks. Even the difference between coming out just $500 ahead each year rather than $500 behind is the difference, for a 25-year-old who earns 8% after tax on his savings or borrows at 12%, between having $57,000 at age 55—or owing $120,000.

Think of your budget not as your albatross, but as your secret weapon.[3]

3. Is the following passage prescriptive, in your opinion? Is it an argument in the loose or strict sense?

Basically, I require two things of an author. The first is that he have something interesting to say—something that will either teach me or amuse me. If he doesn't I stop reading. The second requirement is that he not waste my time getting out what he has to say. If he idles, I conclude that I can be taught quicker elsewhere.

Beyond these two basic requirements, what I find most appealing in a writer is an authentic personal manner. I like to see him come across as a living, companionable human being, not as an emotional eunuch or stuffed shirt. I like to have an author talk to me, unbend to me, speak right out to me. If his prose has a natural, conversational rhythm to it, if it's forged out of basic, idiomatic English rather than pretentious Highbrow English, if it's stamped with the mark of his quirky personality, if it carries the ring of honesty and passionate conviction, then he's my man. What I'm saying, I guess, is that I like an author to be himself, warts and all. It shows me that he trusts me with his vulnerability, isn't afraid of me, and isn't afraid of himself either.[4]

NOTES

1. Norbert Elias, *The History of Manners, The Civilizing Process* (New York: Pantheon Books, a division of Random House, Inc., 1978), 1, p. 148. This book was published again in 1993 under the title *The Civilizing Process,* by Blackwell Publishers, London.
2. Bertrand Russell, *The Conquest of Happiness* (New York: Bantam Books, a division of Grosset & Dunlap, Inc., 1968), pp. 56–59. This book was published again in 1971 by Liveright Books, New York.
3. Andrew Tobias, *The Only Other Investment Guide You'll Ever Need* (New York: Simon & Schuster, Bantam Books, 1989), pp. 32–33. Copyright © 1987 by Andrew Tobias. Reprinted by permission.
4. John Trimble, *Writing with Style: Conversations on the Art of Writing* (Englewood Cliffs, NJ: Prentice-Hall, Inc., 1975), pp. 69–70.

8

Evaluating Alternative Arguments in Light of Their Evidence

REVIEWING THE STRUCTURE

At this point you have learned all twelve fundamental argument features, as shown in Figure 8-1. Not bad! If you had never thought in this way, you've greatly improved your critical thinking skills. The more you practice, the more adept you become.

Although the foregoing chapters touched on the evaluation of arguments, their major purpose was to help you get used to these twelve main features. Now that you know them, these next seven chapters will concentrate on judgment—how to build arguments and insulate them from holes.

EVALUATE BY COMPARING

Toward the end of Chapter 4, in the section titled "Comparison of the Evidence for Alternatives," I mentioned that the best method is to watch for alternative arguments on an issue and to compare the evidence. This advice to "comparison shop" holds for the evaluation of any argument. **Critical thinking is the consideration of alternative arguments in light of their evidence.**

What if you don't know an alternative argument? At least stop for

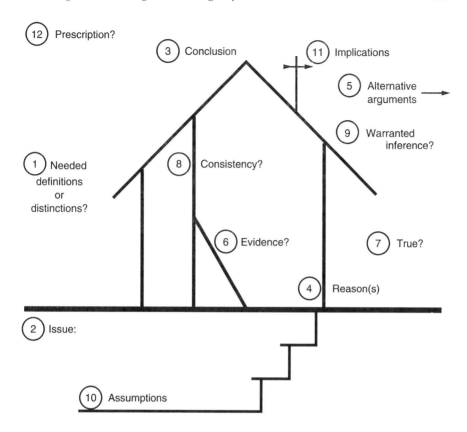

Figure 8-1   The Twelve Basics

a minute and try to conjure one up (this gets easier with practice, wide reading, and age).

STRENGTHEN EVALUATIONS WITH "BETTER," "CLEARER," "MORE"

With your understanding of argument structure, think of how an argument could be made more persuasive in light of an alternative. Three major evaluative terms are "better," "clearer," and "more." Could an argument, say, define "justice" or "pleasure" more clearly than it does, thus comparing more favorably to comparable arguments that you know? Likewise, could the argument be strengthened by better reasons or more evidence in light of your knowledge of alternative arguments, or spell out implications more clearly (see Figure 8-2)? Like insulation, "better," "clearer," and "more" can be used anywhere that you think they're needed in the structure.

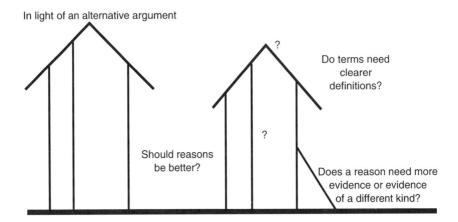

Figure 8-2   Strengthening an Argument

Be Explicit

The more helpful you can be to an argument, the better your criticism. For instance, rather than stopping with the easily made remark, "That argument needs better reasons," be helpful by actually coming up with better reasons:

> That argument **could be supported by better reasons, such as** . . .
> **There are more central reasons is favor of the argument. They are** . . .
> Hacker's argument **needs better substantiation in the form of** careful cross-cultural studies.

If possible, go on to explain why your reasons are better:

> **These reasons would provide better support for the author's conclusion, because** . . .
> **Such evidence would result in a stronger argument, because** . . .

This same explicitness should be the hallmark of your suggestions for clarity. If you cannot understand the author, you should show what feature(s) of the argument you don't comprehend. If you think that a term is unclear, you should show by a distinction how it could be interpreted in two different senses, each of which alters the meaning of the argument. If you want additional reasons, evidence, or an explicit assumption, you should explain how these will help the argument.

CREATE A BETTER ALTERNATIVE ARGUMENT

What if you think that the author should have offered more reasons, but you can't come up with any? Remember that an alternative argument or a counterargument can be quite revelatory of what could improve an argument. Consider the following:

> Modern technology, such as telephones, television, cars, and airplanes, has been a tremendous factor in uniting people and creating what has been called the "global village." Instead of communicating over a few hundred yards—the farthest that most people could afford to wander throughout the history of the world until this century—people now maintain communications over hundreds and thousands of miles.

But consider:

> The excellence of modern technology keeps people apart as never before. We are now so fixated by long-distance communication that most of us don't even know our next-door neighbor. We have lost the far more important and potentially supportive "local village" to the cold, anonymous "global village."

In light of each argument, it will be easier to see where the other needs fleshing out with "better," "clearer," "more." Perhaps your class could discuss these arguments and make helpful suggestions for both, then vote on which side convinces you more. For a review of counterarguments, see Chapter 3.

Define for Clarity

Don't forget the importance of defining the crucial terms in all arguments. By now you've noticed that good arguers do a lot of defining. "Define" comes from the Latin verb *definire,* to set bounds to. If bounds are not set for the more abstract terms, then we're all over the block rather than inside the one argument structure where we're supposed to be.*

Don't Abuse the Request to Define   As always, balance and a sense of fairness are crucial. If one wished to be abusive, one could attack nearly all terms in an argument by going after the definitions ("What do you mean by 'attack'?" "What do you mean by 'definition'?")

---

*Edward de Bono argues that sloppy definitions can play a very important part in critical thinking at times, because they keep the mind free and creative. I'd be a bit more cautious to the extent of claiming that we should know when we are being sloppy and use sloppiness deliberately but not sloppily.

We've all probably done our share of irritating and stalling someone by this tactic. To the request to "Go study," for example, "What do you mean by 'study'?" The chances are excellent that the person responding was not in the least interested in the philosophy of education. The tack of asking for definitions should always be taken when you have the interests of truth in mind; but it should be taken *only* when you have the interests of truth in mind. So the desire to know the truth is a necessary and sufficient condition for requiring a more precise definition. For more on definition, see Chapter 1.

Novel and Unnecessary   It is usually a compliment to say that an idea is novel. If an argument has unusual but relevant and persuasive reasons, by all means give it that compliment. If the reasons are not relevant, then they are unnecessary. Remember to think about what might be better removed from an argument (see Chapter 1).

SUMMARY

Mulling over the major features of an argument, you should ask which of them could be better, more fully explored, or clearer.

A quick counterargument is an excellent tack for discovering what else an argument needs.

Don't abuse the request to define. Use it and all critical techniques with a will to get at the truth.

Critical thinking is the consideration of alternative arguments in light of their evidence.

EXERCISE

Is watching the news a waste of time or is it worthwhile? Use your knowledge of the twelve basics to make a rough draft of arguments on both sides. Identify the parts of the argument (reason, conclusion, etc.) in the margin. Then, using a different-colored pen, go back and improve on each argument in light of the other.

READINGS

1. No doubt you have noticed that arguments are messy. They are messy because, as indicated in Chapter 3, arguers don't use the tools of argumentation in any prescribed order. Arguments are also messy in the sense that even good arguments leave themselves open to improvements in a lot of places.

This disagreement between Eric and Sherry on advertising has many arguments and contains every critical thinking phrase in the book—almost. Follow along, noticing how each has to define and improve his or her arguments as a result of the other's response. Please do not assume that you should be arguing this well!

Eric argues:

Advertisements are in general misleading. Advertisers are notorious for misrepresenting their products to the public. For instance, how many ads have you seen in which the woman smoking is tall, slim, beautiful, and—as if that weren't enough—dressed gorgeously? **The implication is that** if you smoke, you will be all of these things too (unless you happen to be male, in which case you'll be instantly transformed into a handsome cowboy).

Not only are the users of advertisers' products supposed to be beautiful people, but they are eternally happy. We are constantly treated to the sight of men and women in ecstasy over one product or another, be it dish soap or laxatives. Further, the images of men and women are often sexist: It's the woman who beams at her "whiter than white" wash, the man who delights in his brand of motor oil.

Finally, **the most serious objection** to advertisements is the outright falsity of many of the claims made.

Next, Sherry's argument:

Advertisements are not in general misleading. Eric's argument is **based on a questionable assumption.** Is there a soul alive who seriously believes that he or she will be magically transformed into a beautiful woman or a cowboy upon lighting a cigarette? That would certainly be an **unwarranted inference.** Eric's particular **argument** against smoking advertisements **could be better if he offered** health reasons against such advertisements. But this argument against cigarettes **is not relevant to the issue whether** advertising is generally misleading.

In what sense can it be said to be "misleading" for advertisers to show attractive people using their products? **Why must** an advertiser have to show normal or even unattractive people using a product? It's obvious that if someone who is "easy on the eyes" is demonstrating a product in a beautiful setting, we're more interested in watching. An advertiser should not be criticized merely for playing along with human nature.

The **same type of counterargument applies** to images of happy people using a product. Since we all live on this planet, we know that not everyone is thrilled while using a scouring pad. But why criticize an advertiser for doing all she can to create a positive impression of her product—a "you'll-be-glad-that-the-grime-comes-off-easier" type of impression?

The assumption beneath Eric's agrument is that an honest advertiser would show only the average user in an average situation. Some ads actually seem to do this, but **my point is that** they shouldn't *have* to show "average" people. Furthermore, **even if** the poor advertiser did show the average user of his product, he would **still** be subject to the criticism of sexism leveled by the argument above. So the advertiser is stuck in an impossible **contradiction:** should he show the "average" person (i.e., a woman) using a scouring pad, or should he adopt Eric's *nonsexist fantasy* and show a homely man using a scouring pad?

Eric's **point** that outright false advertising should be stopped **is well taken,** however. I agree that the FCC should fine or even imprison advertisers who make verbal fraudulent claims. I would, however, argue that such cases constitute a small percentage of all advertising.

In essence,* ads are attention-getting devices to remind people that certain products are for sale and that people should think about buying them. **Even granting that** ads create brief fantasies in order to get our attention, ads are not misleading, since we all know very well that they are just that: fantasies.

Eric comes back:

First of all, I think that the actual number of outright lies in ads is far greater than the "small percentage" that Sherry claims. On that issue, I guess we shall have to **agree to disagree** until we can **find some evidence for either case.** Even then, we may well need to discuss **how "lie" is defined** by those compiling statistics on the number of advertisers who lie about their products.

Now, regarding Sherry's **main argument** that ads are just "attention-getting" devices: This argument is naive. It **fails to take into account** the fact that advertising images have tremendous power to persuade and that this persuasion exists on both conscious and unconscious levels. So people are in fact misled into **the mistaken inference that** certain products are wonderful because beautiful and happy people are using them.

As far as the use of homely and unhappy people is concerned, I would argue that Sherry has **overstated my case.** It is not necessary

---

*This phrase often signals both a conclusion and a definition.

for advertisers to show unattractive people. In fact, it is arguable that if an advertiser just showed a product being used in a normal manner by normal people, the ad would be so unusual as to cause a sensation. As things stand, however, advertisers are taking advantage of the public. Therefore, they are not acting in a socially responsible manner.

Sherry responds:

I disagree with Eric's claim that advertising images persuade on an unconscious level. Let's discuss conscious and unconscious persuasion separately and **see whether the distinction holds.**

To the extent that ads consciously persuade they are no more dangerous or pernicious than Eric himself, who is trying to persuade us to his point of view. **I assume that** we are both fully conscious at the moment!

Let's **more carefully define** "unconscious persuasion" by asking what, in fact, it would involve. **I infer that** if we were really persuaded on an unconscious level we would find ourselves buying mattresses and packs of cigarettes without having any inkling why we were doing so. Now, whom do you know who does that? No one in fact acts that way! I have never met a person who has said, "I just found myself in the department store buying a sofa, and it wasn't until later that I remembered the furniture ad I saw the night before." While ads certainly *lure* a person to buy something, I believe that the temptation is conscious and I don't believe that ads ever overpower our will to resist their temptations. **The distinction between** being unconsciously persuaded and being tempted **is crucial to my argument**. My evidence is that no one is stepping forward and admitting to being overpowered. What most people who make this type of argument claim is that everyone *else* is being overpowered. Yet after seeing an attractive ad, as after any temptation, we can and do usually modify our desires with a little conscious thought.

Finally, Eric's argument **implies that** any ad is powerful enough to get me to buy. But I would **claim that this is not true**. If I am not interested in motorcycles, no ad in the world is going to "persuade" me out of hand to buy one. Other factors would have to come into play; for example, friends would be discussing getting motorcycles or I'd have to read that this was a great way to commute to work. And **to take the strongest case, if** I happen to think that motorcycles are quite dangerous, an ad showing glamorous people on motorcycles could not overpower my fears.

In sum, it is not clear that we can be unconsiously persuaded by any means, and certainly not by ads.

Eric responds:

I agree that people are not being misled in the crass sense that Sherry describes. Nobody walks away from the TV and into the motorcycle shop like a zombie. But that is not the type of influence I am talking about. Sherry **has created a false dichotomy between** conscious and unconscious states.

    What I mean by "persuasion" is the daily bombardment of ads that eventually wears down our resistance to products and that turns us into the consumer culture that we have become. As Sherry says, no one steps forward and admits to being overpowered because we're not even aware of the influence that ads have on us!

    Furthermore, Sherry's entire **counterargument is predicated on the false assumption that** everyone constantly acts just as rationally as she does (or perhaps, as she *thinks* she does). Hasn't she ever heard of hypnosis? Or Freud?

Sherry finishes up:

It seems that **the argument has shifted from** the question whether advertising is misleading **to the issue whether** one can be unconsciously influenced. The **argument** whether advertising misleads by an appeal to our unconscious now **hinges on the question whether** we can be unconsciously influenced. I think that there are important **differences between** advertisements, on the one hand, and hypnotic states and Freudian repression of traumatic events on the other. Frankly, the bald assertion that we are influenced but we don't know it is really odd. If we don't know that we were influenced, how can we be certain that we were, in fact, influenced? If Eric answers, "We know that we were influenced because we bought the sofa," then the reasoning is circular: We're influenced because we buy the sofa because we're influenced!

    In any event, advertising is far closer to other "normal" events in life and is therefore no more persuasive than any other normal life event. I wonder what is **at the base of** this special condemnation of advertising—is it **predicated on the assumption that** free enterprise is itself evil? Or that wanting material things is evil?

    As to the question whether the advertiser bears more responsibility than others to "mold" public attitudes toward sex roles, **I would suggest that it would be better** in the long run if advertisers reflected society's larger values about sex roles rather than attempting to create them. In fact, I think that's what advertisers do now. For instance, many advertisements reflect women having careers, men doing housework.

I doubt that ads influence people as much as Eric says, but especially if ads do have an unconscious effect, he should agree that we'd be far safer if advertisers restricted themselves to reflecting the values that society consciously holds.

2. *Here is a novel argument about gossip by Sissela Bok. Can you make an alternative argument—say, against gossip—and use it to suggest ways that Bok could improve her argument (with "more," "better," or "clearer")?*

Cheap, superficial, intrusive, unfounded, even vicious: Surely gossip can be all that. Yet to define it in these ways is to overlook the whole network of human exchanges of information, the need to inquire and to learn from the experience of others, and the importance of not taking everything at face value. The desire for such knowledge leads people to go beneath the surface of what is said and shown, and to try to unravel conflicting clues and seemingly false leads. In order to do so, information (gossip) has to be shared with others, obtained from them, stored in memory for future use, tested and evaluated in discussion, and used at times to encourage, to entertain, or to warn. Everyone has a special interest in personal information about others. If we knew about people only what they wished to reveal, we would be subjected to ceaseless manipulation; and we would be deprived of the pleasure and suspense that comes from trying to understand them. . . .

Consider the many harmless or supportive uses of gossip: the talk about who might marry, have a baby, move to another town, be in need of work or too ill to ask for help, and the speculations about underlying reasons, possible new developments, and opportunities for advice or help. Some may find such talk uninteresting, even tedious, or too time-consuming, but they can hardly condemn it on moral grounds. . . .

Bok's argument grows more complex as she works out the distinctions she has in mind between harmless and harmful gossip. She claims that "three categories of gossip should be singled out as particularly reprehensible: gossip in breach of confidence, gossip the speaker knows to be false, and unduly invasive gossip." Although, as the author states, each of these involves uncertain borderline cases, most people would agree that betraying secrets and lying about others are immoral acts (though you're always entitled to disagree). But we need to know what "unduly invasive" means in order to distinguish it from the helpful kind of gossip-invasion, and that is where Bok is the most interesting. Notice the distinctions she makes while reasoning out "unduly invasive":

Is any gossip, then, unduly invasive whenever it concerns what is private, perhaps stigmatizing, often secret? If so, much of the gossip about the personal lives of neighbors, co-workers, and public figures would have to be judged inexcusable. But such a judgment seems unreasonable. It would dismiss many harmless or unavoidable exchanges about human foibles. . . .

How then might we sort out what is unduly invasive from all the gossip about private and secret lives? To begin with, there is reason to stop to consider whether gossip is thus invasive whenever those whose doings are being discussed claim to feel intruded upon. But these claims must obviously not be taken at face value. . . . While such claims should give gossipers pause, they are not always legitimate. People cannot be said, for instance, to own aspects of their lives that are clearly evident to others and thus in fact public, such as a nasty temper or a manipulative manner, nor can they reasonably argue that others have no right to discuss them. Least of all can they suppress references to what may be an "open secret," known to all . . . a topic treated in innumerable comedies about marital infidelity. Similarly, more concealed aspects of their lives may be of legitimate interest to others—their mistreatment of their children, for example, or their past employment record. . . . At such times, gossip may be an indispensable channel for public information.

Merely to *say* that gossip about oneself is unduly invasive, therefore, does not make it so. I would argue that additional factors must be present to render gossip unduly invasive: the information must be about matters legitimately considered private; and it must hurt the individuals talked about (e.g., result in the loss of a job).[1]

3. *Read the following article, "Class Struggle: Should Schools Permit Searching of Students for Weapons, Drugs?" by Anne MacKay Smith. Locate the major arguments, and evaluate them.*

Detroit high-school student Lynn Bittner says she was standing around with three of her friends outside school, waiting for their first class, when a policeman demanded their student ID cards. He herded them into the school security office, and without waiting for a woman security guard, stood them against the wall and frisked them.

"It was incredible. Thrown up against the wall like a criminal, when we hadn't done anything," Miss Bittner, 17 years old, says.

Students like Miss Bittner, who has since transferred to a Catholic school, dislike being subjected to searches. But not all searches are fruitless. Since the beginning of the year, special squads carrying metal detectors have found 59 guns and 69 knives and other weapons on Detroit students. Parents, concerned about their children's safety, generally support such efforts.

The situation in Detroit illustrates a dilemma faced by schools nationwide: how to protect students and the learning atmosphere without infringing on students' rights to be free of unreasonable searches. The issue is emotional. Proponents of the right to search note that when weapons are available, schoolyard scuffles have become matters of life and death.

Differing Views   "What's reasonable for someone standing on Main Street might be different from what's reasonable in school. We are dealing with children and the state has the responsibility to protect them," says Allan J. Nodes, deputy attorney general in New Jersey.

But Barry S. Goodman says, "The real issue is whether students shed their rights when they enter school." The two are arguing a New Jersey suit now before the U.S. Supreme Court as to whether a staffer's search of a teenager's purse constituted illegal search.

Until now, the courts haven't been of much help in resolving the conflicts. Rulings in dozens of cases have been complex and contradictory. Many school officials are hoping that the Supreme Court will lay some ground rules. The court is expected to rule in the New Jersey case before its term ends in July.

The case started when a Piscataway High School teacher found a girl, identified in the suit only as T.L.O., smoking in the bathroom, and an assistant principal demanded a confession. When T.L.O. refused, he checked her purse for cigarettes. He removed the cigarettes and saw rolling papers, then turned the contents of the purse over and found marijuana. The student was convicted of possession of marijuana with an intent to distribute it, and her appeal of that conviction is before the Supreme Court.

Issues in Appeal   At issue are whether the assistant principal had a right to search the girl's purse and whether the evidence obtained that way should be admissible in court. Mr. Nodes argues that it is, and that there should be a less stringent standard for searches in schools than elsewhere. But Mr. Goodman believes the search violated the most lenient standard for searches because there wasn't any reason for it: Smoking was permissible in some areas of the school, so finding cigarettes wouldn't have proved the girl was smoking in the bathroom. The plaintiff argues that suppression of the evidence would deter such illegal searches in the future.

Increasingly, schools and some courts have tried to carve out a middle ground between giving school officials full rights to search and the stricter "probable cause" standard for police officers, requiring that there be strong evidence to believe the person to be searched has committed a crime.

Search conflicts occur across the country. In Bridgeport, Conn., teachers are working to expand their right to search; teacher DeOla Jones Barfield says her interest was spurred by finding a high-school student carrying a gun in a gym bag. Nancy Demartra, a Louisville, Ky., fifth-grade teacher, says that there have been two shootings in city schools this spring and that teachers should have the right to search students and their property at any time.

But in the last two years, strip searches of students to find stolen money have prompted a spate of angry newspaper articles in Rockford, IL, and two lawsuits in New York. Nationwide, dozens of suits have been filed questioning school searches.

Killings in Brooklyn   The debate as to when to search becomes most emotional when violence breaks out. Two students at the Samuel J. Tilden High School in Brooklyn, NY, were knifed to death in incidents six weeks apart this spring, the second in full view of students streaming out of the building after classes. Tilden, which prides itself on its academics and its winning football team, exploded with pleas from teachers, parents and more than 100 students that metal detectors be used to search students at the school doors.

Two weeks after the second death, the issue was heatedly debated at a meeting of the Parent-Teachers Association in the school's auditorium. Stephen Dorf, a resources teacher at the school, dismissed the civil-liberties concerns. "The good kids have to suffer with the bad sometimes. Sometimes we have to pick the lesser of two evils," he said.

But others argued that mass searches would erode students' rights. "We will become the school that has our children pass through these portals and be presumed guilty. That is not the principle on which this society is founded," Agnes Green, president of the PTA, said. "I ask you to reconsider."

Mrs. Green says it took some agonizing thought to come to her position. She says she still worries about both physical danger to her 15-year-old son, and the scarring effect of close association with violence. As PTA president, she received early notification of the second stabbing, and she vividly recalls her son's reaction when she told him the victim had died.

"He said, 'You know, I figured as much, because of the way the blood was coming out of her body, and the way she fell to the sidewalk,'" Mrs. Green recounts. "Within a few weeks, my son has seen more death and destruction than I have in my whole life."

Her position against metal detectors seems to have triumphed. While the school has set up a task force to discuss ways to improve school security, metal detectors aren't likely to be one of them, the school's assistant principal says.

Parents of some third graders at P.S. 282 in Brooklyn sued school officials over a strip-search. They charge that the officials, who were looking for about $50 stolen from a substitute teacher's purse, stripped most of the class in spite of the fact that most of the stolen money was found on the first child they examined. Among the charges is that "all students who had been searched . . . were forced to stay outside the search chamber and listen to their classmates crying as they were being searched."

Two of the officials, a school guidance counselor and the district superintendent, filed a response in U.S. District Court in New York denying the allegations. Counsel for the school principal declined to comment on the charges, but said he believed the suit would be settled within a few weeks.

Richard Emery, a lawyer for the New York Civil Liberties Union representing the plaintiffs, says the effects of such a search are lasting, and that all searches are unsettling. "Very few of us can maintain a feeling of innocence and confidence when official authorities are searching, or even inspecting," he says. "The best people at maintaining a composed demeanor are usually the worst criminals."

J. L. Skelton, a senior at Detroit's Finney High School, has a scar at the side of his nose from a knife thrust during a school argument two years ago. Nevertheless, he agrees that the increased presence of security guards with metal detectors has a chilling effect.

"You could be walking by, and you don't have nothing, but you shut up, boom," he says. "I've seen plenty of students walking by using regular slang language, and they numb up. Go straight as a board."

Guards' Procedure Security guards say they search only when they have "reasonable cause" to believe a student may be carrying a forbidden item. Causes might include smelling marijuana on a passing student, or a report, usually from another student, that someone is carrying a weapon.

But some students say that searches are less reasonable and more random than that implies, and they are aware that some are legally questionable. Suzanne Koten, a teacher at Detroit's Denby High School, says discussion erupted in her class on Basic Law when they began discussing search and seizure practices. "At that time, the police were in the building all the time, and the kids wanted to know why the police could just search them at any time," she recalls. "They feel that it's an infringement on their privacy to just be stopped like that. I do, too."

But students say weapons are common in Detroit schools. Finney senior Skelton says, "I know plenty of girls that have things on them— knives, box cutters, razors, scissors, nail files. As for the guys, some of them could sneak a .22 in here, any type of gun, if they really wanted to. I don't see how they could prevent it, unless you put bars on every door and every window."

Hiram McGee, a security guard in Philip Murray Wright High School, says he found a student making a gun stock for a rifle in wood-shop class. He checked his locker and found all the other parts except the firing mechanism ready for assembly.

Self-Defense Argument   For students who live in dangerous areas, carrying weapons for self-defense is a way of life. In Detroit, some parents gave their children knives last fall after a number of girls were attacked and raped on their way to school.

Others say weapons are a status symbol, while Taris Jackson, a 17-year-old Denby student adds, "The reason some of them bring them is to protect things they've got on. Two-hundred-dollar chains, and $60, $70 track shoes. I said, why would you bring something that people would kill you to get, and they say they got to look sweet."

Lawrence Boyer, sharp-eyed after nine years as a guard in Detroit schools, has taken knives, drugs, and other contraband from dozens of students so far this year. At 10 paces, he spots a three-inch, cylindrical leather case, half-concealed in the hand of one of a stream of passing students. It holds a canister of Mace.

"You know you're not supposed to have this in school?" he asks.

"I need to get home!" the student exclaims. "There's two German Shepherds on my block. Loose," he emphasizes.

Nevertheless, Mr. Boyer impounds the Mace. In one hour and a half on duty, he tells a dozen students to take off their hats and asks eight others why they are in the hall during a class period. One student, who was trying to sneak back into the building after a trip outside, is taken to the assistant principal's office for a search. He is subsequently suspended for carrying 10 marijuana cigarettes.

Teachers' Perspective   Most teachers and principals believe that the threat of violence outweighs erosion of student rights. Arthur Jefferson, Detroit's superintendent of schools says he believes rights violations are kept to a minimum. But if they do occur, he says, "I'm not apologizing for that." He adds, "The stakes are too high, in our schools and in our community."

Paul Richards agrees. He is principal of Detroit's Philip Murray Wright High School, a normally quiet school that exploded in violence on April 19 that ended in a threat to Mr. Richards's life. It came from two brothers who were fighting with a former student and chased him into the school. There, at least 10 of the former student's friends joined the fray, wielding a hammer, nightsticks and umbrellas. The former student fled, guards captured one of the brothers, and the other was beaten unconscious. "When I got there, he was motionless, lying in a pool of blood," Mr. McGee, the security guard, says.

The violence may continue. "Supposedly, they have a contract out on me. I've been looking over my shoulder for the last few days, because you never know." Mr. Richards says. "I think that if they do it, it'll be a shooting, because there are so many guns around."

Not surprisingly, Mr. Richards is a proponent of strong measures to keep the schools safe. "Until we get serious about a few things, like handgun control, metal detectors don't bother me. If it keeps weapons out of the school, I'm for it," he says. "You have folks saying it's like a prison. But hell, if it saves one life, to me it'd be worth it."[2]

4. The Supreme Court announced its opinion on January 15, 1985. A majority of the justices held that searches of students could be conducted by school officials as long as they have reasonable grounds for suspecting that such a search will turn up evidence of a student's violation of school rules or of the law. The court found that the school officials had had reasonable cause to search T.L.O.'s purse for cigarettes; then the discovery of rolling papers gave reasonable cause to search further for marijuana. The justices held that all searches of students by school personnel fall under the protection of the Fourth Amendment, which guards against unreasonable search and seizure; yet school personnel are not subject to the strict standard of probable cause for search, only reasonable cause.

The following are excerpts from the justices' reasoning. Note the language of critical thinking:

A search of a child's person or of a closed purse or other bag carried on her person, no less than a similar search carried out on an adult, is undoubtedly a severe violation of subjective expectations of privacy.

Of course, the Fourth Amendment does not protect subjective expectations of privacy that are unreasonable or otherwise "illegitimate." . . . To receive the protection of the Fourth Amendment, an expectation of privacy must be one that society is "prepared to recognize as legitimate." . . . The State of New Jersey (appellate court from which this case came) has argued that because of the pervasive supervision to which children in the schools are necessarily subject, a child has virtually no legitimate expectation of privacy in articles of personal property "unnecessarily" carried into a school. This argument has two factual premises: 1) the fundamental incompatibility of expectations of privacy and the maintenance of a sound educational environment; and 2) the minimal interest of the child in bringing any items of personal property into the school. Both premises are severely flawed.

The justices conclude that children do have legitimate rights to privacy. Then they bring in the argument of the need for order:

Against the child's interest in privacy must be set the substantial interest of teachers and administrators in maintaining discipline in the classroom and on school grounds. Maintaining order in the classroom has never been easy, but in recent years, school disorder has often taken particularly ugly forms: drug use and violent crime in the schools have become major social problems. . . .

How then, should we strike the balance between the schoolchild's legitimate expectations of privacy and the school's equally legitimate need to maintain an environment in which learning can take place? It is evident that the school setting requires some easing of the restrictions to which searches by public authorities are ordinarily subject.

Some of the justices agreed only partially with the ruling. Justice Brennan felt that it gave school officials too much leeway, endangering students' right to privacy. He wrote a scathing rebuttal to the notion of the "balancing of governmental and private interests." Note the use of definition and distinction:

Today's decision sanctions school officials to conduct full-scale searches on a "reasonableness" standard whose only definite content is that it is not the same test as the "probable cause" standard found in the text of the Fourth Amendment. In adopting this unclear, unprecedented, and unnecessary departure from generally applicable Fourth Amendment standards, the Court carves out a broad exception to standards that this Court has developed over years of considering Fourth Amendment problems. . . .

I therefore fully agree with the Court that "the underlying command of the Fourth Amendment is always that searches and seizures be reasonable" [but hold that] seizures are reasonable only if supported by probable cause.[3]

Thus we have three different views: those of the appellate court, the Supreme Court, and Justice Brennan. The implications of the Supreme Court decision would seem to be that school officials have a freer hand in searching students but still have to be sure the searches are reasonable. Do you agree that this is a good idea? Why or why not?

NOTES

1. Sissela Bok, *Secrets: On the Ethics of Concealment and Revelation* (New York: Random House, 1989), pp. 90–97.
2. Anne MacKay Smith, "Class Struggle: Should Schools Permit Searching of Students for Weapons, Drugs?" *Wall Street Journal* (New York), May 30, 1984.
3. *The United States Law Week,* "Opinion Announced January 15, 1985," The Bureau of National Affairs, Inc., Washington, D. C.

9

How to Follow Complex Arguments

LIKE SIMPLE ARGUMENTS, LIKE COMPLEX

A complex argument is no different in its basic features than the simple ones we've looked at so far. It has the basic three and most, if not all, of the other main features we've investigated. The difference is that a complex argument is a larger structure, containing smaller arguments whose conclusions usually function as the reasons for the complex argument. The smaller arguments are called "subarguments."

The easiest way to follow complex arguments is to locate the overarching issue, conclusion, and reasons, saving any details of the subarguments for later.

Three Examples

Consider the following argument:

> Americans are less likely than ever to use public transportation, such as buses, subways, or trolleys. These systems handle scarcely 5 percent of all commuting, down from 9 percent in 1970, according to the 1990 census. In cities, less than 4 percent of local trips, such as commuting or shopping, occur by public transit. The percentage is even lower in the suburbs. Meanwhile, 87 percent of commuters take cars to work—up from 78 percent in 1970. Why this heavy auto usage when public transportation is less

polluting, more cost-effective, and three-quarters of urban freeways are congested at rush hour, up from only half ten years ago?

First of all, public transportation is not convenient for multiple household tasks, for instance picking up a young child at daycare, then dropping by the dry cleaners, then going to the grocery store. How could anyone easily juggle a child and all the packages on a bus, perhaps transferring several times? A related reason is that even the humblest car affords a privacy impossible on the subway.

A further complication is that public transportation is often useless. Not only are people's homes spread over large suburban areas, but workplaces now range over broad areas as well. In contrast, public transportation systems of necessity use a hub-and-spoke system: They bring people to a main station in a city. This is useless for large numbers of people, who commute from their home suburb to a work suburb. At the moment, only the car has the flexibility necessary to follow this mind-boggling number of routes. And in comparison to the bus or train which one must wait for and "catch," the car waiting ever faithful in the garage will always be perceived to be a more useful object, despite its greater cost.

Here is a description of this complex argument:

Overall conclusion: Americans are less likely than ever to use public transportation.
Subconclusion 1 It is inconvenient.
Reason 1 During a trip people often need to collect packages or toddlers
Reason 2 It is not private (a kind of emotional inconvenience for those used to cars)
Subconclusion 2 It is often useless.
Reason 1 People's homes and work are spread too thinly for the hub-and-spoke system necessary for a public transportation system
Reason 2 The car is always more accessible, and so perceived as more useful than public transportation

THE SUBARGUMENTS ARE THE REASONS FOR THE MAIN CONCLUSION

Americans are less likely than ever to use public transportation because it is inconvenient and because it is often useless.

Many complex arguments are not laid out this neatly. Consider the following excerpt from a funny book by one of the world's greatest physicists, the late Richard Feynman:

> I *don't* believe I can really do without teaching. The reason is, I have to have something so that when I don't have any ideas and I'm not getting anywhere I can say to myself, "At least I'm living; at least I'm doing something; I'm making some contribution"—it's just psychological.

When I was at Princeton in the 1940's I could see what happened to those great minds at the Institute for Advanced Study, who had been specially selected for their tremendous brains and were now given this opportunity to sit in this lovely house by the woods there, with no classes to teach, with no obligations whatsoever. These poor bastards could now sit and think clearly all by themselves, OK? So they don't get any ideas for a while: They have every opportunity to do something, and they're not getting any ideas. I believe that in a situation like this a kind of guilt or depression worms inside of you, and you begin to *worry* about not getting any ideas. And nothing happens. Still no ideas come.

Nothing happens because there's not enough real activity and challenge: You're not in contact with the experimental guys (the physicists who test out the theories that the theoretical physicists have come up with). You don't have to think how to answer questions from the students. Nothing!

In any thinking process there are moments when everything is going good and you've got wonderful ideas. Teaching is an interruption, and so it's the greatest pain in the neck in the world. And then there are the *longer* periods of time when not much is coming to you. You're not getting any ideas, and if you're doing nothing at all, it drives you nuts! You can't even say "I'm teaching my class."

If you're teaching a class, you can think about the elementary things that you know very well. These things are kind of fun and delightful. It doesn't do any harm to think them over again. Is there a better way to present them? Are there any new problems associated with them? Are there any new thoughts you can make about them? The elementary things are easy to think about; if you can't think of a new thought, no harm done; what you thought about it before is good enough for the class. If you do think of something new, you're rather pleased that you have a new way of looking at it.

The questions of the students are often the source of new research. They often ask profound questions that I've thought about at times and then given up on, so to speak, for a while. It wouldn't do me any harm to think about them again and see if I can go any further now. The students may not be able to see the thing I want to answer, or the subtleties I want to think about, but they *remind* me of a problem by asking questions in the neighborhood of the problem. It's not so easy to remind *yourself* of these things.

So I find that teaching and the students keep life going and I would *never* accept any position in which somebody has invented a happy situation for me where I don't have to teach. Never.[1]

Here is how I saw Feynman's argument, after reading it carefully several times:

Overall Conclusion: Feynman needs to teach.

Subargument 1 He feels a sense of accomplishment even when he doesn't have any new ideas. (no reasons offered: it's a loose argument)

Subargument 2 Professors without teaching responsibilities become guilty and depressed.

   Reason: They can't think up new ideas.

"Subreason": There's not enough activity and challenge from other students and scientists.

Subargument 3 Teaching is good for him.

Reason: He can rethink elementary problems.

Reason: Students are the source of new research.

"Subreason" 1: They often ask profound questions.

"Subreason" 2: They remind him of problems he wouldn't think of on his own.

This complex argument even sports some "subreasons," although that term is never used. Can you see why they are dependent on the reason above them?

A LONGER EXAMPLE

This final example is an abridged article by mathematician John Allen Paulos. He makes an important argument, and I highly recommend its fuller explanation in his book, *Innumeracy: Mathematical Illiteracy and Its Consequences.*[2]

There are notes on the right-hand side of the text below; cover those notes the first couple of times you read through the argument. Jot down questions and sketch what you believe to be the major argument and its subarguments. Then check your results against the annotations.

The Odds Are You're Innumerate

By John Allen Paulos

Innumeracy, the mathematical analogue of functional illiteracy, afflicts far too many literate people, even widely read and articulate men and women who might cringe if words such as "imply" and "infer" were confused. They generally react without a trace of embarrassment, however, to even the most egregious numerical solecisms. Once I was at a gathering of writers in which much was being made of the difference between "continually" and "continuously." Later that evening, as we were watching the news (another measure of how enjoyable the occasion was), the television meteorologist announced that there was a 50 percent chance of rain for Saturday and a 50

Would seem to be the main conclusion, but is a subconclusion

Innumeracy defined; subconclusion: the "highly literate" suffer from it

Literate people defined

Story offered in evidence of how very literate yet very innumerate some people are percent chance for Sunday as well, and concluded that there was therefore a 100 percent chance of rain that weekend. I grant the mistake was not hilarious, but no one even smiled.

The recent "Mathematics Report Card" released by the Educational Testing Service indicates that more than weather reports are at risk. The rampant innumeracy of our high school students and of the educated public in general is appalling, and since this innumeracy can and does lead to muddled personal decisions, misinformed governmental policies and an increased susceptibility to pseudosciences of all kinds, it's not something that can be easily ignored.

Evidence for high innumeracy rates among high school students

A bigger (the main) conclusion offered here: innumeracy is the cause of large social problems (The odds are that you and many others are innumerate is a subconclusion)

I'm not primarily concerned with esoteric mathematics here, only with some feel for numbers and probabilities, some ability to estimate answers to the ubiquitous questions: How many? How likely? With megaton warheads (equivalent in explosive power to a million tons, or two billions pounds, of TNT) and trillion dollar budgets a reality, people should have a visceral reaction to the difference between a million, a billion, and a trillion. (It helps to note that a million seconds takes less than 12 days to tick by, while a billion seconds requires approximately 32 years, and 32,000 years must pass for a trillion seconds to elapse). They needn't be aware of how fast human hair grows, expressed in miles per hour, or of how many basketballs would fit in the Grand Canyon, but they ought to know roughly the population of the United States, the percentage of the world's population that is Chinese, the distance from New York City to Los Angeles, the odds of winning their state lottery, and a host of other common magnitudes.

Second definition of numeracy: to estimate numbers and probabilities

Prescription and third definition of numeracy: we should be numerate, defined also as having a gut reaction to difference between a million, billion, and trillion

Distinction between numeracy and concern with trivial mathematical problems

Fourth definition: to know common magnitudes

Without a grasp of such basic numbers, just to cite one example, it is impossible to appreciate the silliness of canceling a European trip because of fear of terrorists. In 1985 when, out of the 28 million Americans who traveled abroad, 17 were killed by terrorists, you were

Evidence that many Americans are

almost 25 times as likely to choke to death (one chance in 68,000), about 300 times as likely to die in a car crash (one chance in 5,300), and nearly 2,000 times as likely to die from the effects of smoking (one chance in 800, the equivalent of three fully loaded jumbo jets crashing each and every day of the year).

innumerate: not flying because of terrorist threats

Still, what do numbers, probabilities and mathematics in general have to do with books and literature? A couple of minor points first. In addition to the usual reasons for innumeracy, avid readers of fiction sometimes have an extra vulnerability to numerical myopia. Their habit of reading about individuals in extreme and dramatic circumstances may exacerbate the natural tendency we all have to give considerably more weight to unlikely but gripping events than we do to more mundane ones [for example, news reports of grisly accidents or killings compared to the many people who successfully lived out the day].

A switch here, back to literate innumerates

Subargument that readers of a lot of fiction are innumerate (give unwarranted weight to likelihood of gripping events)

Reason: they read about extreme situations

. . . Although the numerical imprecisions and distortions associated with fictional (and other) writing may be a trivial matter, they're symptomatic of something much more fundamental. The most obvious causes of innumeracy are poor education and "math anxiety," but the deeper sources are prevailing cultural attitudes, in particular misconceptions about the nature of mathematics. These attitudes and misconceptions lead to an intellectual environment that welcomes and even encourages inadequate mathematical education and pride in ignorance ("I hate math." "Hah. Math was always my worst subject"); they also lead, at least in part, to anxiety when quantitative thinking is required.

The distorted perspective of fictional writing is evidence for the subargument that negative cultural attitudes towards mathematics are the reason for poor math education, pride in ignorance of math, and fear of math

The proverbial disparagement of the English as "a nation of shopkeepers" persists as a belief that a concern with numbers and details numbs one to the big questions, to the grandeur of the natural world. Mathematics is often taken to be mechanical, the work of low-level technicians who will report to

Subargument
The nature of mathematics is misunderstood because

the rest of us anything we absolutely must know. Alternatively, mathematics is sometimes thought to have a constraining character that somehow limits our freedom and self-expression.

1. it's thought trivial and
2. it's a hindrance to big questions
3. it's thought to be mechanical
4. it's thought to limit our freedom

From Wordsworth to present-day New Agers,the romantic idea of communing directly with nature without the distorting aid of any intervening formalisms has also contributed to a vague distaste for mathematics. Sentiments such as these are unfortunately quite prevalent among literary people and ultimately help bring about the abysmal test scores. . . .

Subargument
Students suffer from innumeracy because literate people [presumably teachers and parents] hold these mistaken views of mathematics

Innumeracy and the attitudes underlying it provide in fact a fertile soil for the growth of pseudoscience. Linda Goodman's *Star Signs* and *Transformation* by Whitley Strieber are simply two of the latest examples of the many books on astrology, numerology, visitations and the like that fill bookstore shelves (annoyingly often in the philosophy sections), and appeal disproportionately to those who have little interest in or knowledge of numbers, probability or basic science.

Evidence for main conclusion:
pseudoscience is rampant, as indicated by a number of popular books

Others that attract the same people are Budd Hopkins's *Intruders* and Mr. Strieber's earlier *Communion* (on U.F.O.'s and aliens), the Shirley MacLaine books on reincarnation and psychic communication, J. Z. Knight's "Ramtha" books (on channeling and ancient spirits), George Anderson's conversations with the immortals, New Age books on auras, crystal power and chakras, traditional best sellers like Tarot books and the I Ching, and the collection of volumes on the paranormal that Time-Life Books has recently been hawking on television. Even the Harvard-educated physician and author Michael Crichton, who should know better, claims in his book *Travels* that mentally bending spoons is no big deal, and that virtually everybody at a party he attended was gently rubbing spoons, thereby causing them (bowls too) to flex like rubber. And if many of the diet books, get-rich-quick books, medical fad books and books on how to calculate the appropriate tip in a restaurant are added, one begins to feel it may be a blessing that so few Americans read the books they buy.

Microargument: It's good people don't read books they buy because they buy so much junk!

In *Pseudoscience and Society in Nineteenth-Century America,* Arthur Wrobel remarks that belief in phrenology,* homeopathy** and hydropathy*** was not confined to the poor and the ignorant, but pervaded much of 19th-century literature. Such credulity is not as extensive in contemporary literature, but astrology is one pseudoscience that does seem to engage a big segment of the reading public. Literary allusions to it abound. . . . A 1986 Gallup poll showed that 52 percent of American teen-agers subscribe to it. . . .

Historical claim, that pseudoscience was popular among the literate in the 19th century

Given these figures, it may not be entirely inappropriate to note here that no mechanism through which the alleged zodiacal influences exert themselves has ever been specified by astrologers. Gravity certainly cannot account for these natal influences, since even the gravitational pull of the attending obstetrician is orders of magnitude greater than that of the relevant planet or planets. Nor is there any empirical evidence; top astrologers (as determined by their peers) have failed repeatedly to associate personality profiles with astrological data at a rate higher than that of chance. Neither of these fatal objections to astrology, of course, is likely to carry much weight with literate but innumerate people who don't estimate magnitudes or probabilities, or who are overimpressed by vague coincidences yet unmoved by overwhelming statistical evidence.

Subargument
Astrology is not credible because:
1. No mechanism (model) is offered to explain it (See chapter 11 for a discussion of models).
2. Gravity cannot explain astrology.
3. No astrologers have been able to do better than random at guessing at personality on the basis of star signs.

Arrayed against fatuous books on stars, the mind and numbers are some excel-

Prescription to read these books instead

---

*predicting character traits by the size of bumps on various places on the head
**use of minute amounts of a disease-causing substance (for instance, bacteria) to cure that disease
***the use of water as a cure

lent expository works on the same top-
ics. These include, among many others,
A Brief History of Time by Stephen
Hawking; Rudy Rucker's *Mind Tools,*
Martin Gardner's many books and
essays; James Gleick's *"Chaos";*
"The Blind Watchmaker" by Richard
Dawkins; *"The Cosmic Code"* by Heinz
Pagels; Timothy Ferris's *"Coming of Age
in the Milky Way";* Stephen Jay Gould's
books; Douglas Hofstadter's *"Gödel,
Escher, Bach";* Carl Sagan's *"Cosmos";*
"The Loss of Certainty" by Morris Kline,
"The Mathematical Experience" by
Philip Davis and Reuben Hersh. With a
few exceptions, however, such books
don't reach a big readership and,
because they are difficult, they preach
to the converted and inform the
informed.

In regard to mathematics at least,
something more is needed—books, articles, and columns that address a much
larger audience and deal not so much
with the subject proper as with critical
appraisals of the way it is applied and
of the misunderstandings and confu-
sions that arise naturally from these
applications. Such writings would not   *Prescription to educate*
change cultural attitudes towards   *the public to*
mathematics, of course, but by making   *innumeracy problems*
its effects concrete and by relating it to *through daily*
matters that are important to all of us, *newspapers and*
they might help significantly. An over- *magazines*
looked, yet natural, forum for these discussions is the daily newspapers and
the general circulation magazines. (If   *Microargument: They*
they can carry regular horoscopes, why   *should carry articles on*
not entertainingly written articles on   *innumeracy because*
the consequences of number numb-   *they carry regular*
ness?). . . .   *horoscopes*

It is distressing that a society and culture that depend so critically on mathe-
matics and its uses should nevertheless *"Loose" prescription:*
seem so indifferent to the innumeracy   *People should know*
and general mathematical ignorance of   *who Gauss was*
even its brightest citizens. Gauss* will
never touch us the way Flaubert** does,
but people should at least recognize his
name.[3]

---

*Carl Friedrich Gauss (1777–1855), one of the world's greatest mathematicians.
**Gustave Flaubert, one of the world's greatest novelists, who lived in the 19th century.

SUMMARY

A complex argument has the same features as a simple one; but it is a larger structure containing subarguments whose conclusions usually function as reasons in support of the major conclusion.

EXERCISES

1. Diagram and analyze the reading "The Case for Limited Animal Rights" at the end of this chapter.
2. Diagram and analyze the excerpt from "Gossip," at the end of Chapter 8.
3. Construct a complex argument about the death penalty, then diagram it. (Remember, a complex argument does not consist of one argument for and one argument against a position; it is an argument with a main conclusion supported by smaller, strict arguments.)

READING

Challenged by Singer's argument for animal rights (Chapter 2), I set out to construct an alternative position, which became this complex argument. In light of my argument, can you think of ways to strengthen Singer's—and vice versa?

The Case for Limited Animal Rights

The question of what rights animals should enjoy is a vexatious one, involving a Gordian knot of ancillary issues. The problem, too, is not without significance, because hundreds of thousands of animals are put to death for human use each year.* About four hundred animal rights groups have been mounting publicity campaigns which range from appeals for increased restrictions on scientific experimentation and animal farming to the admonition of strict vegetarianism and discontinuance of all animal experiments. These groups have as their end the prevention of what they perceive to be needless suffering of helpless victims. Were it clear what "needless suffering" means, and were there no serious ramifications to the imposition of further restraints on scientific research and animal husbandry, the solutions would be clear. But there are problems.

---

*Of course, humans are animals too. But to avoid the cumbersome phrase "nonhuman animals," the term "animals" in the rest of this essay will refer to nonhuman animals, with the distinction understood to be an artificial one.

It is not well appreciated, for example, that slowing down scientific research would retard discovery of antidotes to diseases such as cancer which kill humans and animals alike. Given the bureaucratic snarl in England that has resulted from overseeing "animal handlers," it is certainly unrealistic to expect that regulation would not have a slowing effect. Thus, many thousands more people and animals would die through delays in research than would have died if a few thousand animals had been put to death in the course of discovering an antidote. Furthermore, the benefits to the many at the expense of the few are even more impressive if one calculates future years. The death, say, of 500,000 animals in the course of cancer research will make possible the prolongation of the lives of many millions of animals and people into the foreseeable future. Ironically, it may be the very success of hard-won discoveries in warding off disease that makes this trade-off difficult for animal rights advocates to appreciate. Yet as recently as the 1930s, deformity, pain, and disability were far more common, even in the developed countries. A partial listing of vaccines acquired through animal research which have saved millions of animals' lives would include anthrax, distemper, typhoid, cholera, plague, and recently, feline leukemia.

The list for humans would include polio and measles vaccines, antibiotics, immunizations for diphtheria, smallpox, dramatic strides in surgical techniques, and treatments for cancer. Even current knowledge of effective hygiene and good nutrition is in large part the result of animal experimentation. But many health problems are still unsolved: chronic neurological disease, schizophrenia, senile dementia, most forms of cancer, deafness, blindness, arthritis, and autoimmune diseases. Without animal experimentation, there will be no end to these diseases.[4]

Of course, a catalog of advantages does not end the discussion. A counterargument could be raised that these comparatively few experimental animals are killed or made to suffer without their consent; so the end of prolonging the lives of many does not justify employing the means of deliberately hurting the nonconsenting few.

This counterargument contains two important assumptions: that animal life is as important as human life, and that animals have absolute rights to life and freedom from suffering. But these principles, if applied in all interactions between humans and animals, would lead to monstrous results in daily life. A minor infestation of house mice would, unchecked, spread across an entire city, mice and their droppings creating great health hazards. To respond that cats could be brought in to kill the mice is odd, since if animals have absolute rights to life, then cats would have no more right to kill mice than humans (and surely humans would be "accessories after the fact" in putting cats up to it). This brings to light another problem: What will animals eat if all animals have rights to life? If animal life is as important as human life, do humans have a moral obligation to try to put all animals in the world, wild and domestic, on a vegetarian diet? Even if one counters that animals are entitled to kill other animals because it is their instinct, while humans should be above killing animals under any circumstances, the problem of overpopulation by rodents or other animals remains, as does the problem of feeding pets. It would be cruel to turn out domesticated pets to forage for themselves. Many millions would die in fights with others or from lack of food. It therefore seems wise, for the sake of animals as much as humans, to retreat from the extreme view that all animals have an absolute right to life. Most people would also shrink from the practical implications of the conclusion that animal life is as important as human, since such implications would entail more animal and human misery than now exists.

But that is not to say that animals should have no rights whatever. Currently, legislation exists in all states to protect animals from senseless abuse. There are sanctions against tormenting an animal with no other object in mind. The question now being raised, however, is whether this is enough. Proponents of animal rights, such as Peter Singer, have answered in the negative, doing much to remind us that even when using animals for other ends than just to be cruel, we are still using sentient beings, perhaps as capable as we of feeling pain. For the most part, activists' concern is limited to mammals because of the similarity of their nervous systems to that of humans. (Reptiles and so-called lower forms of life are not at issue, thus raising the specter of future accusations of "mammalism"—that mammals have been unjustly singled out over, say, arachnids and plants as worthy of concern.)

Staying with those animals who have offered evidence of an ability to suffer, such an ability would seem to count as important for reasons of fellow feeling. Were I a mouse about to be killed, I would far rather die painlessly than in agony. An argument might therefore be made on the basis of compassion that a homeowner should use mouse traps rather than poison, supposing that the former is less painful for the mouse. (Trapping a house mouse and releasing it in the backyard or nearby hills will not rid that area of the problem, but pass on the need to kill to someone else. Or is it incumbent on the homeowner to make a trip far out of town with the mouse?) It is thus not hard to argue that animals, be they house mice or deer, should be dispatched as painlessly as possible if they are so numerous that they would starve. The point here too is that for reasons of animal or human well-being, mice, deer, or any animals not facing species extinction,* should forfeit their lives.

---

*A distinction can be made in cases of endangered species on the grounds that their very uniqueness gives their lives greater weight against larger numbers of nonendangered species, including human, because although humans are more important, all species are *close* enough in worth to merit their survival.

The assumptions beneath this argument have been, of course, that humans are more important than animals, and humans may kill animals under certain circumstances. Thus baldly put, these attitudes bother people who recollect a worldwide history of cruelty and prejudice by humans against other humans. Isn't the assertion that humans are more important than animals yet one more instance of chauvinism?

Cases of prejudice against other humans are not analogous to the issue at hand. No other species has the ability to be the steward of the planet's animals. And since a great deal of human and animal misery would result if humans were to abdicate this stewardship, they should retain it. Further, humans can't share the job of animal-management with animals. Humans can, however, share such jobs as choosing leaders and formulating guidelines for animal experimentation with other humans. The very absurdity of extending equality of opportunity for jobs, the vote, and animal-management to animals points to the vast difference in these situations. (An interesting note is that although humans have often behaved badly towards animals, even driving some species into extinction, no other species has demonstrated the altruism which mankind has in fostering other species. Were another species intelligent enough to actually participate in decision-making about other animals, it is not clear that its members would show other than the narrowest self-interest.)

But difficult questions remain. Even though animals don't share equal status with humans, is it justifiable to inflict pain on them? In cases of scientific research, and given the argument of the greater importance of the many, the answer should be yes. Yet out of respect for fellow sentient beings, experiments should be performed only under these conditions: that there is no good alternative procedure; that good science is being done; that no experiment already performed is needlessly repeated; that any experiment should be conducted with the least possible infliction of suffering; that there be open scrutiny of the experiment and its results among the community of scientists. These standards should be prerequisites for all experiments. But how often are they honored, and who should enforce them in their breach?

In fact, severe pain is very rare in animal experimentation, partly because scientists are as humane as anyone else, partly because severe pain would kill the animal or otherwise destroy the experiment through the physiological disturbances it causes. Animals are anesthetized for more severe invasions and then killed. The most the average laboratory animal feels is the passing discomfort of a shot. Of course, the ideal would be to develop technologically to the point of using cells instead of animals, but for the moment animals are required in a great many cases. Such technological transcendence of animals might be achieved, but ironically, only after more animal experimentation reveals how to do so.

On the premise that no one is better able to judge the value of a research proposal than a scientist's colleagues in the area in question, scientists should continue to judge whether an investigator's proposal is worthy of funding; in so doing, they will also continue to judge whether the animal research involved is appropriate. Were someone outside the field of expertise to have power to halt research, many important, life-saving projects would suffer because of ignorance.

As an additional safeguard for animals, many universities have set up animal boards, consisting of several licensed veterinarians. The scientific investigators submit their research proposals to the boards each year. More safeguards might be built with the formulation of ethical guidelines for scientists, as well as the creation of required short courses in which more experienced researchers pass on practical advice to less experienced colleagues. For example, an inexperienced researcher might struggle with guinea pigs as he tried to decapitate them. A more experienced researcher could point out that the guinea pigs might be made unconscious with carbon dioxide, then killed, thus ensuring that they wouldn't suffer.

Basically, what is now being done within the scientific community involves the warranted and nonabusive use of animals. Moreover, it is important to remember that of all the animals put to human use each year, a very small percentage are used in scientific research—most are eaten.

It would seem that a movement to forbid any work on animals, thus permitting the death of many more animals and people, reflects a prejudice against laboratory experiments as in themselves horrifying incarnations of evil. Or it may reflect a desire for absolute moral perfection, even painlessness, in a world that is full of pain and whose biological basis depends largely on killing to eat. And even now, despite the many medical breakthroughs, there remains much pain. It is odd that the comparatively minimal animal suffering which carries the hope of reducing immense amounts of future suffering should be so bitterly attacked.

The case against permitting animals raised for food to suffer is harder to counter, because here the infliction of discomfort does not result in a diminution of it somewhere else. Furthermore, humans can, with some effort, be perfectly well nourished without eating animals. So animals are raised for bringing additional pleasure and variety to the human diet, rather than to forestall future suffering, as in scientific experiments. If it is true that hundreds of millions of factory farm animals are, every moment of the day, denied such elementary freedoms as the space to walk a few steps or stretch their limbs, that seems unwarranted cruelty to sentient beings. Learning that pigs and chickens are frequently raised in such close quarters that they cannot turn around, and that this is done solely for finanical reasons, is disturbing. Farmers may need to strike agreements with one another to undertake the expense of providing more room in which to raise animals. Or perhaps legislation is needed. The results would be higher production costs and the passing on of higher prices for humane animal husbandry to the public, but an informed and understanding public should be willing to pay the price. To the argument that animals should not be raised for food at all, one might counter that the animal farmer is the domestic animal's best friend, since it is only because of the farmer—and his client, the meat-eater—that so many cows, chickens, and pigs have had the privilege of living at all. The question, however, is whether the farm animal, pen-raised for slaughter, is better off for having lived. If conditions under which the animals are raised are humane, the answer would seem to be affirmative.

A sticky, middle issue is research conducted for the consumer. It is in between the foregoing issues in this sense: Like food-animals, new products bring pleasure to humans; but as with scientific research, failure to experiment with animals could result in the injury of many unsuspecting humans. So for the sake of the consumer, millions of animals are sacrificed each year to meet the public demand for safety—not to advance science, but to make sure that substitutes for sugar will not cause cancer, or that mouthwashes will not irritate the skin. Since myriad such consumer products now exist, one might well ask why the chance must be taken of inflicting pain on animals merely to give the world a product such as a new after-shave lotion.

Experiments for consumer products should be carefully distinguished from scientific experiments. Humans choose new consumer products. They do not choose to get neurological diseases. Further, consumer products are for pleasure; products of scientific research are for the prolongation of life. Perhaps, then, humans should bear the risk of using caustic products-for-pleasure, rather than subjecting animals to it. But the public might not approve of the implications of this solution. No company would be willing to take the financial risks involved in developing new products unless those burned could not readily sue a company that put untested products on the market (or not collect the huge damage awards now granted). Yet the ability to sue for injury from a product up to now has been a far more sacred cow in this country than the regard in which experimental animals have been held. It will be interesting indeed if animal rights activists can change these priorities.

In sum, not one but three quite different situations exist which demand consideration of animals' rights. In cases of future betterment of animals and humans through scientific experiment, animals may be made to suffer, but the minimum amount necessary. Animals bred and raised for food should be better off alive than if they had never been born. And since human use of a number of products is only for pleasure, yet testing these products involves pain to animals, humans should be willing to knowingly bear these risks. Beneath all three conclusions lie the principles that animals are not as important as humans but should not suffer unless that suffering might forestall future unavoidable suffering of other animals and humans.

Even though the aforementioned solutions seem better than the alternatives, are they truly fair to animals? What if superintelligent beings from Alpha Centauri landed on earth and decided to use *us* for their experiments, arguing that they could save far more of our, and their, lives by so doing? Would the same arguments apply against humans as have been used to give animals fewer rights? If our intelligence were at all within the realm of theirs, then the foregoing argument that we should share decision-making and exemption from experimentation could apply. But what if they countered that their intelligence was so exquisitely refined compared with ours (say as ours is to that of mice) that we couldn't even begin to help them in their stewardship of the galaxy? Would that entitle them to raise us (humanely) for food and use us (as painlessly as possible, but occasionally in pain) for the betterment of our life spans and the lives of others in the galaxy? Let us hope that such advanced beings would have the technological ability to transcend the need for experimental animals.

NOTES

1. Reprinted from *"Surely You're Joking, Mr. Feynman!" The Adventures of a Curious Character,* Richard P. Feynman, as told to Ralph Leighton, edited by Edward Hutchings, pp. 165–166, by permission of W. W. Norton & Company, Inc. Bantam Books, 1989 Copyright © 1985 by Richard P. Feynman and Ralph Leighton.
2. John Allen Paulos, *Innumeracy: Mathematical Illiteracy and Its Consequences* (New York: Hill and Wang, a division of Farrar, Straus and Giroux, 1988).
3. John Allen Paulos, "The Odds Are You're Innumerate," *The New York Times Book Review,* January 1, 1989. Copyright © 1989 by The New York Times Company. Reprinted by permission.
4. See William Paton, *Man and Mouse: Animals in Medical Research,* second edition (New York: Oxford University Press, 1993), pp. 45–72.

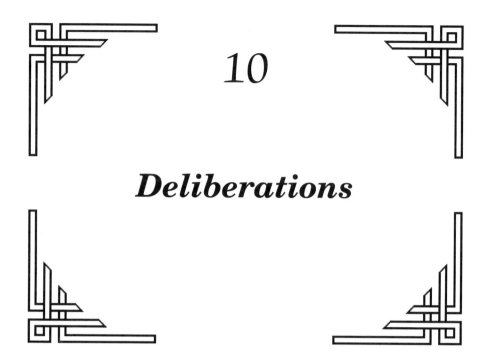

10

Deliberations

ARE DELIBERATIONS BETTER THAN DEBATES?

This is a chapter on how to "un-debate."

The trouble with debates is that the participants so rarely seek the truth—each is seeking to win, and in attempting to win, it is all too easy to bend the truth. Furthermore, in a debate it is a mark of failure to concede that the other side is right.*

Another objection to debates is their bruising quality. We've probably all been shellacked by somebody whose only merit was to be more persistently belligerent than we were at driving home a point. Unless one suffers from sadomasochistic tendencies, therefore, it is best to avoid debates.

Both Sides Win

On the other hand, we need to interact as members of the community of thinkers. The stance of the balanced critical thinker is, as Karl Popper put it, "I may be wrong and you may be right, and by an effort, we may get nearer to the truth."

---

*In *The Republic,* the ancient Greek philosopher Plato warned against the trap of being one who "when he thinks that he is reasoning . . . is only disputing . . . and he will pursue a merely verbal opposition in the spirit of contention and not of fair discussion."

To work this idea out practically, you can use a scheme which is a cross between a debate and a discussion. Two or more people start out on opposite sides of an issue, but for the purpose of consulting with one another to reach a decision. They argue as persuasively as possible at the beginning, but then they really listen to the other side(s) and decide whether to change course. They are deliberating over an issue, not debating with one another. It's fine if by the end they've decided to stay on the same side of the issue that they began on; it's fine if both end on one side; it's perfectly fine if they end up having switched positions. The emphasis here is on *getting at the truth* as best one sees it.

PLAY "THE DEVIL'S ADVOCATE"

Everyone should play the devil's advocate from time to time. This means to counterargue some position that is put forward, not because you necessarily believe your counterargument (you probably don't), but for the fun and enlightenment of seeing where this argument will take you. Again, you don't hang on to the death, but try to take this counterargument towards the truth of the matter. Here is some language to get you into the game:

> **Let me play the devil's advocate and argue that** . . .
> **One could make the argument that** . . .
> **A case could be made that** . . .

If you hit upon an idea and want to try it out, playing the devil's advocate in the middle of a deliberation is perfectly acceptable.

FORMAL DELIBERATIONS

The more you deliberate and play the devil's advocate with others, the more quickly you'll become skilled in critical thinking. Make arrangements to meet fellow classmates to practice, or train some loved one in the sport.

You might also want to hold formal deliberations in class. Here is one possible system of points. The numbers represent the maximum possible points you can receive for each category.

Points for

20 points for using critical thinkers' language and twelve tools of argumentation during the deliberation.
20 points for producing a cogent, well-supported opening argument.

5 points each time you request a definition of a pivotal term or make a distinction.

10 points for trying to harmonize the other side's claims with your point of view. It may work or it may not, but the idea is to try.

10 points for playing the devil's advocate.

Then points for one of the following:

20 points for changing your position if you give an argument why you're changing that takes the other side into account (e.g., explain the specific point or points the opposite side has that seem true and can't be taken into account by your argument).

or

20 points for not changing your position if you give an argument why you're not changing that takes the other side into account (e.g., "despite the other argument that," or "even granting the argument, my argument still holds, because").

That makes a total of 75 points (more if you request more definitions or distinctions as often as the deliberation genuinely needs them).

Points off

20 points off for being sarcastic or otherwise uncivil (distinguish "sarcasm" and "incivility" to one's partner from showing frustration at not getting one's point across).

Whatever Is Right

As in a debate, you are rewarded for coming up with strongly supported arguments. If you believe it is right to maintain your original position, you are rewarded as long as you show you've considered the other side. Unlike in a debate, however, if you start to become convinced by the other side you are rewarded for being flexible and altering your position.

AN EXTENDED EXAMPLE

This should give you a flavor of how a deliberation might go. Because the participants are arguing on their feet, you can't expect the close rigor of a written dialogue, nor even that of a written argument, unless those participating are very skilled. The language and tools of this deliberation over which method of verbal argument is better (debate or deliberation?) are in boldface. First, Jennifer presents her prepared remarks:

> **I will argue that** debates are a much better way to argue than deliberations. **By definition,** debaters are supposed to argue their sides right to the end. **That implies that** they're going to argue just as hard as they can. With a deliberation, **on the other hand,*** it is too easy to give up on your side earlier than you should. If you can get as many points for "caving in" as you can for pushing your point, why go to the trouble?
>
> **As evidence to support my claim that** debates are the best way to argue, the debating style is used in all crucial arguments: In life-and-death matters, attorneys debate in courts of law; in deciding the future leader of our country, we have the presidential aspirants debate; in determining whether to vote a bill into law, Congress debates its pros and cons. Just because somebody gets his or her feelings hurt once in a while **is no reason** to eliminate this valuable means of getting at the truth.

Mike then presents his prepared remarks:

> **My argument is that** deliberating is the best way to argue. So often in a debate the flashiest argument is the one that wins. It often happens that in a debate the arguers get backed into maintaining positions that they don't even believe, just to save face or to try to win the argument. With a deliberation, **on the other hand,** there are no "winners" or "losers," just two people working together to decide on the likeliest conclusion of an issue.
>
> **I would further argue that** debates have harmed the cause of argument rather than helped it. **In support of this claim,** I ask you to consider how rarely you and the people you know want to get into "arguments" about topics that they care a great deal about, because argument in their minds implies a painful debating session.
>
> Getting at the truth is much more important than winning, and **on this assumption I base my argument that** deliberations are the best choice for argument.

Jennifer's and Mike's extemporaneous remarks follow (look for critical thinking language and counterarguing strategies):

> Jennifer: I'd like a definition of "flashiest arguments."
>
> Mike: Um . . . they are the ones where people are more dramatic or forceful.
>
> Jennifer: Okay, but haven't you created a false dichotomy? I mean, couldn't somebody be very dramatic and right?
>
> Mike: Yes, they could, but my point is that in trying so hard to be dramatic and to win the debate, they can easily lose track of being right. I mean, haven't you gotten into a debate with your mom or dad about staying out

---

*points out a distinction

late at night, and because you've wanted to so badly you've said things that even you don't believe?

Jennifer: Yes, but would a deliberation really solve that problem? I mean, since I want to stay out so badly, how is a deliberation going to make it less of a scene?

Mike: Well, if you go with the attitude of figuring out the best course of action and argue your case as hard as you can at the beginning, I'd still count that a deliberation.

Jennifer: What do you mean by "at the beginning"?

Mike: That's a tough one to call. I'd say that it's when the sides both pretty much understand each other. Then it's time to really look at what the other side has said and consider it.

Jennifer: Don't you think people would look like fools if they changed their minds in the middle of an argument? What if it's a presidential debate and the Democrat suddenly says, "Oh, I see you've been right all along, I'm going to go out and register Republican."

Mike: I see your point. We've come to expect political candidates and leaders not to change their minds, which is weird. Why should *we* get to change our minds and they don't get to change theirs?

Jennifer: Well, they say they're going to do a thing, and we vote for them because they're going to do it.

Mike: Maybe that's the problem. Maybe we should just accept a candidate's assumptions and . . . I mean, accept one candidate's assumptions as better than the other's and vote for her on that basis. Then if she changes her mind, that's O.K.

Jennifer: [a bit impatient]: Look, you can't hope to change the world. It's just a fact that most people vote for a candidate on the basis of how strong a leader he is. If he can't decide what to do and shows that in a debate, I don't think he should be in office.

Mike: Well, I'll agree with you that it would take a long time for people to expect deliberations rather than debates out of candidates. Let's accept that that won't happen soon. But what about our daily lives? I think that we don't talk about the things that really matter to us because we don't want to get into a debate over these issues.

Jennifer: I don't think that's why we don't talk about these things. It's because we're afraid of being wrong and having to change. If I believe that abortion is right and suddenly am confronted with some ideas that throw this into question, then I'm not going to be comfortable. It has nothing to do with whether I have a deliberation to find out these uncomfortable ideas or if it's a debate.

Mike: I'll grant you that all types of arguments can turn up some uncomfortable ideas. Aren't we missing a central piece of evidence? We don't know whether people would be more willing to deliberate than debate. Would you be willing to try an experiment? We could poll whatever number of people you think would make a convincing sample to at least see what people *think* they'd prefer.

Jennifer: Or how about just trying both methods out on a group of people?

Mike: That's O.K. with me too. (slyly) You know, Jennifer, you worked this deliberation out very well.

Jennifer: Heck, no! This was a debate!

SUMMARY

A deliberation is a form of discussion in which two people begin on different sides of an issue. Each person argues his or her position with the best, most truthful means possible. Then each decides, in light of the other argument, whether to adopt the other position, to change his or her position somewhat, or to maintain the same position. Both sides realize that to modify one's position is not to lose; the point is to get closer to the truth of the matter.

EXERCISE

Get a classmate, family member, or friend to deliberate with you on any issue of mutual interest.

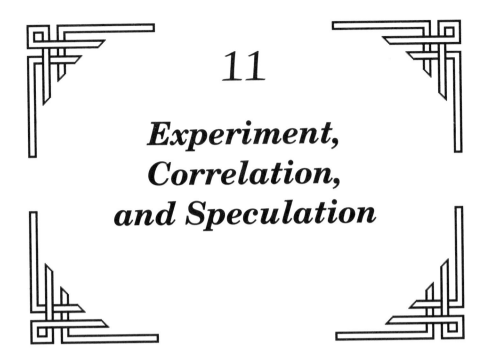

11

Experiment, Correlation, and Speculation

Experiment, correlation, and speculation—your appreciation of how these types of evidence differ will greatly enhance your critical acumen. This chapter elaborates upon the information presented in Chapter 4.

It's best to grant *any* argument only provisional status pending a better argument, no matter what the nature of the evidence. You will often find a critical thinker's favorable assessment of an argument in such terms as *"the best argument on this subject to date."* The rule of faith here is that a better argument, theory, or hypothesis may appear on any subject, thanks to the community of thinkers.

Experimental evidence is frequently used in science to get at underlying mechanisms in the material world. Experimental evidence is gathered in the social and behavioral sciences too, whenever possible and whenever doing so would not endanger the subjects' well-being. In cases where experimental evidence can't be obtained, correlation or evidence gathered after the fact is used. Finally, evidence based on reason and shared experience is speculative. Following are more detailed examinations of each type of evidence.

EXPERIMENT

One of the most important aspects of knowing about anything is to know what caused it.

Until recently in human history, people were stuck with trying to understand how things were caused by just looking at some situation and fishing for cause-effect connections. They would see W happen, and then Y would happen. They would infer that W had caused Y. The argument is "because W (reason), therefore Y (conclusion)."

Some of the beliefs arrived at in this fashion now strike us as weird or unfair; for example, the notion that applying leeches and bleeding people would cure fevers, or that witches could make others do evil. Those who believed these causal connections were quite intelligent, presumably just as intelligent as we are. But the problem they faced was that there are usually many more factors than just a W and a Y in a situation. There are all sorts of other events.

As the arrows in Figure 11-1 indicate, each object is acting or moving in a different way. There are many possible causes for any given event (Y), be it a poorly running car, increased hormonal activity, or anything else. The problem is how to sort out those factors that don't matter and find the cause of Y's motion or behavior. Scientific method

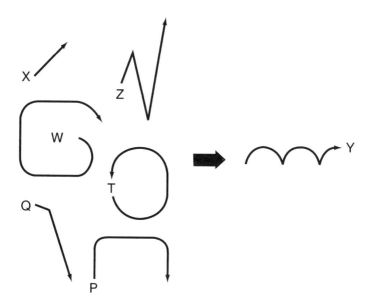

Figure 11-1   Which of these moving objects is the cause of Y's motion?

has given us a way to deal with this problem and gain good evidence for cause and effect.

There are two sides to the methodology of science. The first is that of model-building. The second is that of experimental setup.

Model-building

Although we may have identified causal factors, we don't yet necessarily know the mechanism whereby X causes Y to move. With a combination of careful yet creative thinking, the scientist gets an idea about the way that some process might work. That idea, or model (also called hypothesis, or theory), outstrips the available evidence. The model should also obey two rules:

Rule 1: It should be the *simplest explanation* of the expected evidence. Another way of stating this is that, given a choice between two theories which explain some evidence, the simpler theory would be superior. This principle was first enunciated by William of Ockham in the twelfth century, and is known as Ockham's razor. The simplest plausible hypothesis is better, since it is much easier to work with.

Rule 2: The model should have *high predictive power*. It should help us to see many other connections: "If this is the case, then X and Y and Z facts should be found in the future."

Once we have a theory, we can test its predictions with the experimental setup.

An Example   Model-building to get at causation is not the same as speculation. The scientific origin of the atomic theory, that is, the idea that everything is made up of atoms, began with the work of John Dalton, Joseph Louis Gay-Lussac, and Amedeo Avogadro. This idea was actually speculated upon by the ancient Greek philosophers. They debated the question whether tiny, invisible particles might compose all matter. However, they had a serious objection: How could the complexity of nature be explained by atoms, which they believed differed only slightly from one another? That is, how could living things, rocks, and air be made of the same components? Unfortunately, these ideas of the Greeks lacked the essential feature of a scientific theory: They were not supported or tested by experiments. These ideas were not tested against the realities of the world. Since they were the product of conjecture, they could be demolished by more conjecture.

Two thousand years after the Greeks' atomic speculations, Dalton formulated the first atomic theory. The scientists of that time had found that chemical compounds, regardless of their source, were always made up of the same ratios of the same elements; for example, that mercuric oxide was always made up of a certain proportion of mercury for a certain amount of oxygen (for instance, say, 200 grams of mercury always combined with 16 grams of oxygen). No matter how much mercuric oxide scientists decomposed, they always found the two components, mercury and oxygen, in the same proportion (Figure 11-2).

Then they realized that the same components could be joined in different proportions and yield quite different chemicals. "Different" here means different smells, color, etc. For example, three combinations of nitrogen and oxygen were known, each with different properties. At zero degrees two of these chemicals are colorless gases; the third is a yellow liquid. Furthermore, at very low temperatures one of the gases becomes a colorless liquid, the other a blue liquid. Each combination was made up of different ratios of oxygen and nitrogen (e.g., one is 14 g of nitrogen with 16 g of oxygen; another is 14 g of nitrogen, 32 g of oxygen; the third is 28 g of nitrogen and 16 g of oxygen) (Figure 11-3).

A simple explanation for these and other findings was that the elements (oxygen, nitrogen, etc.) were made up of atoms, basic particles which could combine in different ratios to yield molecules with different properties. This is the beginning of atomic theory. So the model that everything is made up of atoms explains how we can have such a diversity of compounds. This, of course, got around the problems the Greeks had about the multiplicity of things they saw. Furthermore, the atomic theory gave rise to many successful and important predictions which

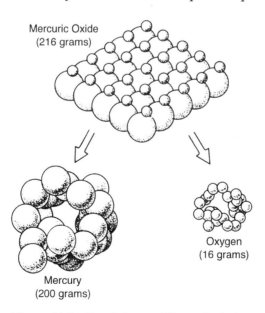

Mercuric Oxide
(216 grams)

Oxygen
(16 grams)

Mercury
(200 grams)

Figure 11-2   Breakdown of Mercuric Oxide

Nitric Oxide $\left\{\begin{array}{l} \text{14 g of Nitrogen} \\ \text{16 g of Oxygen} \end{array}\right.$

Nitrogen Dioxide $\left\{\begin{array}{l} \text{14 g of Nitrogen} \\ \text{32 g of Oxygen} \end{array}\right.$

Nitrous Oxide $\left\{\begin{array}{l} \text{28 g of Nitrogen} \\ \text{16 g of Oxygen} \end{array}\right.$

Figure 11-3   Combinations of Nitrogen and Oxygen

comprise modern chemistry. One of the most dramatic examples that comes to mind is the probing of the structure of the atom which eventually led to the ability to release atomic energy.

All of the foregoing exactitude about the ratio of grams in mercuric oxide is data upon which scientific model-building depends. Early chemists obtained these data by using the experimental setup.

The Experimental Setup

Rather than just looking at one situation and trying to fish out a cause from any number of candidates, the procedure here is to take one possibility at a time. Taking the example shown in Figure 11-1, we systematically go through and allow only *one* of these factors to operate at a time and see whether Y moves or not.

The factors (letters on the left) are not allowed to move. Only X is permitted to move (Figure 11-4). This is the experimental situation. One of two things is going to happen here. Either Y will move or it won't. Say that Y doesn't move. Then we can rule out the possibility that X caused Y to move. But suppose that Y does move. Even if Y does move, we *still* can't be sure that X is the cause until we hold X (and all the others, Z, W, T, Q, and P) motionless and see that Y in fact does not move under those circumstances. We have to be sure that Y moves only when X does.

As Figure 11-5 shows, an almost identical situation, called the *control,* is set up. The only difference between the experimental and the control situation is that in this latter case everything is held down, including Y. Now if Y doesn't "perform," we can conclude that X is the cause. In effect, when X is in play, Y is affected (experiment). When X is out of play, Y is not affected (control).

The scientist can proceed to systematically try each variable

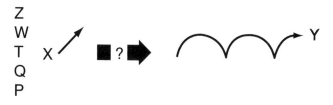

Figure 11-4 Experimental Setup for Figure 11-1

(Z,W,T,Q,P) in the same way as X, always comparing that result with the control situation. We always want to be assured that when a factor is out of commission the effect is, too.

Experiment-Control at Work Let's consider two examples of the experimental method, since this duality of experimental and control systems is part of every scientific experiment. To take a simple example, say we want to test for the ability of blood to catalyze (carry out) a chemical reaction, transforming compound A into compound B. If we want to find out whether blood could carry out this transformation, we would mix compound A with some blood, wait several minutes, and then look for the presence of B. But even if we found B, we would need to do the control experiment, mixing A with water to see how much, if any, B accumulated after the same period. Why would we have to do the control experiment? We want to be certain that it is the blood, and not some property in A itself, that is causing the change (see Figure 11-6).

As a second example from a different scientific area, consider the extraction of oil from oil shale. Engineers are constantly testing new methods against old methods of extraction, the new methods being the experimental methods, the old functioning as the control. They extract many samples with both methods and compare the results. Small differences in the two methods carried out with large amounts of material make enormous differences in terms of cost or amount of oil obtained or pollution generated, among other things.

This tactic of discovering causes by means of two systems (experimental and control) has to be one of the greatest discoveries in history.

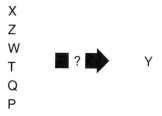

Figure 11-5   Control for Figure 11-1

Figure 11-6   Example of Experiment and Control

It has literally put us on a rocket ship, compared with the slow walk of former times to gather strong evidence.

Improving Models, Improving Experiments

The model and consequent experiment don't exist in isolation. They are part of an ongoing building project. Think of a constant cycle by which our understanding improves through thousands of orbits from model to experiments to model (Figure 11-7). The theory gives rise to predictions. These predictions are used to design the experiments, which test the predictions. The new experimental data that is generated will cause the model to be accepted, rejected, or—what is usually the case—modified to better fit the data.

This cycle has given birth to an enormous number of refined, related offspring in physics, chemistry, and biology. When a sufficient amount and complexity of powerful evidence exist, a separate discipline emerges. In engineering, for instance, chemical engineering, structural engineering, and, recently, genetic engineering are the practical application of scientifically derived theories.

The existence of an elaborate engineering—this power to manipulate the phenomenon in very intricate ways—is good evidence that the

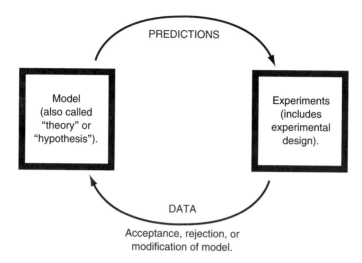

Figure 11-7 Ongoing Cycle of Model to Experiment

models in a particular scientific area correspond with what's out there in the world.

The Cycle at Work

A model can be abstract and represented in mathematical terms. Or it can actually take the shape of a structure, much as a plastic airplane model is a miniaturized image. Let's take the example of the genetic material, DNA. The scientists who determined its structure had originally expressed their hypothesis in the form of a physical model. Of course, unlike an airplane model, this model was more than a million times larger than the original.

Experiments before 1953 showed that DNA could give bacteria new genetic traits. Thus it appeared to be the material that stores the information of inheritance. In 1953, James Watson and Francis Crick proposed a model for the structure of the DNA molecule. Figure 11-8 shows the operation of the cycle. The experiments focused scientists' attention on the possibility that DNA stores genetic information.

First, this new model for the structure of the DNA molecule explained the well-known rules of inheritance, such as that a woman has an almost equal chance of having a boy or girl baby. Furthermore, it predicted something new—the existence of a DNA genetic code, that is, a blueprint for inheritance. The experiments to test for the existence of a DNA genetic code ultimately gave scientists the ability to "read" this

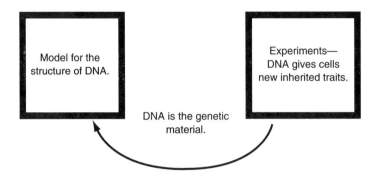

Figure 11-8   Cycle for DNA Experiments

code (see Figure 11-9). Today, not only can we read the genetic code, we can rewrite it as well, a phenomenal achievement of our time.

Support for Other Sciences

We've dealt with physics and chemistry as disciplines supported by strong evidence. Other areas derive great benefit when they can rest on evidence from these disciplines. For example, physics has given astronomers insight into astronomy. They know a great deal about the physical reactions taking place in the sun without ever having been there or experimenting with the sun itself. Physics has also been of help to cosmology (theories of origin and development of the universe); physics and chemistry likewise support geology.

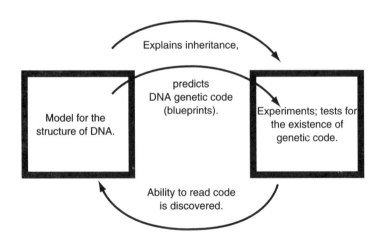

Figure 11-9   Experiments, Model, and Outcome of DNA Research

Controversial Areas at the Forefront

Although all theories stand ready to be supplanted in the future, some areas are "hot"—most of the research is based there. These controversial areas are rapidly changing as evidence mounts to push the frontier forward. For instance, the cellular theory of sexual reproduction, with its hypotheses of gametes, fertilization, and zygote, was at the forefront of scientific thinking in the nineteenth century but is now not in dispute.[1] Of course, on the cutting edge of scientific thinking, many conflicting theories will remain controversial until exhaustive experimentation points to the more likely theory. For instance, is there an influence of attitude on the causation of disease? Even if a strong correlation were found between those with serious disease and depression, the depression could be the result of being ill, not vice versa. Eventually, better information will strengthen the likelihood of this theory, or it will fail for want of evidence.

CORRELATION

Case Study—A Correlational Tool

As discussed in Chapter 4, oftentimes for moral and practical reasons, social, behavioral, and medical scientists cannot run experiments on humans. Researchers have to rely on evidence gained after the fact. We can look through records to find a situation where all variables were held constant except the one we're interested in. The validity of the results will depend on two factors. First, any variables besides the one in question must have in fact stayed constant. Second, many instances of this situation must be found, which often requires sifting through an enormous number of records. Researchers who use this kind of evidence look for correlations between variables.

Correlation Compared to Causation

What is the difference between correlation and causation? With a correlation one can see that there is a relationship between two variables. The relationship can be of two types: It can be a direct (causal) relationship, such that changes in X will bring changes in Y, or it can be the case that X and Y change in response to a third variable, say, W. There is not a direct relationship between X and Y in this second case. That is, if we change X, we will not necessarily see changes in Y (Figure 11-10).

The difficulty of after-the-fact, or case, studies is that although one finds a correlation between variables, this does not mean that a causal

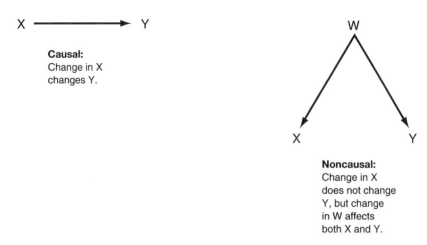

Figure 11-10   Causation

relationship has been found, although that might turn out to be the case. It is much more difficult to be sure that only the variable X in which you are interested is changing while all other important variables, including W, have been held constant. Experiments, however, allow you to manipulate the environment precisely so that you can exclude the possibility that X and Y are moving in response to a third variable.

For example, say that one discovers a correlation between the automobile accidents and their proximity to the drivers' homes. Is being close to home causing people to have accidents? The problem is that other variables may be at work. For instance, once it is realized that out of all the miles driven, more would be near home (especially if a person makes many short trips), the causal explanation no longer seems plausible.

Here are three more examples which illustrate the quandary we sometimes face in trying to decide whether a relationship is just a correlation or actually causation.

You recall the brief discussion about smoking and lung cancer in Chapter 4. When the correlation was originally found, two possibilities could have explained it. First, smoking could actually cause lung cancer; second, people who had a susceptibility to lung cancer (for some unknown reasons) could also be the same group of people who were heavy smokers (Figure 11-11). One might fish around for any number of possibilities to explain this correlation. For instance, it is *possible* that people who smoke a lot also drink a lot, and drinking might be the cause of lung cancer. Or perhaps nervousness causes lung cancer, and people who are nervous smoke.

Additional correlation studies between these factors and lung can-

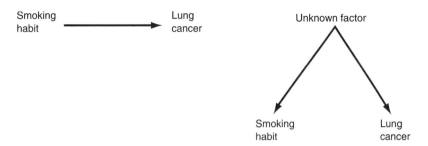

Figure 11-11   Correlation Studies Between Smoking and Lung Cancer

cer could be made. But far more powerful evidence is an understanding of a direct mechanism whereby cigarette smoking could be causing cancer. Laboratory experiments with the substances found in cigarette smoke have shown these substances to change normal animal cells into cancer cells. Furthermore, experimental evidence strongly suggests that a chemical change in the DNA causes this malignant transformation. In sum, a strong correlation is vastly reinforced by direct experimental evidence.

There is some correlation between milk consumption and the incidence of cancer in various societies. The milk *might* be causing the cancer, but this correlation is probably explained by the relative wealth of these societies, which allows more people to buy milk as well as to live longer (the longer one lives the greater the chance that one's body will on its own make the "mistakes" in cell division that lead to cancer).

As a third example, there is a well-known positive correlation between the number of Baptist ministers and the per capita liquor consumption in cities with populations over 10,000 in the United States. We can either blame the Baptist ministers for this lamentable condition, or search for some other more likely cause of these two phenomena occurring at the same time (Figure 11-12). The most likely explanation is probably trivial: More Baptist (and other) ministers and higher per capita liquor consumption occur in larger cities. However, there is not necessarily any causal relation between liquor consumption and number of Baptist ministers.

In short, strong correlations are important in pointing out possible causal relationships but in themselves aren't definitive evidence of a causal relationship.

The Significance of Increasing Knowledge

We tend to forget the amount of knowledge we have accumulated over the centuries and how our everyday lives have been affected. The follow-

Figure 11-12   Correlation Studies Between Number of Baptist Ministers and Higher Alcohol Consumption

ing reconstruction of the mental outlook in Europe six hundred years ago should be enlightening.

Imagine that you live in fourteenth-century Europe. Suddenly, half your family and neighbors develop strange black swellings about the size of an apple or egg in the armpits and groin. These swellings ooze blood and pus and are followed by spreading boils and black blotches on the skin from internal bleeding. Many in your town are suffering severe pain and dying quickly after five days, or sometimes overnight. The disease spreads. Then other symptoms, continuous fever and the spitting of blood, appear instead of the swellings. Everything that issues from the sick—breath, sweat, blood from the swellings, bloody urine, and blood-blackened excrement—smells foul. You and everyone around you are terrified, desperately seeking an explanation in order to save yourselves from pain, deformity, and death.

Alas, given the lack of knowledge at this time in the areas of physiology, biology, and pharmacology, the explanations available to you will not help. You are used to living among rats and fleas, so nothing in your understanding would lead you to ascribe the cause of the disease to these creatures, since people lived with them before the bubonic plague began. Your most acute observation of rats running down the gangplanks of cargo ships that carry diseased sailors would therefore not enable you to make the mental jump (hypothesis) to rats as disease-carriers, because no understanding of animal and insect-borne contagion exists. To further complicate matters, there is also a pneumonic form of the disease, carried by microorganisms in the air, but of course you don't know about microorganisms.

Here are some of your fourteenth-century contemporaries' attempts to explain the plague:

1. Poisoned air and stinking mists from stagnant lakes are poisoning people.
2. People fall ill by looking at sick people, who "dart death from their eyes."
3. The planets are conjoined in a way that causes the plague.
4. God is visiting His wrath on mankind for its sins.
5. The Jews are poisoning the wells, hoping to murder all Christians.

Here are the accompanying remedies, in the same order:

1. To draw poison from the body, bleed it, purge it with laxatives, or apply hot plasters. In addition, give these medicines: powdered stag's horn, compounds of rare spices, powdered pearls or emeralds mixed into potions. Other recommendations: Eat a bland diet, avoid excitement, go to the public latrine, and smell the foul odors, which are curative (avoid swamps, however, which cause the plague).
2. Avoid anyone suffering from the plague, even your parents or child. Don't visit the sick or bury the dead.
3. Wait for the planets to change their positions.
4. Join a penitents' procession, lasting up to three days and attended by as many as two thousand people, to pray for God's mercy. Stop doing anything that could anger Him, including gambling, cursing, and drinking. Or join the flagellates, whose members go from town to town whipping themselves for mankind's sins and exhorting others to atone.
5. Attack the Jews.

Unhappily, all of these expedients were attempted. The second, cruel as it was, probably worked best. Many realized that the charge against the Jews was ridiculous (Jews were dying at the same rate as Christians), but even the pleadings of the Pope could not stop mobs in many cities from burning thousands of people to death.

The medical faculty of the University of Paris, and doubtless many others, realized that the cause of the plague was not known. It would be five hundred years before its cause, the microscopic bacillus *Pasteurella pestis,* was discovered. It lives alternately in the stomach of the flea and the bloodstream of the rat—the bite of flea or rat transmits the disease. It is now believed that caravans carried rats with the bacillus out of Central Asia, where it was further spread by rats on cargo ships. When the plague raged, India, China, North Africa, and Europe suffered huge casualties, possibly 30 to 50 percent of their populations. Because they were not understood and thereby checked, the plague and other epidemics returned for centuries, racking Europe, Asia, and Africa.[2]

A Modern Contrast

The discovery of a virus involved in Acquired Immune Deficiency Syndrome (AIDS) within three years of its detection makes a startling contrast with the half-millenium required to understand bubonic plague. The contrast is especially impressive, since the mechanism underlying AIDS is more complicated. This initial understanding was not achieved, however, without a monumental collaboration of thousands of scientists and $80 million in research grants to abet scientific understanding of the immune system. Compared to the five hundred years it took to cure bubonic plague, one can only assume that a cure for AIDS is right around the corner, relatively speaking.

VITAL SPECULATION

Thanks to science, we have longer life spans, better health, bigger bridges, and more powerful weapons. But what on earth should we do with them?

Science and its consequent technology have increased human capabilities enormously, creating an ever-enlarging blank slate for our pleasure. Decisions about whether and how to use our new techniques are value judgments that we must make. Value judgments which arise out of controversial, subtle arguments in the social sciences and humanities enable us to "write" on that ever-expanding blank slate of human capabilities. In the social sciences, for example, historical arguments can suggest national policy; evidence from anthropology and sociology help us rethink our cultural assumptions. Besides sheer enjoyment in studying them, the humanities afford us a range of life options that we could never have invented as individuals. World literature is a window into possible or actual states of awareness and ways of life. And philosophers thrive on arguments, speculating about the basic assumptions of other disciplines and even the nature of philosophy itself.

All of the readings in this book are speculative arguments. Four will appear at the end of this chapter. Two are about the nature of literature, one about science, and the last about the nature of the major subject areas.

EVALUATION

The foregoing chapter was a second sketch, an overlay to Chapter 4. The significant point is that as you evaluate an argument, keep the general subject area in mind. Is this an argument about the material world? Then wherever possible its evidence should be founded on the scientific method. Is it an argument about the "social world"? Then usually expect correlative studies and evaluate their adequacy. Is it a prescriptive or values argument? Look for a general principle and persuasive examples from common experience.

Remember that no matter what sort of evidence is presented, you're not forced to accept or reject an argument totally, but have a range of options (review "Good Arguments and Their Evidentiary Limits," in Chapter 4). An argument might present little evidence, some evidence, good, or even very strong evidence, compared to alternative arguments or hypotheses.

Outside the Pale

What about a study such as astrology? Is it mere academic prejudice that this subject is not included as a serious pursuit? After all, many people have been surprised to learn that their behavior matches what their sign predicts about them. Isn't this good evidence that astrology is onto the truth about human nature and should be carefully studied?

It can be argued that astrology is rigid where it should be flexible and flexible where it should be more rigorous. It's a dogma, not a hypothesis, that anyone born between March 21 and April 20 is, as an Aries, going to be more aggressive than a person born under another sign. (One piece of evidence—Hitler was an Aries.) This is a *dogma,* not a hypothesis, because astrologers, unlike scientists, are unwilling to modify their notion of an Aries upon receipt of evidence, say, that many people born during this time are not more aggressive.

An astrologer might counterargue, "Well, that's just the point. Every Aries is in fact more aggressive! You can't find any evidence to the contrary. Show me an Aries and I will show you a more aggressive person." We would cite as counterevidence the poet William Wordsworth, also an Aries (April 7), but not a person known to be aggressive.

In the spirit of balance let's reply, okay, maybe you're right. But this aggression could still be in the eye of the beholder-astrologer and not in the Aries person. Let's adopt the scientific stance and take the "Aries notion" as a hypothesis to be tested. Thus we will put the predictive power of astrology to the test. If those born under the sign of Aries are in fact more aggressive, astrologers should be able to detect that aggression without being told the person's sign. In that spirit of inquiry, how about the following experiment:

A number of people present themselves to an astrologer. The one thing that they may not tell the astrologer is their birth dates; however, the astrologer may conduct any sort of personality test, with the subjects doing their best to answer truthfully. Now, can the astrologer successfully predict which people are born under the sign of Aries? Even a 50 percent success rate that could be repeated any time would be impressive. It would be impressive, but only as a beginning. For instance, it has been claimed that people often like best the season in which they were born. If this is true and if the astrologer asks what a person's favorite time of year is, he or she has improved the chances of guessing a person's sign from one in twelve to one in three. The way around this possible leak would be to prohibit the subjects from telling their favorite season. The question always remains whether there is some other variable at work helping the results along, but that is what the community of thinkers is for.

Even after numerous successes, more carefully controlled (correlative) tests would have to be run to detect what this "aggression" actually is, in order to define it narrowly enough so that one could successfully predict behaviors that an Aries would engage in and those that he or she would not. Then those predictions would have to be traced, preferably without the subjects' or the "aggression" evaluator's knowing the purpose of the experiment.

Finally, what is the precise causal connection between the planets and personality? The dogma of astrology does not (yet?) rest on physics or astronomy, and it doesn't (yet) fit into the body of established knowledge hard-won through scientific method. Current theories of physics would have it that the doctor at the newborn's bedside exerts a gravitational pull many times greater than that of the nearest planet. No relationship between gravitation and personality has been established to date. (See also John Paulos's objections to astrology in Chapter 9, pages 129–134).

SUMMARY

The three major types of evidence and their characteristics are:

1. *Experimental:* Evidence gathered by cycling from scientific experiment to model change to new experiment.
2. *Correlative:* Evidence gathered by detecting relationships between two variables which may or may not be causally related.
3. *Speculative:* The use of a general principle and persuasive examples from common experience as evidence.

Our increase in knowledge has resulted in startling changes in the way we live and view the world.

To assess evidence (review Chapter 4), ask the following questions: What *kind of evidence* does the argument provide—experimental, correlative, or speculative? Given the kind of evidence possible in that subject area, is the evidence in this argument appropriate? If you know of any alternative arguments, do you find the evidence in the argument at hand to be *nonexistent, slight, good, strong, or compelling?*

If you give any evidence more credence than it deserves, little harm is done as long as you maintain the balance discussed throughout this book.

EXERCISES

1. What kind of evidence would you expect in the following arguments: experimental, correlative, or speculative?

    That crime is caused by a bad environment

    That human nature is evil

    That growing cacti can reward you

    That Roosevelt knew that Japan would bomb Pearl Harbor

    That supply-side economics reduces inflation

    That philosophers should deal with the language contained in factual claims, and not with values

    That treating moths with a certain pheromone (insect hormone) will make them sterile

    That the origin of the American slang term "copacetic" probably came from the Yiddish *kol ba seder,* meaning that all goes well.

2. What if the astrologer countered that he couldn't predict who would be an Aries because their entire astrological chart had to be taken into account? The Aries with, say, lots of passive Pisces in her chart would not emerge as an overall Aries. Everyone has a rising sign, a moon sign, and signs in twelve houses, which represent areas of life such as "marriage" and "career," as well as planets distributed in various houses. Can you come up with any ideas to test this more complicated hypothesis?

READINGS

1. *The following article might better be titled "The public misunderstanding of science." The authors surveyed stratified random samples of 2,041 American and 2,009 British adults in 1988. Their results offer surprising findings. Perhaps the most amazing is that in the United States and Britain the public says it is more interested in science than sports. Yet the public seems to have a dim view of the way that science works. Might it also be true that the public has little notion of how the humanities work?*

The Public Understanding of Science

Why should anyone care about the public understanding of science? First, science is arguably the greatest achievement of our culture, and people deserve to know about it; second, science affects everyone's lives, and people need to know about it; third, many public policy decisions involve science, and these can only be genuinely democratic if they arise out of informed public debate; and fourth, science is publicly supported, and such support is (or at least ought to be) based on at least a minimal level of public knowledge. Whether or not the difference between public understanding and public science is, as Isaac Asimov has claimed, "the difference between respect and admiration on the one side, and hate and fear on the other," common sense suggests that the scientific community would be unwise to presume upon the continued backing of a public that knows little of what scientists do.

So, how much science does the general public understand? The answer that emerges from our research in Britain and that of Professor Jon Miller and his colleagues in the United States is "not much." According to the results of two parallel national surveys, carried out in the summer of 1988, levels of interest in science, technology, and medicine are relatively high; but levels of knowledge of each area are far lower. Although an impressive 66% of British and 62% of American respondents clearly understood the implications of simple probabilistic statements, only 34% of Britons and 43% of Americans appeared to know that the earth goes round the Sun once a year, and just 28% of Britons and 25% of Americans know that antibiotics are ineffective against viruses. Equally striking, in the context of current public and political concern about technology and the environment, is that only 34% of British respondents knew that nuclear power stations are not a source of acid rain, whilst a mere 23% recognized a link between the burning of fossil fuels in coal-fired power stations and the problem of global warming. . . .

We begin with [the question of public] interest, because this represents a basis for an individual's cultivation of understanding and the formation of attitudes. Respondents were asked to say how interested they were in six different issue areas in the news. Easily the highest level of self-reported interest is that for new medical discoveries; next come the levels for new inventions and new technologies and scientific discoveries; and after these (in descending order) come those for sport, new films and (predictably, perhaps) politics. The pattern in the United States is broadly similar, except that there are consistently slightly higher levels of self-reported interest in science, technology, and (especially) medicine.

These results are quite surprising. As a check on their reliability, British respondents were asked to say how likely it was that they would read newspaper stories under a variety of different headlines. Medical stories are clearly in the lead, together with an item on government cuts; and once again, scientific and technological stories have a very strong following.

In general, one would assume that people who are interested in a particular issue will tend to be relatively well-informed about it. We asked respondents to say how well-informed they were about each of the self-report interest issue areas. As we had expected, self-reported interest and "informedness" match pretty well for sport, politics, and films; but for science, technology and medicine there is a substantial discrepancy: Here, only a minority of those who report that they are very interested also claim that they are very well informed. As before, the pattern is broadly similar, with self-reported levels of informedness running consistently at a slightly higher level than those in Britain. For science, technology, and medicine, it appears that many people perceive a gap between themselves and a world of learning about which they would like to know more. . . .

The independent assessment of understanding is at the heart of our inquiry. We measured scientific understanding on two main dimensions: understanding of the processes of scientific inquiry (henceforth, process) and knowledge of the elementary findings of science (henceforth, knowledge). In combination, we believe that process and knowledge provide a reasonable index of scientific understanding. Of the two, process is by far the trickier to deal with—the issues are more abstract and less clearcut, and the task of formulating sensible and serviceable questions is inherently difficult.

We adopted a two-part question . . . British respondents were asked whether they had a clear, a general, or little sense of what it means to study something scientifically; and respondents falling into the first two categories were then asked to state in their own words what it means to study something scientifically. The resulting statements were recorded verbatim and then placed into one of four categories. The results make rather gloomy reading for anyone who takes seriously the conventional, quasi-popperian model of scientific method. For in their answers less than 14% of respondents made any mention either of theory construction and hypothesis testing, or of the experimental method. . . .

Before concluding that only a small minority of British adults had any grasp whatever of the roles of theory and experiment in science, we should reflect on the sheer difficulty of this item. Arguably, the question measures linguistic as much as scientific skills; certainly, it ignores the possibility of tacit public understanding of the processes of science.

To get round this problem, we devised a number of questions which required respondents only to recognize and not to state the right

answers. In general, the results point to considerable tacit public understanding of the processes of scientific inquiry. Although fewer than 14%
of respondents mentioned experimentation unprompted, more than 56%
opted for the experimental approach when given a choice between
alterntive methods of investigating a problem [see insert below]; and
although fewer than 4% mentioned theory construction and hypothesis
testing unprompted, more than 55% disagreed with the proposition that
"All of today's scientific theories will still be accepted in a hundred
years' time" . . .

1. What does it mean to study something scientifically? Percentage of
   answers including reference to:

Theory construction	3.2
Experimental method	10.5
Other answers	43.1
Don't know/Not answered	43.2

2. Suppose a drug used to treat high blood pressure is suspected of not
   working well. On this card are three different ways scientists might
   use to investigate the problem. Which one do you think scientists
   would be most likely to use?

   (a) Talk to patients to get their opinions   12.5
   (b) Use their knowledge of medicine
         to decide how good the drug is   26.5
   (c) Give the drug to some patients
         but not to others, then compare
         what happens to each group   56.3
   (d) Don't know   4.4

How do these results, briefly sketched here, speak to the reasons
for caring about public understanding of science with which we began?

On the question of science as a cultural achievement, there is clear
cause for concern. Some of the questions about knowledge addressed elementary but fundamental aspects of the scientific world picture, yet
they defeated a majority of respondents. That most of the public do not
know of the achievements of J.J. Thomson, Robert Millikan, and Niels
Bohr may perhaps be explained on the grounds of the relatively esoteric
nature of atomic physics; but what excuse shall we give (not for the public, but for ourselves as scientists and educators) to account for the fact
that most of the public appears not to have caught up with Nicholas
Copernicus and Galileo Galilei? If modern science is our greatest cultural achievement, then it is one of which most members of our culture
are very largely ignorant.

As regards practical reasons for caring about the public understanding of science, we find a similar picture. Although our survey was not intended primarily to discover how well the British workforce is equipped for life in an economy dependent upon science and technology, the fact . . . that only between a quarter and a third of our respondents were able to give a minimal account of the difference betwen computer hardware and software does not augur particularly well. Even more worrying, in the quiz more than half our respondents asserted that antibiotics kill viruses as well as bacteria, while almost 70% believed that natural vitamins are more efficarious than laboratory-made ones.

We turn next to what might be termed the democratic argument for promoting the public understanding of science. What are the prospects for informed public debate and decision making when a large proportion of the public is confused about most of the relevant facts? For example . . . we asked whether nuclear powerstations cause acid rain. Almost 50% of respondents said they did, and only 34% said they did not.

This result is strongly related to scientific understanding. Only 11% of respondents in the top quartile of scientific understanding believed that nuclear powerstations cause acid rain, whereas the figure for the bottom quartile is 62%.

. . . Finally, there is the question of the relationship between public understanding and public support for science. Our survey contains a large number of measures of attitude. Preliminary analysis of results on these measures indicates that there are important relationships between public understanding and public attitudes, with a tendency for better-informed respondents to have a more positive general attitude towards science and scientists; at the same time, however, it indicates that it is unwise to generalize to any particular conclusions concerning public attitudes towards specific scientific or science-related policy questions. This being the case, we shall say no more here about Asimov's image of a largely uninformed public caught between hatred and fear of the scientific community. The results we have provided indicate that although the public is largely uninformed, it is also largely interested in science. This is surely a cause for optimism about the scope for improving the public understanding of science.[3]

2. *In this excerpt from a revealing essay, Czech novelist Milan Kundera argues that the purpose and greatness of the novel lie in its asking questions about human experience that only the novel can ask. Unlike science, however, there are no precise answers, and to interpret one character's experience as closer to the truth than that of another character is to distort the novel's understanding of life's complexity.*

The rise of science propelled man into the tunnels of specialized knowledge. With every step forward in scientific knowledge, the less clearly he could see either the world as a whole or his own self. . . .

If one accepts as a hypothesis that philosophy and science have ignored man's being, then it is even clearer that Cervantes gave birth to a great European art which is nothing other than the perpetual investigation of the being ignored by science. . . . The novel discovered the different dimensions of existence one by one: with Cervantes and his contemporaries, it questioned the nature of adventure; with Richardson, it began to examine "what happens inside" and to unmask the secret life of feelings; with Balzac, it discovered man's rootedness in history; with Flaubert, it explored the *terra* previously *incognita* of the everyday; with Tolstoy, it focused on the role of the irrational in human behavior and decisions. It measured time; the evanescent past with Proust, the evanescent present with Joyce. With Thomas Mann, it queried the role of the myths that control our movements from the remote past of man. And so on, and so on.

The novel has accompanied man uninterruptedly and faithfully since the beginning of the Modern Era. It was then that the "passion of knowing," which [the philosopher] Husserl considered to be the essence of European spirituality, seized the novel and led it to observe man's concrete life closely, and to protect him from "the forgetting of [his own] being." . . . The only *raison d'être* [rationale] for a novel is to discover what can only be discovered by a novel. A novel that does not uncover a hitherto unknown segment of existence is immoral. Knowledge is the novel's only morality. . . .

Kundera goes on to define the "knowledge" that the novel gives. Note how it contrasts with scientific knowledge:

To take the world as relative, as Cervantes does, to be obliged to face not a single absolute truth but a heap of contradictory truths (truths embodied in *imaginary thinking selves* called characters), to have as one's only certainty the *wisdom of uncertainty,* requires . . . [heroic] courage.

Who's right and who's wrong? Don Quixote or the [other characters]? Much has been written on the question. Some see in Cervantes' novel a rationalist critique of Don Quixote's wooly idealism. Others see the novel as a celebration of the same idealism. Both interpretations are mistaken because they both try to find at the novel's source not a question but a moral judgment.

Man desires a world where good and evil are clearly distinguished. He has an innate and inextinguishable tendency to make judgments before he understands. Religions and ideologies are founded on this desire. But they can cope with the novel only by translating its language

of relativity and ambiguity into their own . . . dogmatic tongue. . . .
Either [Kafka's character] K., crushed by an unjust court, is innocent, or
the court stands for divine justice and K. is guilty.

This "either-or" encapsulates an inability to bear the essential relativity of human affairs. This inability means that the novel's wisdom
(the wisdom of uncertainty) is hard to accept or to grasp.[4]

3. *John Gardner's argument about the purpose of literature differs some-*
   what from Kundera's. In your opinion, are their views compatible?

The writing of fiction is a mode of thought because by imitating we come
to understand the thing we imitate. Fiction is thus a convincing and
honest but unverifiable science (in the old sense, knowledge): unverifiable because it depends on the reader's sensitivity and clear sense of
how things are, a sense for which we have no tests. Some people claim
our basic human nature is vicious, some claim otherwise. The cynic can
be shown, by definition, to be a cynic, but he cannot be proved wrong.
(So far, unhappily, it cannot even be proved conclusively that he grows
ulcers more quickly than do nice people.) Therefore, the kind of knowledge that comes from imitation depends for its quality on the sanity and
stability of the imitator. Clearly no absolute standard for sanity and stability exists, but rough estimates are possible. If a writer regularly
treats all life bitterly, scorning love, scorning loyalty, scorning decency
(according to some standard)—or, to put it another way, if some writer's
every remark strikes most or many readers as unfair, cruel, stupid, self-
regarding, ignorant, or mad; if he has no good to say of anything or anyone except the character who seems to represent himself; if he can find
no pleasure in what happy human beings have found good for centuries
(children and dogs, God, peace, wealth, comfort, love, hope, and faith)—
then it is safe to hazard that he has not made a serious effort to sympa-
thize and understand, that he has not tried to guess what special circumstances would make him behave, himself, as his enemies behave.
. . . Whatever some possible divinity might say of such a writer's fictions,
the nonomniscient can say this much: he is not using fiction as a mode
of thought but merely as a means of preaching his peculiar doctrine. . . . [5]

4. *Compare the foregoing arguments about literature with this one about*
   the nature of science:

[Scientific] objectivity is closely bound up with the *social aspect of scien-*
tific method, with the fact that science and scientific objectivity do not
(and cannot) result from the attempts of an individual scientist to be
"objective," but from the *friendly-hostile co-operation of many scien-*
tists. . . .

Two aspects of the method of the natural sciences are of importance in this connection. Together they constitute what I may term the "public character of scientific method." First, there is something approaching *free criticism*. A scientist may offer his theory with the full conviction that it is unassailable. But this will not impress his fellow-scientists and competitors; rather it challenges them: they know that the scientific attitude means criticizing everything, and they are little deterred even by authorities. Secondly, scientists try to avoid talking at cross-purposes. (I may remind the reader that I am speaking of the natural sciences, but a part of modern economics may be included.) They try very seriously to speak one and the same language, even if they use different mother tongues. In the natural sciences this is achieved by recognizing experience as the impartial arbiter of their controversies. When speaking of "experience" I have in mind experience of "public" character, like observations, and experiments, as opposed to experience in the sense of more "private" aesthetic or religious experience, and an experience is "public" if everybody who takes the trouble can repeat it. In order to avoid speaking at cross-purposes, scientists try to express their theories in such a form that they can be tested, i.e., refuted (or else corroborated) by such experience.

This is what constitutes scientific objectivity. Everyone who has learned the technique of understanding and testing scientific theories can repeat the experiment and judge for himself. . . .[6]

5. *This last passage is a rich series of arguments about the nature of various disciplines. It deserves a good deal of thought and affords any number of comparisons with the foregoing three arguments.*

Value and meaning traditionally have been the preserve of the humanities, which depict their nature, present instances, describe or inspire their pursuit, and portray their role or their absence in our lives. Philosophy, too, can fall within this domain. Before describing how philosophy can be carried on as part of the humanities, we must pause to describe the intellectual and imaginative landscape.

The sciences aim at truths and explanations; it is the highest ambition of current scientists to discover and formulate new important truths, laws, and explanations that will be incorporated into the textbooks of the future. No physicist, biologist, or economist now expects or even hopes that the articles or books he writes will themselves be read one hundred years from now. These are not designed to be read or experienced directly; the truths they discover and laws they formulate can just as well be present in other people's words—and they will be as they are incorporated into the larger edifice of scientific truths and textbooks. When, occasionally, an elder scientist writes his autobiography or presents general thoughts on the nature of his scientific activity, he is well aware that he is not doing science.

Works of art and literature, on the other hand, are produced with the intention that they will be experienced directly. No one now thinks it is unnecessary to read Shakespeare because everything important in him has been incorporated into current literature. However, although these works of art are produced with the intention that they will be read or experienced directly, it is not intended usually that they present truths or explanations, unless "imaginative" ones—truths of another sort. Since the "truths" they contain are not extractable or paraphrasable without loss, it is not surprising that these works must be experienced directly and so cannot merely be incorporated into future texts or re-presentations. . . .

There is a body of writing, however, which intends both to present truths, explanations, and so on, and to be read directly rather than merely incorporated into other writings. Here fall the great works of political philosophy (of Plato, Aristotle, Hobbes, Locke, Rousseau), of social theory (Marx, Tocqueville, Weber, Durkheim), of moral theory, of religious thought, of philosophy generally. The writers of these works strive after truths, yet view it as important and write with the intention that their works themselves will be read, that their own voice will be heard. With an aim of science (to produce truths and explanation) yet an intention of artistic works (to be experienced directly), these works present a puzzle. Why should it be important that works presenting truths be experienced directly? What accounts for this phenomenon in works of the humanities?

The humanities are marked by (the nature of) their concern with value and meaning. . . . Yet, not every concern with value and meaning falls within the humanities; for example, consider the way an anthropologist can study the values of different cultures or tribes, make cross-cultural comparisons of value, and so forth. The anthropologist studies values by placing them in quotation marks, telling us: "they believe it is wrong to eat meat, marry one's uncle or aunt, allow an insult to go unavenged." The anthropologist's report of these beliefs neither endorses nor condemns them; from the anthropological report no value statement follows. Values can be the subject matter of the anthropologist's study, but as a social scientist his standpoint toward these is external. He could just as well be describing (or trying to explain) different values, or things other than values. He does not respond internally to them; he does not respond to values qua values. The quotation marks are the fence that keeps him external to the values.

[On the other hand,] a work of the humanities responds to value as value, to meaning as meaning, and it is concerned with these in relation to humanity, as they guide or inspire human affairs; so, the humanities are concerned with . . . the value and meaning we bring into the world and exhibit through our free choices. . . .

The poet, painter, or critic is responding to value as value, meaning as meaning, and he also has an audience in mind; he intends that through the object he makes (poem, painting, essay) or the activity he performs, the audience will also respond to the values and meanings he is responding to. . . . Also, the artist (often? always?) intends that his product have a value of its own that will be responded to by the audience. . . .

The search for explanations itself lifts us out of our narrow concerns; and the free consideration of possibilities, placing a matter within a wider matrix of possibilities, not only increases understanding but enables us to transcend the limits of the actual. . . .

Cannot scientific explanations also be offered in a quest for valuable theoretical unifications in nature, as a vehicle whereby we can respond to that value as the scientist does, and to the value of his so responding? Why cannot science be carried on as part of the humanities? The motivation of scientists often is to discern and uncover the deep unifying principles underlying diverse phenomena, and their motivation even can be to remove unsightly theoretical blemishes, coincidences, tensions, rather than to account directly for observed facts. . . .

To investigate the ways science is or can be humanistic, to discern its humanistic strands, is not to recommend *transforming* it further, against its grain, into a humanity or into something with humanistic veneer. Yet the investigation is worth making, for the sciences are a dominant part of the modern intellectual world, and the scientific picture of the world, the "scientific outlook," appears to leave no room for value and meaning, and so threatens the very legitimacy of the humanities. . . . It is ironic that one of the most glorious achievements of the modern mind, science, seems to leave no room for its own glory; that the reduced image of man toward which it seems inexorably to lead—a mean and pitiable plaything of forces beyond his control—seems to leave no room even for the creators, and the creation, of science itself.[7]

NOTES

1. Ralph W. Lewis, Letter, Scientific American, April 1984, p. 6.
2. Adapted from Barbara Tuchman, *A Distant Mirror: The Calamitous 14th Century* (New York: Ballantine Books, 1987), pp. 92–126.
3. "The public understanding of science," *Nature* (London), 6 July 1989. The article contains more tables than the one shown here in abbreviated form.
4. Milan Kundera, "The Novel and Europe," *New York Review of Books,* July 19, 1984, p. 15.

5. John Gardner, *On Moral Fiction* (New York: Basic Books, Inc., 1978), pp. 116–17.

6. Karl R. Popper, *The Open Society and Its Enemies* (Princeton, NJ: Princeton University Press, 1971), II, pp. 217–18.

7. Robert Nozick, *Philosophical Explanations* (Cambridge, MA: Harvard University Press, 1981), pp. 619–21, 625–27.

12

Flimsy Structures

This chapter could have been titled " *Un*warranted Inferences." The following are certain infamous reasons given to support arguments—infamous because they mimic real support. There are two basic replies to these inferences: "So what?" or "What else?"

Abusing arguments may be among the world's older professions. Proper names for many types of abuse are in Latin. I'll deal only with the seven deadliest: inconsistency, ad hominem attacks, appeal to pity, begging the questions, post hoc ergo propter hoc, appeal (only) to the many, and straw man.

INCONSISTENCY

Two main ways of being inconsistent come to mind:

1. Offering reasons that are contradictory. For example, arguing that most people who strive for success do so out of hunger for love and admiration they didn't get when growing up; and in the same book arguing that most people strive for success because they can afford to take the risk of failure, having been given a lot of encouragement and attention as children. Since encouragement and attention are tantamount to love and admiration, this argument is foundering on inconsistency unless the arguer makes a careful distinction between the pairs of terms *love-admiration* and *encouragement-attention* to explain this disparity.

2. *Offering reasons that contradict the conclusion.* For example, We should conserve on fuel because many of the elderly poor are dying from lack of heat in the winter. Given that reason, the conclusion would appear to be the opposite: that we should expend more fuel, at least on the elderly poor (unless some fiend is advocating killing off the elderly poor).

Enjoy Being on the Lookout

You can enjoy ferreting out inconsistencies (rather like the children's game "What's wrong with this picture?" in which the flag and the wind sock are flying in opposite directions, with the rabbit upside down under the hedge).

Discoveries can be fascinating. For instance, employers frequently advertise themselves as an "equal opportunity affirmative action employer." But the only case in which an employer could be both is when the minority candidate or woman applying is more qualified than any white male applicant. In cases of a tie, or when a white male is better qualified, something has to give. Think about whether these two often-connected terms, "equal opportunity" and "affirmative action," can be reconciled.

Reconciling Differences

Anyone who is at cross-purposes with his or her own ideas has just shot him- or herself in the foot, argumentatively speaking. The hearer's appropriate response to inconsistent arguments is "So what?"

One can let the argument drown in its own juices. But, depending on how interested one is in the subject, a lot of fun can be had trying to reconcile these differences ("What else would reconcile these inconsistencies? Is that something else true?").

Carefully check your work to make sure you're not involved in major inconsistencies. Students sometimes say, "I know my major reasons look inconsistent on paper. But I had such-and-such other idea in mind when I wrote this, so the reasons really do fit." For heaven's sake! Don't expect your reader to be a mind reader as well. It's only fun to ferret out inconsistencies when they're subtle. Those that glare are painful.*

---

*For a discussion of consistency, its relationship to warranted inference, and language with which to point to inconsistencies, review chapter 5.)

AD HOMINEM ATTACK

Ad hominem argument is the formal name for name-calling. Ad hominem literally means "against the man."

> The author was **guilty of an ad hominem argument** when he impugned Ms. Manners's reputation instead of discussing her ideas.
>
> It's a shame that the discussion **sank to the level of ad hominem argumentation.** Dislike of a person's affiliations **is not relevant** to the issue.

An ad hominem attack is the discounting of another person's ideas by *discounting the person* instead of showing why the idea is not good. The name-caller is off the issue.

Varieties of this logical sin can be blatant. For example: "Don't listen to Betty; she's a real dope." The answer should be something like "So what if you think she's a dope? What is her argument?" Other times ad hominem attack can be subtle: "Politicians are busy at this time advocating reduced taxes as a way to improve their image with the public." So what is their argument to reduce taxes?

The salient points should have been *what* Betty's and the politicians' arguments are and *why* these arguments should be discounted or accepted. So what if the counterarguer thinks that Betty is a dope and politicians are image-polishers?

The assumptions beneath the conclusion that name-calling is a pitfall are, as always, that everyone is a member of the community of thinkers and no one should be excluded. Of course, the people we want to exclude are the people whom we dislike. With so many juicy things we can say against our neighbor, it's often easier to backbite than to bother with the argument at hand.

In defense of name-calling, one might argue that life is short, the tasks are many, and name-calling is a kind of a shorthand ("consider the source") which helps us make quick decisions and eliminate silly notions. Even granting that, every time we use this shorthand we've robbed ourselves of the reward of some intellectual discovery, perhaps why a Communist's advocacy of state ownership of the means of production is not a good idea. Although dealing with the unpleasant ideas of unpleasant people involves facing the fear that they may end up convincing us that they're right, we can only act as fair-minded critical thinkers in the hope that they (who doubtless also find us unpleasant) will be similarly moved by *our* alternative arguments and that the best approximation of the truth will out.

APPEAL TO PITY

It is all right to appeal to pity when it is directly related to the issue. Here is an example: "The Lilliputians are in great pain and starving. Please take pity on them and give money to the Fund for the Lilliputian people." Of course, before we dig into our pockets, we might want to check whether the Lilliputians are in fact starving and whether the fund is reputable. Still, the argument that we should help fellow human beings out of pity because they are in pain offers a *relevant* reason, even if it turns out that the whole thing is bogus—Lilliputians, fund, and all.

What is neither ethical nor logical is switching tracks, evoking sympathies for one issue and transferring them to another.* Say, for example, that a professor tells her students to write especially favorable evaluations of her because she's coming up for tenure and really needs the job. While it may be a piteous thing indeed for all concerned if she is fired, the only relevant reasons for good evaluations must lie in the professor's performance as a teacher.

These are, it is hoped, clearcut cases. There are others in which the distinction between legitimate and illegitimate appeal to pity is blurred. Let's consider the current debate on affirmative action ("affirmative action" here defined as the deliberate hiring of qualified women and minorities, these women and minorities not necessarily being the best qualified among all applicants). The first argument is one in favor.

> Since many white males unavoidably perceive women and minorities as less capable than themselves, there must be affirmative action in hiring. As things stand, most white males enjoy positions of greater money and power than most minorities and women. These historically disadvantaged groups will continue to suffer from job discrimination unless a mandatory affirmative action policy is instituted in all businesses. Out of compassion and fellow feeling (on which, after all, justice is founded), we should have affirmative action.

The next argument is one against affirmative action.

> Most people, white males included, now perceive women and minorities as having capabilities equal to those of white males. Granting that white males enjoy many more positions of money and power, the reason is that minorities and women have not until recently striven for these positions. Hard work and demonstrated ability should be the determinants in all hiring decisions, not sympathy for past disadvantages. After all, strict equality of opportunity (on which true justice is founded) is color and sex blind; affirmative action is highly color- and sex-conscious, to the deliberate disadvantage of one group.

---

*The Latin name, *argumentum ad misericordiam,* is rarely used.

What is a compassionate and fair-minded person to do?

In such cases, proceed to the question "What else?" Here there is a basic conflict over whether white males perceive women and minorities as equally capable. And it is on this disagreement that the further disagreement whether an appeal to pity is relevant rests. So what else in the form of evidence is there that might resolve this conflict? Public opinion polls or sociological studies of attitudes towards women and minorities? What else is there in the way of values assumptions beneath each of these arguments? And what are the implications of both positions? These arguments were quite brief. What additional reasons might support each position?

In sum, when you feel the tug of an emotional appeal, *ask whether the emotion is relevant (so what?).* If you can't decide whether the pity is relevant, look at other aspects of the argument and its counterargument (*what else?*).

Language with which to complain about irrelevant pity is:

> The professor's **appeal to pity was irrelevant to the question whether** her performance as an instructor was good.

BEGGING THE QUESTION

You've already encountered this fallacy in Chapter 5. It is asserting reasons which are the same as the conclusion. Remember Woody Allen's "Money is better than poverty, if only for financial reasons" or President Calvin Coolidge's remark, "When large numbers of people are out of work, unemployment results." It's fairly easy to spot the fallacy in these one-liners; it's harder to detect in longer arguments, where the conclusion may be separated from the reasons by a number of other claims. A bit of thought comparing the conclusion and reason will reveal this pitfall, however. The conclusion should not be the reason dressed in another form. Here are a few illustrations of how to point out this fallacy:

> **When the author argued that** we should no longer have grades because standards of evaluation ought not to exist, **he begged the question why** we should no longer have grades.
> **To argue that** we are happy because we are content **is to beg the question why** we are happy.

An answer that is completely off the subject is also called begging the question:

> When they asked him why he committed the murder, he asked them what right they had to know, **thus begging the question** of his motives.

In the case of arguments for which evidence can be obtained, we should take a dim view of people wasting our time with question-begging arguments. One exception which might earn our indulgence, though not necessarily our acceptance of their conclusions, is the case of arguments about God.

Strong evidence demonstrating anything about God is notoriously scarce. Yet in his excellent text on fallacies, author S. Morris Engel asserts that the following is fallacious because circular:

> The world is good because God is good. God is good because the world is good.[1]

Since we have no way to get universally agreed-upon evidence, this argument should not be considered fallacious, since it is a good try under the circumstances. And certainly the arguer didn't beg the question entirely, claiming that the world is good because the world is beneficent, or that God is good because God is kind. Or do you agree with Engel? The word "good" certainly begs for definition.

Or consider this case: Painter Salvador Dali is said to have remarked that DNA proves that God exists. Extrapolating from that statement, consider:

> If DNA exists, God exists. If God exists, some organizing principles of nature such as DNA exist.

POST HOC

The post hoc fallacy means to argue that what follows a thing must be caused by it, based on skimpy evidence. The full Latin phrase for this fallacy "post hoc, ergo propter hoc," literally means, "after this, therefore because of this."

Post hoc is an easy trap to fall into, because our experience is often just that: We observe one thing (a car hitting a post) and figure that what follows has been caused by it (fender dented by post). However, many causal connections we make are far more tenuous, and humanity has learned by bitter experience to be cautious in concluding that whatever follows after something must be caused by it. Someone, for example, noticed that during the past fifty years whenever women's hemlines have risen, the economy has improved. Although it is possible that an upturn in women's hemlines causes an upturn in the economy, it is too precarious to come to that conclusion only because the one event has followed the other. Again, the operative question is *"What else* could be at work here besides causation?" One possibility is that the connection exists only in the observer's mind, and the evidence he reports is too sketchy to support his claim. For instance, how long before the economy improves do the hemlines rise and how much must the economy improve to count as "improved"?

On the other hand, if the observer does a lot of research and, say, finds consistently that three months after hemlines rise the gross national product rises at least 3 percent, the consistency of his observation over time pulls it far out of the realm of post hoc speculation and into the tool we know today as statistical correlation. The person who discovered the post hoc fallacy must be forgiven for having lived a thousand years before the notion of correlating many post hoc observations was born. But pointing to the fundamental weakness of jumping to a too certain conclusion on the basis of scant observation is still invaluable.

Recall that even with a strong correlation, an unknown third factor can cause both variables—here, hemlines and the economy—to change (see Chapters 4 and 11.) For an excellent discussion of how often people mistakenly draw causal inferences from random events, see John Allen Paulos's book, *Innumeracy: Mathematical Illiteracy and its Consequences.*[2]

Here is the way people normally talk about this fallacy:

> **In concluding that** Hal left the party because he was pushed into the pool, Sam **is guilty of the post hoc fallacy.** Indeed, Hal was upset, but the reason he left was to catch a train.
>
> The stockbrokers thought that the caviar they served their clients clinched the sale.
> **This is a case of post hoc ergo propter hoc.** The buyers enjoyed the caviar, but they told us that they bought from the stockbrokers because they wanted to reinvest their money quickly.

APPEAL (ONLY) TO THE MANY

If you argue that I should believe something because many people believe it, you've got my attention. But that reason shouldn't on its own convince me or anyone of your argument, since in the past vast numbers of people have believed in one idea, vast numbers of people in the opposite idea. Therefore the sheer popularity of an idea does not guarantee its rightness. The important question to ask is for what reasons (what else?) these vast hordes have been thus persuaded.

> Arguing that we should buy seamless silk jeans **just because millions have done so is to commit the fallacy of appeal to the many.** A decision to buy seamless silk jeans should not be based on that sole reason.

If an advertiser is smart, he or she will go on to give the reasons why so many people have bought this product, telling us how warm and durable silk is and (if it's true) that we need not suffer the expense of dry cleaning it.

A number of situations on the surface seem to appeal only to the many, but in fact don't. Consider *Consumer Reports* magazine. It is a handy guide if you're thinking of buying some product. You just look up the issue that deals with what you want, say a car, and learn what many owners think about their cars. This might seem like mere appeal to the many. But the distinction here is that the articles always explain why owners of various types of products are satisfied, for example, that they found few defects, or didn't have to make any special repairs. An argument such as "Pontiacs are good cars because many thousands of users have found them to have few defects" is persuasive of that point and not fallacious. However, a decision to buy the car would depend on additional factors of price, gas milage, and appearance.

On the assumption that people are more rational than not, it is interesting to learn why many have come to a conclusion. This does not mean that you should come to the same conclusion. Nor should you discount an idea just because few people believe it.

STRAW MAN—DAMNING WITH FAINT PRAISE

People arguing for a position have been known to cast the opposite position in an unnecessarily feeble light. This portrayal of a counterargument as weaker than it is, is making a straw man argument. People who indulge in this fallacy may be fearful or ignorant of a strong counterargument. Detecting this fallacy depends on having already heard a better counterargument, or knowing information with which to construct one. One man's steel can be the other man's straw. Avoidance of straw man arguments is best achieved by full information and rigorous practice arguing against cherished beliefs (see Chapter 3 on alternative arguments).

> The author **set up a straw man argument by alleging that** the only reason for not smoking is to save money.
> In making a strong counterargument at the end of the animal rights essay, the author hoped to **avoid the straw man fallacy.**

SUMMARY

The following are the deadliest types of abusing arguments, or unwarranted inferences.

1. Inconsistency: arguing at cross-purposes with oneself
2. Ad hominem attack: attacking the person, instead of examining the idea
3. Appeal to pity: calling on sympathies not directly related to the issue
4. Begging the question: making the reason the same as the conclusion; or totally sidestepping the issue
5. Post hoc ergo propter hoc: automatically concluding that what follows a phenomenon must have been caused by that phenomenon
6. Appeal (only) to the many: arguing that some idea is good only because many people think so
7. Straw man: damning the counterargument with scant support

EXERCISES

1. Questions
   a. What connection do fallacies have with the ideas presented in the first chapter?
   b. The press frequently offers "image" as the reason a politician advocates some program. Make a noise like a member of the press and counterargue that the press is not guilty of ad hominem argumentation in most of these cases.
2. Spot that fallacy (if you think there is one) in the following:
   a. Someone argues that an idea should be rejected because its proponent is a longtime Democrat.
   b. Someone argues that you should vote Socialist in the next election because the Socialists have taken quite a beating at the polls in the past.
   c. Student to teacher: "Look, you have to give me an A in this class because I need it to graduate."
   d. A close friend rings up and asks you to come right over because he is feeling very lonely and upset.
   e. Sam and Harry are on a hiring committee. Harry argues that the candidate named George would not make a good personnel manager because he was arrogant and hostile during his employment interview.
   f. One scientist says of another, "Don't trust the data about nerve cells that Ted told you he's just gathered. It is faked. Did you know that he had a psychotic breakdown two years ago and has been in a mental institution ever since?"
   g. A great many people are buying a product. They must just be following the herd.

h. A movie star advertises a brand of cologne.

i. Parents abuse their children because they are acting out urges to do violence to their offspring.

j. An actor who has played a doctor on a popular TV series for many years is now advertising medicine for lumbago.

k. In eighteen out of the past nineteen Superbowl football games, whenever the NFL team has won, the stock market has gone up dramatically the next day. So an NFL win makes the stock market go up.

Answers: (a) Ad hominem attack. You may not see the proponent's being a Democrat as a blot on a person's character—after all, there are many Democrats—but the arguer here seems to think so. In any event, the argument is irrelevant: off the issue of the Democrat's argument. (b) False appeal to pity. (c) False appeal to pity. (d) Okay. (e) Okay. The issue is whether George would make a good personnel manager. Arrogance and hostility in George bear directly on the question. (f) This remark is okay; the issue here is the validity of the scientific data, and if it wasn't arrived at by scientific method, that fact is relevant. If the claim about Ted is deliberately untrue, however, call it ad hominem. (g) None of the seven fallacies here, but an unwarranted inference (falsely impugning the many for being mindless). (h) Okay, as long as the actress is seen as an attention-getter and not an authority. (i) Begging the question. (j) False appeal to authority, or close to it. (k) Post hoc ergo propter hoc, unless there is some other digging: How often does the stock market go up dramatically? How about a poll of a representative sample of stock purchasers "the day after," asking what is motivating them to buy?

3. Speculate on this exceptional case.

a. Because the stakes are so high in criminal proceedings, it is kosher to consider the character of a witness as *major* support in another issue (the guilt or innocence of the defendant). Do you think that this is a good exception to the rule against ad hominem argument? Why or why not?

4. What fallacy is implicit in this discussion?

Earlier in American history, in seventeenth-century New England, trouble with cattle and milk had often been the occasion of serious accusations of witchcraft. In some communities, cows and dairying still had a faint aura of magic about them. So mysteriously did the butter either "come" [after churning] or fail to appear, that there was a sense of unseen forces at work.[3]

NOTES

1. S. Morris Engel, *With Good Reason: An Introduction to Informal Fallacies,* fourth ed. (New York: St. Martin's Press, 1990), p. 163.
2. John Allen Paulos, *Innumeracy: Mathematical Illiteracy and Its Consequences* (New York: Hill and Wang, a division of Farrar, Straus and Giroux, 1988).
3. Jack Larkin, *The Reshaping of Everyday Life: 1790–1840* (New York: Perennial Library, a division of Harper and Row, Publishers, 1989), pp. 28–29. This book is part of The Everyday Life in America Series, edited by Richard Balkin.

13

Problem Solving by Way of Review

Since critical thinking is the consideration of alternative arguments in light of their evidence, problem-solving is the consideration of alternative *solutions* in light of their evidence. The solution is equivalent to the conclusion. This is lucky, because it enables us to enlarge the practicality of the book while reviewing its twelve basic features.

THE PROBLEM IS THE ISSUE

Say you're low on money, but you don't know whether to add more hours to your twelve-hours-per-week part-time job while going to school, fearing that working more might jeopardize your education. The initial problem-issue is, therefore, "Should I add more hours to my part-time job?" You have the *alternatives* yes and no to work out first. Write down the possible solutions, followed by the reasons for and against each.

> *Solution 1:* Yes, add hours to my job
>
> Reason(s) working more is good: It would please my boss, who might give me a better recommendation; it would make me feel more independent; I could maintain contact with more people by working more.
>
> Reason(s) working more is bad: If I worked longer, I might become overtired and drop out of school.

Solution 2: No, don't add hours to my job

Reason(s) not working more is good: I'd keep my time to study; I'd keep my time to enjoy myself; education is more important than money.

Reason(s) not working more is bad: Being low on money is irritating and demoralizing.

ORDER THE REASONS

Pick the most urgent reason on each side and label it 1. A bit of thinking will show some reasons to be less significant. For example, more contact with people could be achieved by other activities less time-consuming than additional work, such as study groups or church groups. In fact, more work might not bring you into contact with more people than it does now. Moreover, getting a recommendation from the boss is presumably not nearly as important as finishing your education. And are you thinking important thoughts, studying, and enjoying yourself in the free time you have, or are you more often just passing time?

It is the reasons against on both sides that are the primary considerations in this case. What does it matter if education is more important than money if you get irritated by being low on money and drop out, anyway? Yet the foremost worry on the other side creates a bind, because you might drop out of school from overwork. You are caught on the horns of a dilemma. But now you have a clearer idea of what your dilemma is, so you can work on it. The next stage is to define the dilemma.

DEFINE THE PARAMETERS

How low on money am I, exactly?

So low that I can't pay for my necessities?

How irritating and demoralizing is it? Irritating enough that I am distracted and thinking about it all the time, or just once or twice a day?

Say that I can pay for the basics but am broke at the end of each month. And say that I am not thinking about it all the time but lately have noticed that I am worrying about it more often (five or six times a day).

BREAK GRIDLOCKS WITH EVIDENCE

Sometimes finding out how most people fare in similar situations can cast a surprising light. Consider this claim by Professor Alexander Astin, from UCLA, based on his educational research:

One of the most interesting ways to keep students in college now is through jobs. Students who have part-time jobs while enrolled in college have a better chance of finishing than comparable students who have no jobs. This effect is particularly strong if the student lives on campus. Here we have a case where the facts clearly contradict the folklore: Having to work while attending college does not hamper the student's academic progress but rather enhances it. We should add a note of caution here, however. The beneficial effects of work diminish as the number of hours of work exceeds twenty, and if the student has a full-time job the effect is actually reversed: Students who have to work full-time have a decreased chance of finishing college in contrast to students who have no jobs. In short, it would appear that jobs represent a highly effective way of combatting attrition, *provided* that the number of hours worked is limited to twenty per week.

Students who work up to twenty hours per week tend to get better grades than students who don't work.[1]

Amazing—perhaps in setting up the problem as more work versus a better education, I have created a **false dichotomy.** It looks as though people are managing both. But a bit of caution is in order when considering the **nature of the evidence.** The authority is impeccable, but he had to make a correlational study. Persevering students and part-time jobs are strongly correlated, but ask yourself whether some other factor could be causing both of these results, for instance, love of work. Furthermore, might these working students be the kind of people who, even if they didn't work, would stay in school and get better grades to boot?

Consider this counterargument. On the other hand, what would be lost by trying it for a while? You could always bail out of the additional work if it got to be too much. So:

Solution 3: On the premise that up to twenty hours of work doesn't seem to hurt the average student, one prescription would be to go ahead and add hours up to a total of twenty, if possible getting my boss to agree to let me go back to twelve hours if twenty prove too arduous.

SEEK ALTERNATIVES

So far there are three possible solution-conclusions. But we're just warming up. Brainstorming for a while might produce even better ideas to generate money. For instance:

1. Belt-tightening, budgeting. I am wasting some money now, for example, buying lunch and snacks instead of making them, and buying goods at full price instead of sale price. I compute that savings in these areas alone could add up to $100 per month.

Solution 4: Make a realistic but lean budget and stay within it.

2. Borrowing. Is there some understanding friend or relative who would stand me to a loan, or even better, a scholarship were I to attain a certain grade point average?
3. Selling something I own. Do I own some things I don't particularly want? I should seriously consider whether I might want these valuables in the future! I'll hold off on heirlooms.
4. Getting a job with better pay. What else is there that I could do for more money per hour?* Thus I might either work twelve hours and get more money than at present, or work twenty hours and make a bundle.

Solution 5: Check the want ads and all possible sources for jobs, applying for any likely sounding position.

There are many other places along the list where you could have written in a solution, but chose not to, because that solution—selling your motorcycle, for instance—didn't appeal immediately. Yet you now know that you can return to your list later, choose other options, or generate more.

THE GRAND SOLUTION

Make a list of the possible solutions:

> Same hours at same job
> More hours at same job
> Add hours to total twenty
> Budget
> Check ads and apply for higher-paying jobs

Some of these solutions are mutually exclusive, others compatible. The first two are impossible to act on at the same time, but budgeting can occur with any of the others. It's such a good idea that you might pick it for sure. At this point a good critical question is "Would budgeting be enough?" For the sake of elaborating on the example, say no. You can also check the want ads, and since no harm and a lot of good can come of it, you could pick that solution too.

Now, if there are some possible jobs, you'll need to pursue them.

---

*Notice the **assumptions** that better jobs do in fact exist, that I am worthy of them and could get one, that some of the ones I could get would be no more tiring than the one I now have.

Proceeding from the premise that you're already in school and working twelve hours per week, keeping the fewer hours for the time being will enable you to hunt for a better job. For the moment, therefore, you've eliminated the option of working longer at your present job. And **accepting** Astin's **inference** that working up to twenty hours per week is normally not academically harmful, you will look for jobs with a wider range of hours without worry that it will damage your education.

If you get a better offer you can take it outright; or if you would rather work for your present boss you can use your better offer as a bargaining chip to see if she might raise your hourly salary to match what you've been offered.

If, after four weeks (longer?), you can't get a different job, you can try the longer hours at the same job. If the longer hours turn out to be burdensome, you can go back to twelve per week, perhaps job-hunting again. If that doesn't turn anything up, you can go back to your problem-solving list to seek other solutions.

As this problem turned out, here are all the presently conceived solutions for use in case of need:

> budget plus twelve hours at present job plus job hunt for one month to result in:
> new higher-paying job or old job with higher pay. If not, then:
> old job with more hours plus budget. If unsatisfactory after one month, old job with twelve hours plus job hunt plus budget.

You'll see that with other problems, some solutions that make it to the grand finals are then eliminated.

There is nothing more comforting than contingency planning.

KEEP AN OPEN MIND

Most important decisions are fraught with uncertainty. The **inference** that longer work hours don't hurt an education may be **unwarranted.** But on the **assumption** that money worries will continue, it is reasonable to try working more, based on Astin's **evidence.** The **implications** are uncertain too, but ideally they would include being happier, easier to live with, and more productive. On the other hand, maybe this is not the best solution, after all. The point is to keep an open mind, considering other options and possibilities as they occur.

Working systematically on solutions to major life problems requires a lot of thought and nerve. To fully explore a problem, write, revise, and think at some length. Doing so turns anxiety into an interesting challenge. Further, as with the dialogue and any creative thought, you shouldn't know where your ideas will take you; otherwise, there is no problem.

I hope to have kept faith with the promise in the preface that everything in the book would be practical and that you are more skillfully negotiating your way through the twists and turns of argumentation. More, I hope that you are very curious to know what is engaging the community of thinkers and that you revel in finding out.

NOTE

1. Alexander W. Astin, "Strengthening Transfer Programs," in *Issues for Community College Leaders in a New Era,* George B. Vaughan and Associates, eds. (San Francisco: Jossey-Bass Publishers, 1983), p. 125.

14

The Dialogue

How to Construct Alternative Arguments

BECOME TWO ARGUERS

Another excellent way to generate critical thinking, the consideration of alternative arguments in light of their evidence, is to write a dialogue. Chances are slim that outside of this class you will be required to write a dialogue. Yet dialogue-writing is a great tool for preparing a term paper and invaluable in making a personal decision, such as a career choice.

With the twelve tools already at your disposal, you can construct some rather sophisticated arguments. Now try a kind of dual argument that, because of its greater density, reveals more about an issue than most arguments.

Think of a dialogue as consisting of two parties who disagree.* Both parties will come to life and flesh out their positions in your head. Call your characters A and B, or give them names if you want—but be careful not to get involved in dramatic details.

No writer knows how his or her dialogue will end. This is doubly the case in a well-constructed dialogue. Even as the author, you don't know how either side will progress—one side may convince the other, or a whole new approach to the issue may emerge. For the dialogue to

---

*Dialogues can involve more parties who needn't disagree, but starting this way will help you to avoid pitfalls.

work, you must argue equally strenuously for each side. Don't stack the deck on one side. This point cannot be stressed enough. Don't turn the dialogue into an interview, with one side feeding the other questions which the latter merely gives an opinion about. If that happens, the argument won't deepen and will, of course, be lopsided. Eventually A and B may have to agree to disagree on a point, but only after considerable skirmishing. What you're after is some sort of breakthrough into the deeper layers of the issue.

Think of the dialogue as a thin, tough, and tight construction. You will have several ideas on each side to throw into the ring. But hold back. Feed the ideas in one at a time and have both sides engage exhaustively over one idea before proceeding. Remember, you have no idea where the logic will take you—you have some ideas you think will tie in, but don't force them into the dialogue strand. Their time should arrive in the logical course of the dialogue. To feed ideas in one at a time, restrict yourself to one or two or, at most, three brief sentences per speaker.

Once A has stated a claim, B must directly counter that claim and support the counterclaim. Then A must come right back at what B has just said. Don't break the thread. Chances are you will be able to toss off three or four opening lines. Then, if you're really keeping the thought on target, you will get stumped for a time, and that is good. You'll wonder how on earth you're going to come back against that last brilliant point. Take a break and put the problem in the back of your mind for a while. Do something else and see what comes. Sometimes sleeping on it overnight will produce a mental breakthrough.

Finally, as you work, keep rereading your dialogue from the beginning to ensure that you are staying on a consistent track. Don't get confused and switch your characters' positions!

Here is a summary of the rules:

1. A and B must *disagree*. Don't have one interview the other.
2. Keep each speaker's remarks *brief*.
3. Make each speaker *directly address* the point made by the last.
4. Don't lose your nerve. Adhere strictly to the first three rules; take frequent *breaks* when you get stuck.
5. Constantly *reread* the dialogue as you add to it.

A DIALOGUE

A. Boxing causes brain damage. It should be outlawed.

B. Nonsense! What evidence do you have that boxing causes brain damage?

A. Autopsies of professional boxers have revealed brain scarring. The condition is called "dementia pugilistica," otherwise known as punch-drunkenness, the symptoms of which are permanently slurred speech and slowness of thought.

B. I don't believe that you can measure "slowness of thought."

A. Why couldn't someone have given boxers problems of similar difficulty over a number of years and measured the time it took them to answer?

B. Perhaps the brain scarring does not cause the slurred speech and slow thought.

A. I assume that medical researchers did controlled studies, autopsying any number of nonboxers. Besides, if slurred speech and slowness of thought appear in virtually all professional boxers, and we already know that blows to the head cause brain damage, the inference that boxing causes brain damage seems warranted.

B. Let them wear helmets.

A. Helmets don't prevent this brain damage. Boxing could outlaw the hitting of a person's head.

B. That would ruin the sport!

A. That's what I assumed you and other boxing aficionados would say.

B. Well, even granting that boxing causes brain damage in some people, that's no reason to outlaw it.

A. How can you say that? You admitted that some people are damaging themselves!

B. People damage themselves all the time by doing things that we don't outlaw: They play football, they drink, they ride motorcycles—

A. Wait a minute—let's take those examples one at a time. First, football injuries are rarely brain injuries.

B. What's so sacred about a brain injury that makes it different from the lifelong paralysis suffered by a former football player?

A. It is the rare football player who suffers such a severe injury. It is the frequent boxer who suffers irreparable brain damage.

B. Look, there is frequent and irreparable damage to some part of the body involved in every sport: "Tennis elbow" is common among those professionals, chronic knee and foot injuries among runners. Do you suggest we also outlaw these sports because they injure people?

A. No! Brain damage is far worse than any other type of bodily damage, including paralysis.

B. You are overstating your case. The damage to a person's bodily movement in paralysis is severe; brain damage to boxers is comparatively minor.

A. How can you call slowness of thought and slurred speech minor injuries?

B. Well, it depends on what the boxer wants to do with the rest of his life. If he isn't in the business of writing dialogues or giving public speeches, he could live a very nice life with the millions he's made from the sport.

A. Look, how many boxers make millions? And even the, say, one in ten thousand boxers who does make a lot of money is going to need all his wits to decide how to invest and spend his money.

B. Oh, he can always hire someone to help him with that.

A. You seem to be assuming, B, that a boxer's mind is not a terrible thing to waste.

B. Not if the boxer doesn't care. A, you are just trying to impose your values on other people.

A. Of course; what are laws if not "values imposed on people"? Our criminal law imposes the value that people may not deliberately kill or injure one another, and boxing is a perfect instance of people injuring one another.

B. How is it different from wrestlers or football players injuring one another?

A. Boxing is the only sport that has as its object to damage the opponent's neurological system.

B. Oh, come on. Do you think that's what goes through a boxer's mind in the ring?

A. Those aren't his exact thoughts, of course. But to try to hit the opponent's head as many times as possible and ideally knock him out is to have as one's object the damage of the opponent's neurological system, even if a boxer doesn't realize that his acts will have a damaging effect.

B. But still—that damage isn't different from the neurological damage suffered in other sports.

A. B, you are stubborn. The plain fact of the matter is that far more neurological damage occurs from boxing, since that is the very purpose of the sport!

B. You're no slouch for stubbornness yourself. But another fact of the matter is that more deaths have occurred from football or hang gliding or horse racing than from the sport of boxing. Do you want to outlaw all of these sports because they violate your aforementioned value of our criminal law that "people may not deliberately kill . . . one another"?

A. Hm. But wait—you're not making an important distinction. If the intent of a sport were the death of opponents, were gladiator combats, then that sport should definitely be outlawed. But the intent in football is to put a piece of pigskin over a goalpost; that's not deliberate intent to kill.

B. You're not fair! The poor boxer is just out there trying to win, not trying to injure or to kill, and you want to outlaw his actions. But even though more deaths result from football you say you don't care as long as the football player is out there just trying to win. That's certainly inconsistent and unfair.

A. But don't you see? Boxing is set up with its central purpose that of injury. In football, injury and death are only occasional side effects of the central purpose of the game.

B. I don't see what "purpose" has to do with it. Results are results, and the number of deaths remains greater from football.

A. Purpose is central to the issue: In boxing, everyone is bound to suffer neurological damage; in football only a very few people die.

B. Are you then assuming that the death of a few people is less significant than the slight (okay, moderate) brain damage of many?

A. I am assuming that any sport or activity in which brain damage is a certainty should be outlawed.

B. Then welcome to the prohibitionist cause! It's well known that alcohol kills brain cells, and every drinker suffers "neurological damage," your criterion for outlawing an activity.

A. You are failing to distinguish between the slight damage of the death of brain cells and the moderate to severe neurological damage resulting from boxing. The two are quite different in degree.

B. Well, this is where I need some information. If a person drinks a bottle of gin every day for twenty years, how serious is his neurological damage compared with that of a professional boxer?

A. In that case, I assume, the neurological damage would be severe. But the alcoholic is damaging himself; a boxer damages someone else.

B. That's a false distinction! Obviously both boxers in the ring are consenting to be hit, even though they hope they won't be damaged, just as the heavy drinker consents to drink, hoping, however irrationally, that damage won't result.

A. Your terms "consent" and "irrational" are intriguing. What if there were a law requiring placement of a "warning label" in a conspicuous place on all boxing equipment, describing the neurological damage that results from boxing?

B. I don't know how much boxing it would prevent, but a cigarette-type warning seems more just than prohibiting the sport altogether. Besides, outlawing boxing would create terrible enforcement problems.

A. Yes. I agree that the warning seems more equitable, since it respects freedom of choice. You've shown me that there are other activities people regularly engage in that harm them but are legal. Still, I think boxing should be illegal for anyone under twenty-one.

B. (groan) Here we go again.

Notice that the dialogue has moved forward and that both sides have come to a deeper understanding. But problems remain, one of which is raised at the very end.

THE DIALOGUE DISSECTED

Here is the same dialogue with the various moves explained. (Obviously, your moves are going to come in a different order when you write your dialogue.) Don't be misled; the moves were written the day after the dialogue was finished. You should likewise construct your dialogue and *then* analyze its moves.

A. Boxing cause brain damage. It should be outlawed.	*Brief strict argument*
B. Nonsense! What evidence do you have that boxing causes brain damage?	*Truth of reason questioned*

A. Autopsies of professional boxers have revealed brain scarring. The condition is called "dementia pugilistica," otherwise known as punch-drunkenness, the symptoms of which are permanently slurred speech and slowness of thought.

Evidence outlined

B. I don't believe that you can measure "slowness of thought."

Evidence questioned

A. Why couldn't someone have given boxers problems of similar difficulty over a number of years and measured the time it took them to answer?

B. Perhaps the brain scarring does not cause the slurred speech and slow thought.

Debate over the likelihood that the evidence supports the claim of "brain damage"

A. I assume that medical researchers did controlled studies, autopsying any number of nonboxers. Besides, if slurred speech and slowness of thought appear in virtually all professional boxers, and we already know that blows to the head cause brain damage, the inference that boxing causes brain damage seems warranted.

B. Let them wear helmets.

Solution proscribed

A. Helmets don't prevent this brain damage. Boxing could outlaw the hitting of a person's head.

Factual claim that this isn't a solution; solution prescribed

B. That would ruin the sport!

Implication

A. That's what I assumed you and other boxing aficionados would say.

B. Well, even granting that boxing causes brain damage in some people, that's no reason to outlaw it.

Rejects A's original inference

A. How can you say that? You've admitted that some people are damaging themselves!

B. People damage themselves all the time by doing things that we don't outlaw: They play football, they drink, they ride motorcycles—

Counterexamples

A. Wait a minute—let's take those examples one at a time. First, football injuries are rarely brain injuries.

Counterargues to the main topic: brain injury

B. What's so sacred about a brain injury that makes it different from the lifelong paralysis suffered by a former football player?

Requests distinction

A. It is the rare football player who suffers such a severe injury. It is the frequent boxer who suffers irreparable brain damage.

Distinction between rarity and frequency

B. Look, there is frequent and irreparable damage to some part of the body involved in every sport: "Tennis elbow" is common among those professionals, chronic knee and foot injuries among runners. Do you suggest we also outlaw these sports because they injure people?

Counterexamples of frequent and irreparable damage from other sports

A. No! Brain damage is far worse than any other type of bodily damage, including paralysis.

Brain damage distinguished as worse

B. You are overstating your case. The damage to a person's bodily movement in paralysis is severe; brain damage to boxers is comparatively minor.

Claim that the damage is not in fact worse

A. How can you call slowness of thought and slurred speech minor injuries?

Reminder of definition of brain damage

B. Well, it depends on what the boxer wants to do with the rest of his life. If he isn't in the business of writing dialogues or giving public speeches, he could live a very nice life with the millions he's made from the sport.

Claim that seriousness of effect depends on a person's lifestyle

A. Look, how many boxers make millions? And even the, say, one in ten thousand boxers who does make a lot of money is going to need all his wits to decide how to invest and spend his money.

Argues that money is not a sufficient cause of economic security

B. Oh, he can always hire someone to help him with that.

Factual claim

A. You seem to be assuming, B, that a boxer's mind is not a terrible thing to waste.

Value assumption of B

B. Not if the boxer doesn't care. A, you are just trying to impose your values on other people.

Factual assumption about A

A. Of course; what are laws if not "values imposed on people"? Our criminal law imposes the value that people may not deliberately kill or injure one another, and boxing is a perfect instance of people injuring one another.

A agrees and justifies assumption by argument

B. How is it different from wrestlers or

Requests distinction

football players injuring one another?

A. Boxing is the only sport that has as its object to damage the opponent's neurological system.

Distinction

B. Oh, come on. Do you think that's what goes through a boxer's mind in the ring?

Distinction questioned

A. Those aren't his exact thoughts, of course. But to try to hit the opponent's head as many times as possible and ideally knock him out is to have as one's object the damage of the opponent's neurological system, even if a boxer doesn't realize that his acts will have a damaging effect.

Distinction made between sport's purpose and athlete's intent

B. But still—that damage isn't different from the neurological damage suffered in other sports.

Denies distinction

A. B, you are stubborn. The plain fact of the matter is that far more neurological damage occurs from boxing, since that is the very purpose of the sport!

Factual claim

B. You're no slouch for stubbornness yourself. But another fact of the matter is that more deaths have occurred from football or hang gliding or horse racing than from the sport of boxing. Do you want to outlaw all of these sports because they violate your aforementioned value of our criminal law that "people may not deliberately kill . . . one another"?

Factual claim to refute claim that boxing is the most harmful sport

A. Hm. But wait—you're not making an important distinction. If the intent of a sport were the death of opponents, were gladiator combats, then that sport should definitely be outlawed. But the intent in football is to put a piece of pigskin over a goalpost; that's not deliberate intent to kill.

Intent in football distinguished from intent to kill

B. You're not fair! The poor boxer is just out there trying to win, not trying to injure or to kill, and you want to outlaw his actions. But even though more deaths result from football you say you don't care as long as the football player is out there just trying to win. That's certainly inconsistent and unfair.

Inconsistency

A. But don't you see? Boxing is set up with its central purpose that of injury. In football, injury and death are only occasional side effects of the central purpose of the game.

Purpose and side effects distinguished

B. I don't see what "purpose" has to do with it. Results are results, and the number of deaths remains greater from football.

Claim that results are more important than purpose

A. Purpose is central to the issue: In boxing, everyone is bound to suffer neurological damage; in football only a very few people die.

Distinction: many versus few

B. Are you then assuming that the death of a few people is less significant than the slight (okay, moderate) brain damage of many?

Questions A's assumption

A. I am assuming that any sport or activity in which brain damage is a certainty should be outlawed.

A defines his assumption

B. Then welcome to the prohibitionist cause! It's well known that alcohol kills brain cells, and every drinker suffers "neurological damage," your criterion for outlawing an activity.

Claims implication of A's statement is that alcohol should be illegal.

A. You are failing to distinguish between the slight damage of the death of brain cells and the moderate to severe neurological damage resulting from boxing. The two are quite different in degree.

Distinction between damage to brain from alcohol consumption vs. boxing

B. Well, this is where I need some information. If a person drinks a bottle of gin every day for twenty years, how serious is his neurological damage compared with that of a professional boxer?

Request for fact; meant to eliminate distinction

A. In that case, I assume, the neurological damage would be severe. But the alcoholic is damaging himself; a boxer damages someone else.

Distinction

B. That's a false distinction! Obviously both boxers in the ring are consenting to be hit, even though they hope they won't be damaged, just as the heavy drinker consents to drink, hoping, however irrationally, that damage won't result.

False dichotomy

A. Your terms "consent" and "irrational" just gave me an idea. What if there were a law requiring placement of a

Solution prescribed

"warning label" in a conspicuous place on all boxing equipment, describing the neurological damage that results from boxing?

B. I don't know how much boxing it would prevent, but a cigarette-type warning seems more just than prohibiting the sport altogether. Besides, outlawing boxing would create terrible enforcement problems.

Claims implications are uncertain, but agrees; implications for law enforcement

A. Yes. I agree that the warning seems more equitable, since it respects freedom of choice. You've shown me that there are other activities people regularly engage in that harm them but are legal. Still, I think boxing, like alcohol consumption, should be illegal for anyone under twenty-one.

Assumption exposed; consistency as reason to keep boxing legal

Prescription

B. (groan) Here we go again.

Try It

There are many points in the foregoing dialogue at which you may have thought, "A [or B] gave in too easily there; I would have said. . . ." Pick up the thread at that point and continue the dialogue in your own way.

SUMMARY

The dialogue is a tightly constructed argument/counterargument that is invaluable in plumbing any issue deeply.

The writer must make each side argue one point as strenuously as possible, exhausting that point before proceeding to the next.

The dialogue ends when the writer has thoroughly explored the major features of both arguments. The dialogue characters may end by coming to agreement, or they may still disagree—whatever the writer finds closer to the truth of the matter.

EXERCISES

Any of the topics covered so far in the book are, of course, grist for the dialogue mill. Here are some others. Use these to create your dialogues.

1. A. I want to get into the occupation where I will make the most money. In a choice between money and on-the-job contentment, I'll take the money.

   B. You should follow a career path that brings you the most happiness on the job. Obviously, making a decent salary will contribute to your happiness on the job, but it's better to take job satisfaction over money any day.

2. A. As a prerequisite for graduation, students should have to take basic education courses in all major subject areas. Otherwise, colleges are failing in their duty to students.

   B. I disagree. Forcing students to take certain courses destroys their natural incentive to learn.

3. A. Pornography is violence against women.

   B. That sounds ridiculous. "Violence" is defined as "physical force exerted for the purpose of violating, damaging, or abusing."[1] You may dislike pornography, but it certainly should be carefully distinguished from violence.

   A. I'm using "violence" in another of its definitions: "the abusive or unjust exercise of power; an outrage; a wrong."[2]

READINGS

Here are excerpts from two opposing points of view regarding population.

1. The first, "The Paradox of Population Growth," by demographer Robert W. Fox, emphasizes an explosive growth rate.

For most of mankind's history world population grew slowly, checked by epidemics, famine, and chronic malnutrition. Though the mortality rate was high, the birthrate was slightly higher, and with that small excess our numbers gradually increased.

Human population grows much like a savings account accruing compound interest—greater amounts yield greater amounts. English economist Thomas Malthus cited this fact in his 1798 "Essay on the Principle of Population," warning that human numbers—if unchecked—would soon outweigh the ability of the earth to feed them.

But Malthus was writing on the eve of a new era, when the industrial revolution would transform Europe. The continent's population did rise substantially during the 19th century as medical breakthroughs lowered the death rate, but simultaneous agricultural advances also allowed food production to rise. And emigration to America helped siphon off population excess.

The newly widened gap between birth and death rates gradually began to close as smaller families became socially acceptable. That trend quickened in industrialized countries during the 20th century, and today the gap between births and deaths is once again small.

In the developing countries a far different history prevails. Only in the 1930s did the death rate begin to fall, but it fell dramatically as imported technology improved overall health and dietary conditions. The birthrate, however, remained high. Its decline depends largely on changing cultural norms, and family planning has made substantial inroads only within the past two decades. As the gap between deaths and births widened, the population exploded. Generally speaking, there were not more births—there were more survivors.

With this considerable momentum, population expansion in these countries will continue. Even optimistic scenarios do not foresee a leveling off of growth until late in the 21st century.

Because the traditional birth-and-death-rate relationship has been broken in Third World countries only within the past few decades, they now hold very youthful populations, and the populations will continue to soar because there are more women of childbearing age. Hence the paradox of modern population growth: Even as the birthrate continues to fall, the population will rise.

For every 100 Africans today, 55 are under 20 years of age. Among Europeans, only 30 out of 100 are under 20. In 1975, 93 out of 100 African women were of childbearing age. The birthrate that year in Africa was 47 per 1,000, and 19 million children were born. The UN projects that by 2025 the African birthrate will fall to 25 per 1,000—a reduction of almost half. But by then the number of reproductive-age women will have risen to 430 million, and even with a lowered birthrate 42 million children will enter the world that year.

Rural Exodus Deepens the Crisis [In the Third World] the rural birthrate is consistently higher than the urban birthrate. As children grow and seek work, often their only choice is migration to a city. Most arable farmland is already under cultivation, and millions of small landholdings around the world can no longer be subdivided among large families. Often workers have no clear title to land, and primitive farming methods limit crop yield—and profit. . . .

The struggle to find work is all consuming in Third World cities, where combined unemployment and underemployment rates of 30 to 50 percent are common. Relatively few people find work in industry; the majority fill the service sector, where jobs range from clerical work, to hand-delivering messages across town in phone-poor cities, to washing windows of cars stopped in traffic. . . .

The World's Urban Explosion The upsurge in Third World urban populations has overwhelmed resources. Sprawling slums, massive traffic jams, chronic unemployment, regular failure of electric and water services, strained educational and recreational facilities, and sky-rocketing food and fuel costs are the stuff of daily existence.[3]

2. *This excerpt from the book* Food First, *by Frances Moore Lappé and Joseph Collins, disavows the strong language of "explosion" and "crush," offering a somewhat different set of facts. How does the implied solution differ?*

Are People a Liability or a Resource?

Terms like "tidal wave" and "inundation" can readily lead us to believe we are witnessing a natural and inevitable process [of unemployment-related hunger in the Third World]. Dramatic metaphors can jolt us by the very power of their imagery, but they can also lead us away from real understanding.

This question [whether people are a liability] reflects several wide-ly held beliefs that we have found to be myths.

MYTH ONE: *Agriculture in underdeveloped countries is held back because there are just too many people in the countryside to be produc-tively put to work.*

If too many workers per acre really stood in the way of production, wouldn't countries that have a *more* productive agriculture have *fewer* workers per acre than their less successful neighbors? Yet, what do we find? Japan and Taiwan, both thought of as agriculturally successful, have more than twice as many agricultural workers per acre than the Philippines and India. The value of production per acre in Japan is seven times that of the Philippines and ten times that of India. The overall trend, in fact, seems to show a *positive* relationship between the number of workers on a unit of land and the level of agricultural output. This may be hard for Americans to accept because we are taught to mea-sure productivity in terms of how few people it takes to grow food. Such a measure makes no sense at all in underdeveloped countries with vast, untapped human labor resources. . . .

MYTH TWO: *Since agriculture cannot absorb any more people, the overflow from rural areas must go to the cities where new jobs in indus-try must be created for them.*

It was exactly this analysis of the problem that prompted both the neglect of agriculture and the promotion of industrialization by develop-ment planners during the 1950s and 1960s. The result? A lot of capital investment but remarkably few new industrial jobs. . . .

Foreign corporations with their labor-saving technologies . . . have aggravated the chronic "job crisis." Two hundred fifty-seven multina-tional corporations studied in Latin America employ less than one-half the number of people per unit of sales as do local companies. . . . A new modern factory employing a couple hundred persons might well put thousands of local craftsmen out of business. . . .

Efforts to solve the unemployment problem by creating jobs in centralized, urban areas are misplaced in any case. In underdeveloped countries agriculture and small-scale decentralized workshops serving the needs of local agriculture have the greater potential to absorb workers. China has been able to reduce the percentage of its workforce in full-time agricultural jobs. . . . This was accomplished not by creating urban industries but by developing small factories and workshops throughout the countryside to make farm implements and basic consumer goods. China's large rural, but nonagricultural, population also represents a sizable reserve labor force for agriculture [to help out at harvest]. . . .

Too Many People?   Measured globally, there is enough food for everyone now. The world is producing each day two pounds of grain—more than 3,000 calories and ample protein—for every man, woman and child on earth. A third of this grain now goes to feed livestock. . . . Thus, on a global scale, the idea that there is not enough food to go around simply does not hold up.

But global figures mean little, except to dispel the widespread notion that we have reached the earth's limits. What counts is whether adequate food-producing resources exist in countries where so many people go hungry. The resources do exist, we have found, but they are invariably underused or misused. . . .

According to United Nations Food and Agricultural Organization, less than 60 percent of the world's cultivable land is now being cropped. In both Africa and South America less than 20 percent of the potentially arable land is cultivated. . . .

Barriers to unleashing this productive capacity are, in most cases, not physical; rather, they are economic: Wherever there is unjust, undemocratic control over productive resources, their development is thwarted.

In most countries where people are hungry, large landholders control most of the land. A study of 83 countries showed that slightly more than 3 percent of all landowners, those with 114 acres or more, control a staggering 79 percent of all farmland. But these large landholders are the least productive. Studies in seemingly diverse countries reveal that large landholders consistently harvest lower yields per acre than the smallest farmers. . . . Furthermore, many who hold large amounts of land for prestige or as an investment, not as a source of food, leave considerable acreage unplanted. . . .

In addition, low productivity results from economic and social injustices that obstruct agricultural improvements by small, poor farmers. . . . Moneylenders commonly charge the poor 50–200 percent interest. With no individual or shared ownership of the land, how can tenants, sharecroppers, and landless laborers either be motivated or have the wherewithal to conserve and improve the land for better crops? They realize any improvement will overwhelmingly go to advance the landowners, not themselves.[4]

Use the material in the two excerpts you have just read to continue the following dialogue.
A. *The world is overpopulated.*
B. *It's overpopulated by insects, perhaps, but certainly not by people.*
A. *How can you say that when world population, which reached one billion in the early nineteenth century, went to two billion in 1930, and by the end of this century will top six billion?*
B. *You act as though the rate of growth will continue to increase. The birthrate has fallen, and the total number of people on this planet will peak and remain at the same level by the end of the next century.*

NOTES

1. *The American Heritage Dictionary* (Boston: Houghton Mifflin Company, 1992), s.v. "violence."
2. *Ibid.*
3. Robert W. Fox, "The World's Urban Explosion," *National Geographic Magazine,* 166, no. 2 (August 1984), pp. 179–84.
4. Frances Moore Lappé and Joseph Collins, *Food First: Beyond the Myth of Scarcity* (New York: Ballantine Books, a division of Random House, Inc., 1991), pp. 13–17, 24–27.

15

The Research Paper

A Simple Guide

Writing is easy. All you do is stare at a blank sheet of paper until drops of blood appear on your forehead.

Gene Fowler (1890–1960)

Most people hate to write, with any number of arguments having been launched as to why this is so. My favorite hypothesis is that the trouble lies in the difference between the way we naturally think while *developing* ideas and the way we like to *receive* ideas. Consider everyday speech. In a conversation we are often rather sloppy, repeating ourselves and wandering around a topic, getting at what we mean eventually or perhaps dropping that subject and picking up another as it occurs to us. A perfect metaphor out of India, "the monkey of the mind," captures this play in which we swing from one topical branch to another in the process of talking.

Unlike a conversation, however, we expect a piece of writing to be a *product,* not a process. The ideal today is to be brief and to the point. While no one would think of criticizing a conversation because its participants had dropped one subject and launched into another, that would be reason for criticism of a piece of writing—that is, we in late twentieth-century industrialized countries don't like it. Now, why did I have to add that qualification? The reasons are that for most of human history people had a great deal of time, and there was less to learn.

STANDARDS OF GOOD WRITING DEPEND
ON THE READER'S NEEDS

We wake daily to an avalanche of facts and claims. If we are to absorb a fraction of what is available, it must come to us rather bluntly compared to the past, when an educated elite needed to fill endless days of leisure and hence disgression was met with pleasure rather than impatience. Consider this passage from the classic work of a hundred and fifty years age, *Democracy in America,* by Alexis de Tocqueville:

> When the ranks of society are unequal, and men unlike each other in condition, there are some individuals invested with all the power of superior intelligence, learning, and enlightenment, while the multitude is sunk in ignorance and prejudice. Men living at these aristocratic periods are therefore naturally induced to shape their opinions by the superior standard of a person or a class of persons, while they are averse to recognize the infallibility of the mass of the people.
>
> The contrary takes place in ages of equality. The nearer the citizens are drawn to the common level of an equal and similar condition, the less prone does each man become to place implicit faith in a certain man or a certain class of men. But his readiness to believe the multitude increases, and opinion is more than ever mistress of the world. Not only is common opinion the only guide which private judgment retains among a democratic people, but among such a people it possesses a power infinitely beyond what it has elsewhere. At periods of equality men have no faith in one another, by reason of their common resemblance; but this very resemblance gives them almost unbounded confidence in the judgment of the public; for it would not seem probable, as they are all endowed with equal means of judging, but that the greater truth should go with the greater number.[1]

A quick way of saying this is that in places where a nobility such as kings or queens inherits control of a society, everyone looks to these aristocrats as the source of wisdom and takes no stock in majority opinion. On the other hand, in democracies everyone is considered equal, so each person takes the opinion of the majority as the sole yardstick of truth.

This rendition does away with a number of marvelous phrases, but it uses twentieth century standards of prose to make the profound observation that Tocqueville wrote in 1835—consider how frequently we rely on public opinion polls today!

There is nothing inherently wrong with the way Tocqueville wrote. If one has all the time in the world to come to a point, why get there so quickly? I like to imagine a fifteenth century newscast in which a story about a robbery might last hours instead of one minute, with many digressions about the town where the crime occurred, the clothes people wore, and other details which we would find maddeningly irrelevant, except perhaps in a novel. But enough digressing. In the following outline you will find a summary of steps in structuring a research paper, a letter to the editor, or any piece of writing in which you want to make a clear, convincing case.

If you know in advance exactly what you will say you have my condolences, because much of the interest of writing comes from discovering all the new ideas which will pop into your head if you let them. In any case, the steps in the following outline assume that you have little to no idea of what to write about, or how to put it down.

Steps in Constructing a Research Paper

1. **Prepare: Pick, browse, ask, devour, digest**
   (a) Pick a general subject area.
   (b) Browse with an eye for interesting angles and burning questions.
   (c) Ask your librarian where to find more sources for the angle or two you've found.
   (d) Be greedy! Try to get twenty sources.
   (e) Digest them, and figure out what you think.
   (f) Note any quotes and data which support or contradict your view.

2. **Write: Make the best argument you can**
   (a) Fiddle around (see Rule of Paragraph Three, below).
   (b) Make your conclusion your title.
   (c) Show how your theory or argument is better than one or more alternatives—
      • better evidence?
      • better guiding principle(s)?
   (d) But make the alternatives as strong as you can.
   (e) Quoting others gives them and YOU glory!

MORE ON PREPARATION

A Contrary Way of Getting Going

The thought of researching and writing a long, complicated paper has paralyzed many a fine critical thinker, and if you think too hard about everything that goes into it you may feel overwhelmed. This is one case in which looking at the big picture may be a mistake, inspiring too much fear. The way I approach an elephantine project is by nibbles. The day it is assigned I tell myself that I'll just fool around with it for a while, promising myself that if I'm bored after fifteen minutes, then I will quite for that day. Usually I crawl away hours later, far longer than I ever imagined I could tolerate. It is making a deal with myself to nibble on it only as long as I am enjoyably engrossed that does the trick, and I make myself the same promise every day until the project is finished. Of course, you or your instructor may have much better methods to get started—and finished!

Browse for Angles

Some students flail for quite a while before finding an area that interests them. In my view this is not as unfortunate as knowing exactly what one wants to say; that type of paper is usually boring and one-sided. But it is painful not knowing what to write about. The best way out of the fly-bottle is to go to your library and look in the subject index in the computer or card file. The subjects will be very broad, for instance, "crime," "abortion," "the military," "education," "astronomy," "diet." Each of these headings will have a large number of books, usually with some description of the contents (and remember, lots of titles helpfully betray the book's point of view). You might just read through a number of these descriptions to see what strikes your fancy. Don't forget to note down the author and title of a good prospect, because you may have a terrible time finding it again. Another place you can pick up ideas is the Periodical Index, which lists magazine articles. Many libraries also have vertical files, which contain pamphlets on various subjects.

Now, what is a good prospect to write about? I find an interesting angle to be any idea or evidence that contradicts common thinking, for instance that although the crime rate has fallen slightly in recent years, fear of crime has increased. My burning question becomes, "Is the current fear of crime justified?" In contrast, the question "Are Rain Forests Important?" does not interest me, because I believe that rain forests are very important. If I stumbled on an angle about how those rain forests which the world has lost could be restored, however, that would be intensely interesting.

Another way to produce an interesting paper is to discover little-known facts, such as the surprisingly high number of traffic fatalities which elderly people cause, due to their failing faculties. You could grapple with various ways to deal with that problem, including the possibility of doing nothing.

Your Librarian is the Source of Sources

Because the materials you could use are scattered in many places, your librarian will stun you with places you never dreamed to look, such as U.S. government publications where you could get statistics on the crime rate (or agricultural output, weather patterns, you get the idea). There is no greater treasure than a friendly, helpful librarian.

Stay Greedy

Leave no file unearthed, no periodical index unskimmed, if you want to write the best paper. See if you can amass twenty sources, just for fun. Chances are that this will be time-consuming and you may not use half of them, but you will still have many to repay you handsomely when you go to say something.

Figuring out what sources you can use is often confusing, especially if you are some way into your research and still trying to figure out your angle. My rule is *When in doubt, check it out.* If you take the material home but don't use it, no harm is done. Some students have the odd ethic of believing that they must read any book they check out from cover to cover. Not so! That's what indexes and tables of contents are for—to enable you to go right to page 406 and skip the rest, if it does not pertain to your needs.

Digest Your Information

This is perhaps the most important time. You read, you think, you read some more, checking our additional sources as you learn about them.

I always have to go back and check out more books to follow up some new angle—in my example, I might want information on the crime rate in other countries than the U.S., or rates in populous areas compared to rural areas. I am stunned to learn that in the least populous areas of the U.S., the murder rate is *higher* than that of the most violent populous area—definitely an interesting angle!

Trust yourself to develop your own opinions about what you have learned. They will come. They will probably be a mixture of the opinions you have read, or perhaps you will come up with a new conclusion. The important thing is to try to decide what the truth of the matter is. For example, in the case I picked I would keep in mind the question, "Is our fear of crime in the United States justified?" A good answer to this would entail not only statistics on current crime in the United States, but data on current crime rates in other parts of the world, say England and Japan. The latter would be evidence that even though our crime rate has fallen slightly in the past few years, it is still far worse than that of these two countries, hence fear is more justified here than in those countries. On the other hand, how does our crime rate compare to that of Zaire or Argentina? If you run into trouble finding statistics for these countries, or you read that the reported crime rate may not really reflect the true number of incidents, by all means add that information in your paper by means of showing that the question you are asking is a difficult one. Often what you *can't* find despite diligent searching is as interesting as what you do find.

Noting Quotes

Somehow you need to mine the ideas you found so great, but no method is sacred. Some people jot down the best quotes, along with their author, title, page number(s), publisher, and date, onto 3″ x 5″ index cards or on a separate piece of paper. Those who use index cards swear by them because cards can be shuffled around when it comes times to write the paper. Other people use one piece of paper and color code those quotes which seem to belong together. Another method is to xerox those pages on which there are ideas that you want, and worry about how much to quote directly or whether to summarize the idea in your words. In any case, don't forget to note the book title, author, publisher, publication date on the Xerox, making sure that you have a copy of the page number as well (in the case of journals, note the volume number, date, everything that can help the reader readily get back to your source and you to complete your bibliography).

One lazy person I know doesn't use index cards or paper, but puts post-it notes in the margins of books, right next to the quotes she wants to use. The edge of the post-it note hangs outside the book or article as a sort of flag. As she uses a quote in the course of writing her paper, she types it directly into her paper or rephrases it (in either case, be careful to acknowledge the source! See below.). She thus saves herself the tedious step of writing out the quote beforehand on a separate piece of paper. But that method might drive you crazy or prove impractical in cases where books are on reserve and cannot be checked out of the library.

THE WRITING

The Rule of Paragraph Three

I am amazed that in many case I *think* I know what I think, but when I begin to write it down, I realize that I have a number of ideas about something, but the conclusion is not obvious, or the conclusion seems obvious but my reasons are fuzzy. I can see all sorts of unfinished business, holes in the argument that I need to do more research on or think about some more. Thus, *the process of writing is a more precise process of thinking.* A tongue-in-check way of putting this is to say that it takes roughly three paragraphs of writing on a subject to pull out the nubbin of the argument. Late nights, lots of coffee, and deep thought can drastically alter that initial conclusion or the sketchy reasons, which is the intellectual excitement of the research paper.

Make Your Conclusion the Title of Your Work

You may bitterly resist this, believing that you're giving all the excitement away at the start, but if you've got an interesting angle your reader will be hooked on the spot and will press on, eager to know *how* you came to your view. On the other hand, if you play your cards close to your chest, the reader will give up the game. Check the titles of newspaper and magazine articles. You'll be surprised, not only by the fact that they are so often the conclusion, but also a fully described conclusion at that.

As the Rule of Paragraph Three implies, however, you may do better to think of your conclusion as tentative when you set out to write your paper. It may well change somewhat as you put your paper together (see Sample 1, below).

There is one exception to the notion of making the title the conclusion. If you suspect that your reader is hostile to your conclusion, make your title your burning question, for instance, "Is Fear of Crime in the United States Justified?" or "Annual Mandatory Driving Tests for the Elderly—a Good Idea?" Then begin your paper by arguing your reader's position, followed by your wealth of amazing statistics favoring your position, and finally your conclusion that the evidence compels you to go with that position. This is a bit roundabout, but still a clear format.

Make Each Paragraph Start
with Its Main Conclusion

Each paragraph should be a small mirror of the overall construction. Even if your reader is hostile you should still begin each paragraph with its main point, making that main point as much a common area of agreement as you can think of. (See Sample 2 below.)

Show How Your Theory or Argument Compares
Favorably with Alternatives

The most straightforward way to do this is to present a summary of your major points at the beginning, called the *abstract*. Having clearly shown your reader what you have in mind, you can afford to begin your paper by laying down background information. After this, the directions become murky. The best I can advise is to try to think like your reader, presenting whichever part of your case you think the reader needs— evidence? your assumptions? a definition? alternative arguments? implications? (For more on thinking like your reader, see "Editing Overview", below.) Remember, your reader is like a blind person being led through a forest. As interested as he or she is in what is encountered, you must give him or her some idea of the landscape and alert him or her to every twist in the road.

Resist Telling a Story

Just as arguing is as natural as a three-year-old telling you why he or she should stay up until midnight, so is the story a natural tendency of the human mind. Unlike an argument, however, a story begins at some beginning in time and usually tells what happened next. For example, if I asked you to tell me about your morning, you could give me a narrative "First, I got up, then I had trouble finding the cereal, then I found the Corn Flakes, but then I couldn't find the car keys or the coat I wanted to wear, then . . . " Another way you could tell me about your morning would be to offer an argument about it "I had a hectic time today! I couldn't find things like my keys, my coat, or even the cereal." Notice that even in this brief example it is easier to see where the reporter is going when he or she tells about a hectic morning in the form of an argument. You could write your paper in the form of a narrative of your discovery of sources . . . "First, I learned about the crime rate in Scandinavia, then I saw a book by William Julius Wilson . . ." Don't do this! A research paper makes a bad mystery novel—don't bury the outcome.

Choose a Consistent Documentation Style

There are a mind-boggling number of ways to write footnotes and references. You will need to adopt one and use it consistently to give your paper a beautiful appearance and make your reader's life easy. The style common in the humanities is called MLA, since it was developed by the Modern Language Association. The American Psychological Association devised the style used in most social science research. For instances, the list of sources is called Works Cited in the MLA style and References in the APA style. See how many differences you can note between these variants of the same reference:

Knox, Bernard. *The Oldest Dead White European Males: And Other Reflections on the Classics.* New York: Norton, 1993. (MLA Style)

Knox, B. (1993). *The Oldest Dead White European Males: And Other Reflections on the Classics.* New York: Norton. (APA Style)

You probably noticed that MLA requires the first name, when available, and the APA does not. You can see that the APA wants the date of publication right after the name, while the MLA is content to put it after the publishing information. But did you notice that when a reference runs to the second line, the MLA style requires a five-space indentation, while the APA requires three spaces? Attention to detail is king. Each style has a precise format for referencing a magazine article, an encyclopedia excerpt, and so forth.

To complicate matters, there are a number of documentation styles in the sciences. The manual of the Council of Biology Editors (CBE) offers instructions specific to various scientific fields. Ask your instructor which style you should use. If your instructor has no preference, locate the style manual for the area of your research. The *Simon & Schuster Handbook for Writers* is most helpful, offering detailed examples in the major styles for documenting articles, reference works, and the other types of sources you have used.[2] *The Chicago Manual of Style* is also widely used, and very complete.

Quote, and Quote Boldly

You're alone in the library (at least no one is looking), you're hunched over some musty tome and run across a profound idea of page 368, pleasingly put, most cleverly put indeed! The temptation can be almost overwhelming to say, "I'll just pop this into my paper as if I wrote it. No messy footnotes, no tedious reference-writing, and I bet the author wouldn't mind. I'll look really smart." But in so doing you've done two people a bad turn: Your poor author does not get the honor and glory of being acknowledged for that profound observation; and you don't get the honor and glory of having waded through the book to page 368 to find that profound observation! So a double injustice is done. Further, you run the risk that when your reader runs across your undocumented observation that matter and energy are transferable, he is likely to suspect that the thoughts which you *did* come up with on your own, even your organization of your paper, may well have come from someone else.

Here is how you handle another author's ideas and words:

> **When you really like *the way* the author put it, use her words and put quotation marks around them.**
> **Put the reference in a footnote.**
> **When you want to use an author's *idea*, but could say it just as well or better, use your own words but give credit to him by putting the reference in a footnote.**

Sample 1 This student has done a fair amount of research and is starting to write. His tentative conclusion (paper title): *Destroy the*

Smallpox Virus. He's not sure of everything that he needs in the abstract, but wants to include the following:

Smallpox

is a deadly virus that has killed millions of people worldwide
kills 40 percent of the people who contract the disease.
is now eradicated, except for stocks in two laboratories
could accidentally escape and kill others
could be seized by terrorists or sold as a weapon of biological warfare

He decides to put detailed support for these claims in the background section, which he starts:

Background

Smallpox has proven to be a monstrous killer, perhaps the biggest in history. As recently as a century ago it killed a quarter of a million people a year in Europe alone. *He adds the fotenote [1], realizing that he should document his claim. Then he suddenly realizes that he has no estimate of the world-wide death toll and decides to go back to the library later to see if he can find it. He notes* (World death toll? Death rates in Africa, Asia?) *then continues.* But in 1967, the World Health Organization began a campaign to eradicate the disease, which attacks only humans. Ironically, it is a closely-related but harmless virus, the vaccinia virus, which formed the basis of the vaccine that had been used since 1896 to prevent smallpox.[2] As a result of diligent vaccination, it appears that smallpox no longer exists today outside of two laboratories, one in the United States, the other in Russia.[3] The last reported case of smallpox which anyone caught outside of a laboratory was in 1977, in Somalia.[4] *[He has been careful to footnote his different sources with [2,3,4], and likes what he's done so far. He now wants to discuss the danger which smallpox still poses. In the spirit of leading the reader gently along, he begins the new paragraph by tying it to the previous one, alerting us to this new direction by using "however," and starting with the paragraph's main conclusion.]*

However, as long as smallpox exists it presents dangers. In 1978 a laboratory technician in England died from smallpox because a co-worker had mishandled the virus; as a result, the co-worker committed suicide.[5] It is lucky that the technician did not infect anyone else, because the very success of the war against smallpox has meant that people are no longer vaccinated against it. Vaccination against smallpox was abandoned throughout the world in 1985, and many countries had stopped it much earlier.[6] Had the technician infected other people, roughly 40 percent of them would have died.

He decides to take a break and goes to the library, where he doesn't find figures on the death toll but does find new arguments that the smallpox virus should be saved. Up to this point he had only seen the argument that every species, even one deadly to humans, has a right to exist. But now he learns some stunning new facts, which he excitedly jots down along with their ref-

erences. He liked some of the language the author used so much that he decided to take the quotes down directly, and of course, the reference:

Some researchers believe that more experimentation on the smallpox virus "might provide clues in the battles against other scourges, including cancer." (*New York Times,* Lawrence K. Altman, "Frozen in Labs, Smallpox Virus Escapes a Scalding End, for Now," Dec. 25, 1993, p. 7)

He already knew (and had written in his draft) that the vaccine against smallpox, vaccinia, is a close relative of the smallpox virus. But what he didn't know was that this close relationship could be exploited if smallpox were kept around. He copies the quote:

"In asking for a stay of execution, some experts have expressed hopes that additional research will help explain why one virus was lethal and the other beneficial." (New York Times, same as above)

He is also relieved to learn that the virus stocks are much safer than he had feared. They are not sitting on a shelf somewhere in the labs, as he had imagined, but are
    frozen in liquid nitrogen
    the two laboratories in Atlanta and Moscow are closely guarded. (Atlanta lab: The Centers for Disease Control and Prevention; Moscow lab: Institute for Viral Preparations)

He ends by xeroxing the article and taking it home. Suddenly, everything has taken on a new light. The likelihood of another accidental escape of the virus seems far more remote to him, and the possibilities of a breakthrough in the understanding of cancer, no matter how remote, might be worth the small risk of the virus accidentally escaping, as had happened in 1978. And the new article noted that health officials insisted that there are suffi- cient stores of vaccine to quickly prevent an epidemic. It suddenly occurs to him to speak to someone in the Biology Department, who might know how likely an accidental release would be. He doesn't know anyone, but maybe a classmate or his instructor does. He makes a note:

    See Biology Prof. about smallpox escaping from lab

and pastes it on his textbook. Suddenly, it seems like a good idea to keep the virus around! Taking a break, he switches on the news and learns that political conditions in Russia are unstable. He immediately thinks of the virus in the Moscow laboratory, of the desperate economic conditions, and that perhaps the temptation to sell the virus to a wealthy terrorist would be too great. After pleasurably turning the pros and cons over in his mind over the weekend, he suddenly hits upon a solution:

    Let's Buy the Russians' Smallpox

With this new, tentative title his paper has changed focus a bit, zeroing in on the danger in Russia, which he now needs to document. He decides he will weigh his solution against his earlier alternative, of destroying the virus in both labs. In any case, everything in his tentative abstract can stay; but he needs to make additions. And everything in his opening background paragraphs can remain.

Sample 2 The writer of Sample 1 could confidently assume that his reader would bring no violent opposition to his point of view. But say you want to write a letter to the editor or you undertake research which leads you to a position that you suspect your reader already opposes. There are good and bad aspects to this state of affairs. The bad aspect is that you have to be even more careful to build your case, although that can prove interesting. The good aspect is that if you support your case well, your reader's point of view will be forever changed, at least to the extent that in thinking about the issue, he or she will *inescapably* think of your view, and that is a far more impressive achievement than yet another run-of-the-mill letter or paper.

In this case the student has another course in which an instructor has brought up stereotypes and stereotyping. The term grates on her, but she isn't sure why. She thinks about it a lot, and has long discussions about it with her best friend, telling him that she wants to do her paper in critical thinking on the issue. He warns her not to take on such a dangerous subject. But she decides to tackle it anyway, figuring that she has always been foolhardy and she might as well be consistent. At one point her friend kids, "You don't want all those negative stereotypes about women to be flying around, do you?" And that set her to thinking. Was there such a thing as a *positive stereotype?* She jotted down a note to see if she could find some. And was a negative stereotype necessarily a bad thing? Even a negative view might be helpful, if it pointed out a fault that people could work on. Or was she getting it right? Was a stereotype a crude remark about a group that nobody in that group could change, such as "The goobies are creepy because they all have teeny earlobes"? But rather than responding "That's a stereotype," in that case wouldn't it be more accurate to respond "What's your evidence that they have teeny earlobes and, even if they did, how does that make them creepy?

Suddenly she jumped up and down. That's it! Anyone can say "That's a stereotype," and they kill off all further discussion! Here she was, learning in her critical thinking class that one should decide issues in light of the evidence for alternatives, and in another class language was used, unintentionally she suspected, to block looking at evidence for the offending alternative. Yes! When you say "That is a stereotype" you are saying "I am offended," but you do not get to the deeper question, which is a request that the person to produce evidence and get both parties to critically think the matter through—or so she thought.

She picked as her tentative title, *Avoid the term 'stereotype'.* Then, remembering that she was treading on strange ground, she changed that to *Should we avoid the term "stereotype?"*

When she got to the library and looked in the subject index under "stereotyping" for books, she came across *Unkind Words: Ethnic Labeling from Redskin to WASP,* by Irving Allen. That surprised her. She had not figured name-calling into her notion of stereotype, and certainly didn't intend to argue that it was okay for people to be mean. She jotted down the title, author, and library reference, PE 2846. A46, with the plan to *distinguish* in her paper between a nasty name and a description, which might or might not be correct.

She found some other promising books, and on her way to the checkout counter she passed a table on which a newspaper lay open. Her eye caught the headline, "Sex, Power and a Workplace Reversal," by Christopher Lehmann-Haupt. It was a review of the book, *Disclosure,* by Michael Crichton, in which an evil woman who has won promotion over a man takes revenge on him because he refuses to sleep with her by accusing *him* of sexual harassment. The reviewer writes of his discomfort at rooting for the man against this woman, who he writes is "the embodiment of all those antiquated, chauvinistic stereotypes of the power-hungry woman: she is two-faced, underhanded, manipulative, mendacious, underqualified for her position and delighted to wield sex as a weapon." Why, she wondered, couldn't this fictional character be a bad woman and only that? Why apologize for rooting for the downfall of the bad gal? Then, intrigued by the reviewer's term "antiquated," she tried to think of past power-hungry women she had learned about in school. Maybe Queen Elizabeth I, in the 16th century? Or maybe Lady Macbeth—was she a stereotype? She wasn't sure about any of this or how it would relate to her paper, but just in case she jotted down the quote, the review's reference as well as her thoughts, and left the library confused.

At home, she switched on the radio and caught a news headline that a woman was to be admitted to an elite military academy for the first time. "Finally," she muttered, then paused. Was this a case of a breakthrough in stereotyping, the kind of thing her other instructor had meant? She jotted down the information as best she could remember, and made a note to check the newspapers the next day. While she was writing, on came a talk show. One guest was Ellis Cose, a black journalist who had just written a book on minority people who had achieved middle-class jobs but felt that whites viewed them as tokens of affirmative action, stereotyped as unfit or incompetent no matter how much they achieved. Another guest, a graduate of Harvard Law School and member of a big law firm, sounded so nice but had been excluded from his co-workers' social gatherings and shunned when he tried to get promoted. He had tried so hard, only to end up so lonely! Through her tears she jotted down the title of the first guest's book, the author's name and publisher.[3] The following morning when she woke up, she was still mad. The people around this man sure seemed to be giving him a raw deal, stereotyping him as incompetent! She wanted to go and chew them out. But remembering her gut reaction to the term stereotype and her newfound idea that one should request evidence, she imagined herself going to these lawyers and saying . . . what? She sat down and wrote out a few possibilities, among them:

Are you being fair to Mr. Black?

Your *conclusions* about Mr. Black's abilities *do not seem warranted. What evidence* do you have that his work is inferior to that of his colleagues?

This is how her tentative abstract looks:

Many groups have suffered greatly from unfair characterization *[she's begun by showing that she has a sympathetic understanding of the position she believes her instructor holds],* and it is tempting to call these characterizations stereotypes. But the problem is that accusing a person of stereotyping doesn't advance the discussion, but just makes the person accused feel angry and misunderstood. This paper explores alternative responses, such as asking for evidence and trying to work to . . . *[here she was going to write "change their mind," then suddenly remembered an argument she had had with her brother about boys being stronger than girls, and she had thought he meant stronger in every way, and he had meant only stronger in lifting things, and even then she had objected because she could carry things some other boys could not, but their teacher had explained that in general boys have greater muscle mass, so she had in the end changed her mind—so she finished the sentence with]* to work together to get to the truth.

As we leave her, this researcher is off on an exciting intellectual odyssey which may last a long time after her paper. She will have a lot to say on both sides of the issue. If you choose this path, don't be depressed if, despite your *tour de force,* your reader remains unconvinced. Review the section in Chapter 5 on the many strategies that people have to ward off theory change! You are a great success if you can get the reader to give you high marks, literally and figuratively, for your thoughtful development of your position.

EDITING: YOU ARE ALMOST THERE!

Your research paper now looks like a glorious patchwork, unified by your point of view and sparkling with the ideas and evidence of other researchers whose ideas you have skillfully sewn into your work. All you need is to iron out a few wrinkles. The next section offers an editing checklist for reviewing your work. Much of this you can do on your own, but in addition there is nothing like a friend to help you, someone who can give a different eye to what by now is blindingly clear to you.

Editing Overview

Try to see your work from the reader's point of view. Chop yourself in half! Be half your reader, half yourself. Enlist a friend to show you where you were unclear.

Economize

Uproot and rearrange. Scratch out whole paragraphs if they are superfluous.

Restructure the best argument for your reader and therefore for you.

"Make every word tell," as the writer E. B. White advises.

Use the active voice and personal pronouns where you can.

Have fun!

Don't be discouraged if you have to make several changes! Even experienced writers have to experiment with words and various outlines to get their view to make sense quickly and enjoyably to their readers. This is never easy, but I assure you that it becomes easier with practice.

Try to become your reader   When you write successfully you are on intimate terms with what you think. When you edit successfully you divorce yourself as it were, at least the self you were when you wrote. You now look at your written words with a stranger's eye, and the more you are able to pretend to be the reader, the better your work will be. Of course, you cannot be the reader, and you will be eternally surprised by what others wish you had thought to include or felt you had not made clear, but your sensitive anticipation of their wants will make your work far stronger than it would otherwise have been. Rewriting is tedious, but resist the natural urge to leave your work as it first occurred to you.

Make Your Style Simple and Straightforward   As I mentioned at the start of this chapter, the ideal of writing today is simple and straightforward. So it is with words. Think of big words as crown jewels set into plain sentences. Not that you have to dispense with uncommon words like "dispense" or even "dispensation." But the standards of beautiful writing these days hold that slim sentences are more attractive. In books on effective writing you will read many a disdainful remark about bloated prose, such as "with the possible exception of," instead of "except," or "He totally lacked the ability to" rather than "He couldn't." These may seem minor offenses, but multiplied over pages they deal a death blow to the reader's patience.

There may always have been a strain of thought holding that "brevity is the soul of wit" (Shakespeare's phrase); or people who would agree with Abraham Lincoln's criticism of a wordy man, that "He could put the smallest idea in the greatest number of words of any man I met." The point is to get unnecessary words out of the way, words which readily flow from the lips or the fingers on the first effort, but which must give way to lay bare the pleasure of the idea.

The difficulty in achieving this lean look does not lie just in our wordiness. It's all of those people steeped in the jargon of their respective fields, people whose work you must read to gather your information, who will fill your ears with piles of polysyllabic prose. After days of dosing on them, it is hard to resist writing variants of puffy sentences like this:

> Presently, the regulations are undergoing imminent implementation.

It takes extra work to adjust your language dial to say that the rules will go into effect soon. But take that extra work and your reader will bless you.

Use the Active Voice and Personal Pronouns The most straightforward way of getting an idea across is this: A subject does something to an object. For instance:

> The cat sat on the mat.

This is called the active voice, and it does give an active feel to a description. In contrast, the passive voice has a subject being done to by something. For instance:

> The mat was sat upon by the cat.

This is a more roundabout way of saying the same thing, and notice how much longer the sentence is. There is nothing wrong with that if you want to highlight the mat somehow, as in "I tried to step inside the door quickly to get out of the rain, but could not wipe my feet on the mat, which was being sat upon by the cat." But if you have to read one passive construction after another, it is slow going. For instance:

> Longer and healthier lives are enjoyed by Americans to a greater extent than at any time in their history. Yet preoccupation with risks to health and safety and the environment is experienced by them to a greater degree. It is argued by many advocates, such as industry representatives promoting unpopular technology or by Environmental Protection Agency staffers defending the regulatory agenda, that a bad sense of perspective is experienced by the public. Enormous efforts against small but scary-sounding risks are demanded by Americans while more commonplace ones are virtually ignored by them.

Here is the paragraph that I doctored as it was written in a fascinating article on risk analysis in *Scientific American*:

> Americans live longer and healthier lives today than at any time in their history. Yet they seem preoccupied with risks to health, safety and the environment. Many advocates, such as industry representatives promoting unpopular technology or Environmental Protection Agency defending its regulatory agenda, argue that the public has had a bad sense of perspective. Americans, they say, demand that enormous efforts be directed at small but scary-sounding risks while virtually ignoring larger, more commonplace ones.[4]

A way to see whether you are overdoing passives is to check your sentences to see if you find many instances of "is _____ by," for instance in my mishandling of the paragraph above, you will find "are enjoyed by," "is experienced by," "it is argued by," "are demanded by," "are ignored by,"—all clot meaning. Turn such phrases around, as much as possible.

There is a movement afoot to humanize research papers by letting their authors say "I" when they refer to themselves. Instead of writing "This author believes that. . ." you could write "I believe that . . ." Check with your instructor to see whether this usage is appropriate.

Decide to Have Fun   Maybe this is ridiculous—or worse, impossible—advice. But I think that research can be as fun as skiing or any other activity in which you get better by discovering things about it. If you expect to have a good time, I figure that you will work to dig out an issue that will give you a lot of pleasure.

SUMMARY

1. **Asusmptions about writing:**
   (a) There is no such thing as a "natural, born writer," but anyone can get skilled at it.
   (b) Today a good writer is as brief and informative as possible.
2. **Steps in Research:**
   (a) Pick a subject of devouring interest.
   (b) Read, take notes to develop a point of view that takes into account alternative arguments (if you can't decide among alternatives, make that your conclusion and show in your paper why at the moment you can't decide)
   (c) Write:
       the act of writing will produce new ideas
       try several approaches while imagining which the reader would prefer.
       quote boldly
   (d) Edit:
       see your work from the reader's point of view
       "make every word tell"—keep your style simple and straight forward
       use active voice and personal pronouns
       have fun

NOTES

1. Alexis de Tocqueville, *Democracy in America* edited by Henry Steele Commager, (Oxford University Press, 1947), p. 253.

2. Lynn Quitman Troyka, *Simon & Schuster Handbook for Writers,* Third Edition (Englewood Cliffs, NJ: Prentice-Hall Inc, 1993.)

3. Ellis Cose, *The Rage of a Privileged Class* (New York: Harper Collins, 1994).

4. M. Granger Morgan, "Risk-Analysis and Management," *Scientific American* (July 1993), p. 32.

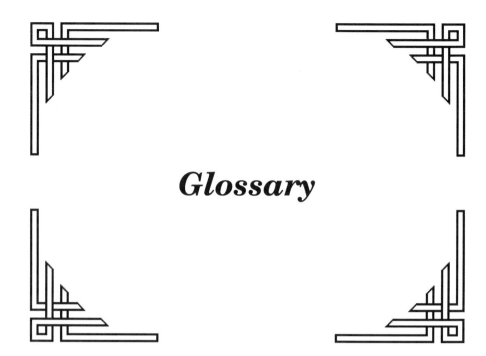

Glossary

The following is a list of frequencly used phrases in argumentation, with some illustrative examples of their use.

agree to disagree   An accord that arguers are at an impasse and shouldn't keep arguing, probably because they will argue in a circle. Arguers should agree to disagree when (1) they need to get more factual evidence, if the argument hinged on a fact, or (2) they need to come up with different approaches or expanded arguments.

assumption   The reason beneath the stated reason(s). Either the author will not state them at all, or the author will announce them by saing, "I am assuming that," or "The assumption here is."

based on the premise that   "Based on the reason (or assumption) that."

based on the presupposition that   Same as "based on the premise that," above.

because   Indicates that a conclusion has preceded and a reason will follow.

cause   See chapter 11.

critical thinking   The consideration of alternative arguments in light of their evidence. Other writers on critical thinking have slightly different definitions. Robert Ennis defines critical thinking as "reasonably deciding to believe or do something;" Richard Paul argues that it is "dialogical reasoning." Harvey Siegel defines it as "being appropriately moved by reasons."

claim   Any statement. Claims are provisional, subject to change with new information.

deduce   To arrive at a particular instance that is entailed in a generalization.

Often found in the form, "from which we may deduce that." "All our parachutes open when the ripcord is pulled, from which you may deduce that the one you buy from us will open too."

definition   All that is meant to be included in a term.

distinction   (between two terms) An important difference between two terms.

draw the inference that   Come to the concluson that.

draw the conclusion that   Same as "draw the inference that."

even granting that . . . still   In a counterargument, a technique for accepting or granting the truth of the other person's reason(s), and yet showing how they are consistent with your argument. "Even granting that it is frightening to speak out in a group and that people may think you're stupid, still it is better to speak your mind because the world needs your ideas just as much as it needs anybody else's."

false dichotomy between   In a counterargument, the claim that a false distinction has been made. He: "In college, you can either have a lot of fun or you can do a lot of studying." She: "You have created a false dichotomy between having fun and studying. By George, you can have a lot of fun studying!"

hinges on   Usually the argument hinges on, or is dependent on, some outside fact or other argument (e.g., "The argument that most societies have suppressed women hinges on the claim that there is no biological explanation for women's failure to hold positions of power").

if . . . then   What follows "if" is the reason; what follows "then" is the conclusion to that statement.

implications   Consequences beyond the conclusion. Either the author does not state them or the author says, "The implications are."

imply   Most frequently found in a counterargument or used by a respondent in a deliberation. It is a request to clarify someone else's conclusion. "You seem to be suggesting a connection between the cultural values held by a group and their average income. Are you implying that most wealth and poverty are the result of these values?" Or you can use it to say what you don't mean: "But I don't mean to imply that." A less frequent but handy use: One idea necessarily involves another (e.g., "Drama implies conflict").

inductive leap   The jump to a general conclusion from a set of particulars. Leaps are necessary, but some leaps are safer than others. Usually used to describe an unsafe one: "In suggesting that . . . on the basis of just a few cases, the author has made too great an inductive leap."

infer   Come to the conclusion that. "From the look of his sweaty body one can infer that he has been doing strenuous exercise," or "We can make the inference that."

inference   The conclusion. "Although he thinks it's right to conclude that we should be patriotic, he doesn't think it right to base this inference on the premise that we are superior to people of other nations."

issue   The topic or subject at hand.

make the argument   Same as "one could argue that." "One could make the argument that."

necessary cause   A factor without which some effect would not occur. "Oxygen is a necessary cause of fire" (no oxygen, no fire). It often takes several necessary causes to create an effect (e.g., to get a rocket into space, or to get to work on time). *See also* Sufficient cause.

necessarily   Must be the case (e.g., "necessarily involves").

not necessarily   Doesn't have to be the case. "Because some people are better at argumentation doesn't necessarily imply (indicate) that they are smarter. These better arguers have probably just been practicing longer"; often found in the phrases, "does not necessarily imply," "is not necessarily the case."

ought   Usually signals the solution a thinker has arrived at as a result of his conclusion. "Because of the rapid rate at which we're polluting this lake, I conclude that we will not be able to swim in it by 2000. So we ought to find a new lake to pollute (just kidding)." *See also* Should.

play the devil's advocate   Take the opposite point of view. Student to instructor: "I'd like to play the devil's advocate to your position that our class should have an in-class final. Think of all the extra love and attention we could give to your questions if we had lots of time to mull over them at home."

premise   Reason. *See also* Based on the premise that.

that presupposes   That requires the assumption (underlying reason) that. "That argument presupposes that everyone is born with equal enthusiasm and talent."

reason   The support for the conclusion; the why. Write, "The reason is," don't write, "The reason is because," because that's redundant. "The reason for her tardiness is her laziness," or "The reason that she is often tardy is *that* the bus schedule is erratic."

should   Signals a solution or a prescription (as opposed to a statement about what the case is). *See also* Ought.

sufficient cause   A cause that by itself will create an effect. "Oxygen is a necessary cause of a fire, but it isn't sufficient. On the other hand, lack of oxygen is a sufficient cause of choking to death."

therefore   Signals that a conclusion must follow and that a reason came before (usually right before, but not always). "She's always up at 4 A.M. Therefore, she's dead tired by 10 P.M."

warranted inference   A phrase to the effect that a conclusion and/or the step from the reason(s) to the conclusion is justified. "Many studies have found a positive correlation between the amount of time students spend on a course and their grades. These studies warrant the inference that sheer effort expended is a central factor in doing well in school."

Index